Public Opinion and Policy Leadership in the American States

Phillip W. Roeder

Published for the

Institute for Social Science Research by

The University of Alabama Press   *Tuscaloosa and London*

Copyright © 1994
The University of Alabama Press
Tuscaloosa, Alabama 35487–0380
All rights reserved
Manufactured in the United States of America

∞

The paper on which this book is printed meets the minimum requirements of American National Standard for Information Science-
Permanence of Paper for Printed Library Materials, ANSI Z39.48-1984.

Library of Congress Cataloging-in-Publication Data

Roeder, Phillip W.
    Public opinion and policy leadership in the American states /
Phillip W. Roeder.
        p. cm.—(Institute for Social Science Research monograph
series)
    Includes bibliographical references and index.
    ISBN 0-8173-0677-3
    1. State governments—United States—Public opinion.   2. Public
opinion—United States.   I. University of Alabama. Institute for
Social Science Research.   II. Title.   III. Series: Monograph series
(University of Alabama. Institute for Social Science Research)
JK2408.R55   1994
353.9—dc20   93-12870
                                                          CIP

British Library Cataloguing-in-Publication Data available

Public Opinion and Policy Leadership
in the American States

Institute for Social Science Research Monograph Series

General Editor, Michael L. Berbaum

Contents

Acknowledgments

As with most research projects, so in the development of this work many individuals have played important roles. First, I want to thank individuals at the Council of State Governments. Carl Stenberg, now at the University of Virginia, was executive director of the Council when this survey project began and was instrumental in supporting the project and ensuring successful implementation. Dag Ryen of the Council worked on numerous aspects of the CSG surveys, including item development and issue identification. Their help and support is greatly appreciated.

At the University of Kentucky, Jim Hougland, Jim Wolf, Shirley Slaton, and numerous interviewers at the UK-Survey Research Center did an excellent job in carrying out the yearly national surveys. Elmer Whitler of the Martin School of Public Administration played an important role in all aspects of the survey project. His experience and knowledge in survey research—including item development, construction of data-sets, and data analysis—are unmatched and played a crucial role in successful completion of all the surveys.

Reviewers for the University of Alabama Press provided excellent criticisms and suggestions for improving the work.

Although all of these individuals helped make the CSG/Martin School State Survey Project and this book possible, I am responsible for any shortcomings which remain. Finally, although it is sometimes impossible to separate work and family, I tried not to make my family accommodate their lives to this book. Without my loving and supportive family, the research and writing would have been much less satisfying and enjoyable.

Public Opinion and Policy Leadership
in the American States

1

Introduction

Abortion, capital punishment, welfare, drug abuse, education, jobs, and taxes are only some of the difficult issues that state governments must confront as America approaches the twenty-first century. Many domestic policy responsibilities have moved from the federal to the state level, and state political institutions have increased their decision-making capabilities and levels of professionalism. Why have these changes occurred? Some contend that state responsibilities have expanded and professionalism has increased because of mandates from the federal government. In this view, state activism and innovation have occurred primarily in response to federal pressures to act, but they often have been unaccompanied by resources necessary to carry out the mandates. Herbers (1990, 11) contends that because of the huge budget deficit and the inability to "adequately deal with the enormous diversity of the country," the federal government has more or less abdicated its domestic responsibilities. This view suggests that suddenly and almost unilaterally, the national government forfeited to state governments the role of chief policy-maker in domestic matters. These governments are now struggling to establish an "orderly and acceptable approach to policy in the briar patch of American federalism."

Regardless of the degree to which the federal government has abdicated its domestic responsibilities or state governments themselves have pushed more aggressively into domestic policy-making and implementation, do contemporary state governments have the political and economic capacity to deal with the many new and complex social problems? Are the American states "laboratories of activism" or obstructionist "captives of the status quo"? As the system of intergovernmental relations and federalism has evolved since the 1960s, many believe the role of the states has changed from that of laggard to leader. Much research suggests that

1

state governments play significant and meaningful roles in our federal system. Although certain centralizing forces continue to operate, states have maintained and even increased their influence and autonomy in the intergovernmental political and policy process. Rather than representing a conservative, backward, invisible, or corrupt level of government, states are now viewed by many as being in the vanguard of governmental reform, innovation, and responsiveness. As states struggle to deal with new or expanded domestic responsibilities, some analysts view them as heroic, while others find them entrepreneurial.

> The states can no longer be considered the weak links of the federal system. Indeed they have become the new heroes of American federalism, implementing national policies throughout their borders in a responsible and responsive manner, while increasingly assuming an active role in the affairs and problems of their local governments. The resurgence of the states represents a new era in U.S. federalism as power and authority are being attracted from the national and the local governments to the state like bits of metal to a powerful magnet. (Bowman and Kearney 1986, 40)

> State government political institutions are infused with an entrepreneurial spirit. No longer passive partners in the federal system, the states are a driving force in American politics. They raise and spend vast sums of money; manage vexing problems; and seek to conquer new policy frontiers. States aggressively set policy agendas for the nation and fashion innovative solutions for stimulating the growth of high technology firms, treating the medically indigent, curbing drunken driving, reforming the schools, and other important matters. (Van Horn 1989, 209)

These effusive views of the American states see strong, active, positive government institutions. Given what some believe to be a key characteristic of the American political culture—distrust or fear of big government—how is it that such activism and strength has developed? To what extent do the American people support or even encourage these "heroic" or "entrepreneurial" roles for state governments?

Basic issues for democratic government are the degree to which congruence exists between the values, attitudes, and policy preferences of political leaders and citizens, and the extent to which public opinion influences government policies. The primary question for this research is, If the American states have become resurgent and activist problem-solvers, do citizens of the states recognize and support this expansive role for state institutions and political leaders? To what extent do individuals hold variable and consequential identifications, attitudes, and preferences concerning levels of government and their institutions and policies? Do political and policy attitudes vary depending on these identifications and depending on where individuals reside?

The two goals of the book are to describe public opinion toward major public policy issues and government institutions as viewed from a state government perspective, and to assess various explanations for these opinions. The major themes of the book include:

the role of government (especially state government)
institutional leadership and intergovernmental relations
national control or decentralization of programs
states as meaningful territorial entities
economic growth and state competitiveness
regulation, equity, redistribution, innovation, and spending in the
   policy areas of education, health, and welfare

This research is designed to assess the extent to which the American state influences individual attitudes and beliefs. First, this concept will be examined at the individual level. What role do individual attitudes and beliefs regarding state government play in explaining other political and policy preferences and evaluations? Are people less interested in, less knowledgeable about, and more removed from power and governing in the states than in the federal or local governments? Can individuals be categorized on the basis of which level of government they prefer? Can people be classified as "state identifiers"? To what extent can this "state electorate" be distinguished from either national or local electorates? What effects do these identifications have on public attitudes?

The American state also will be assessed as a possible contextual determinant of individual attitudes. Does state of residence influence individual opinions or attitudes? In what ways do the varied economic, social, and political contexts of the states affect individual attitudes and preferences regarding state policies and institutions? The overall approach is a multilevel analysis of political attitudes and policy preferences. The impacts of individual-level and state-level factors on public opinion will be assessed simultaneously in multivariate models.

Plan of the Book

The following chapter examines the role of the American states in the intergovernmental system. The primary focus is on the degree to which our system has become nationalized or centralized, as well as on the explanations that have been offered for the varying relationships between the federal and state governments in different periods of our history. The chapter deals with such topics as political culture, constitutionalism, elections and representation, public choice, economic competition between the states, and state policy-making and administration.

Chapter 3 explores several questions related to state electorates and public opinion. The chapter begins by assessing existing research on public opinion in the states and the relationship of state opinion to state policies. The chapter then examines survey items from the State Survey Project (described below) that concern government institutions and policy leadership, develops a composite measure of "level of government identification," and describes the socioeconomic characteristics and political predispositions of government identifiers.

In chapter 4, alternative models of the determinants of political and policy attitudes, preferences, and identifications of the public are examined. The varied types of political and policy attitudes that have been assessed as dependent variables in these models are described, as is the basic model that will be tested in the remaining chapters of the book.

Chapter 5 develops and expands the multivariate model from chapter 4 and tests the effects on political evaluations of the individual-level measure of government identification and contextual measures of state economies and political characteristics, controlling for other plausible determinants. The remaining chapters also use the model to assess state effects on public attitudes toward selected policy issues.

Chapter 6 analyzes public perceptions of program responsibilities of various levels of government and state spending priorities, and the extent to which level of government identification influences these preferences, controlling for other variables such as party identification, perceptions of economic conditions, and the like. Chapter 7 assesses public opinion regarding state economic development policies, perceptions of state business climates and economies, and the degree to which level of government identification and state contexts influence these attitudes. Chapter 8 examines public opinion in the policy area of welfare, including public perceptions of so-called workfare and guaranteed jobs and incomes, while chapter 9 treats education policy, including several recently enacted and proposed education reforms, as well as items comparing public education and the American family in dealing with certain social values. Chapter 10 is concerned with health care issues such as the right to health care, payment for this care, and national health insurance, and the extent to which individuals tend to be self-interested consumers or altruistic citizens regarding these questions. The final chapter evaluates and assesses the role of the states in public opinion formation, summarizes the results of the models tested in the previous chapters, and discusses implications for further research in the area of state public opinion and policy-making.

The State Survey Project

The primary source of data for answering the questions raised above and testing the model is the Council of State Governments/Martin School State Survey Project (SSP). The SSP was designed to provide an assessment of knowledge, attitudes, and evaluations of the public in several areas, including policy choices confronting state governments, the capacity of state institutions to make these choices, the quality of political leadership in the states, and the extent of public interest and involvement in decision-making at all three levels of government. National surveys of public opinion in these areas were conducted yearly from 1987 through 1990.

Many public opinion surveys dealing with citizen evaluation of intergovernmental relations and judgments of the quality and capacity of governmental institutions have been conducted over the past few decades. These surveys have tended to focus on asking people which level of government they believe is better able to deal with current problems or which level of government they feel is most effective or from which they feel they get "the most for their money." These items have some value, but they just begin to scratch the surface of public awareness of the complex intergovernmental system that characterizes the United States.

The instruments developed for the SSP focus on citizen perceptions of state government institutions and public policy issues facing the

American states.[1] In order to achieve some comparability, certain items are identical to those used in other surveys; most questions, however, were devised specifically for this project. Where appropriate, these previous survey items will be compared with items from the SSP. Some of the general questions or themes that formed the basis for development of specific survey items are as follows:

How much confidence do people have in various levels or institutions of government to deal with certain social, economic, and political problems faced in this country?

What type of leadership do people want or expect from governors and legislatures? From the Congress and the president?

To what extent do people participate in various political activities of state, national, and local jurisdictions?

Do people desire increased federal control or the setting of minimum national standards in certain policy or program areas?

1. Telephone interviews were conducted with national samples of adult residents of the United States (1,212 in 1987, 1,199 in 1988, and 1,034 in 1989). The samples were drawn using random-digit dialing, a technique that ensures that every residential telephone number has an equal chance of being selected. The initial sample of telephone prefixes was stratified so the number of prefixes selected from each of the country's four main census regions was proportionate to the region's total population. Clusters of random numbers were then generated from each initial phone number that reached a valid residence. This technique results in a representative national sample of the adult population who are accessible by telephone.

In each household contacted, one adult resident was randomly selected for an interview. Several attempts were made to reach each telephone number and respondent. The margin of error for the total sample for each year is plus or minus three percentage points at the 95 percent confidence interval. The margin of error for smaller groups of the sample such as Democrats or males will be greater than three percentage points.

The interviews were conducted by trained, supervised interviewers employed by the University of Kentucky Survey Research Center. A monitoring device is used to ensure that interviews are conducted in accordance with prescribed procedures. Interviewing was done from 5:30 to 9:30 P.M., Monday through Friday, and on Saturday and Sunday afternoons for each of the time zones across the country. Unless noted otherwise, the percentages used in this analysis are based on respondents who expressed opinions, leaving out those who did not know or refused to answer a question. The exact wording of items is included in the respective chapters. The complete survey instruments are available from the author.

Do people feel their policy views or preferences are better understood or acted upon by state, national, or local elected officials? By governors, administrators, courts, or legislatures? By the president or the Congress?

To what extent do people prefer that a particular level of government be responsible for providing certain types of public goods and services?

2
States in the Intergovernmental System

Although much analysis has focused on the surge of activity in American state governments in the late 1970s and 1980s, views of state governments as entrepreneurial, heroic, or even positive have not been conspicuous in the history of American federalism. Only two decades ago, political scientist Ira Sharkansky wrote a vigorous, systematic defense of state governments entitled *The Maligned States: Policy Accomplishments, Problems, and Opportunities* (1972). Sharkansky felt it necessary to respond to the then widely accepted view that the states were the invisible, corrupt, undemocratic, and conservative element of the intergovernmental system. This negative view was so pervasive that even a defender of the American states wrote that:

> The states are indecisive.
> The states are antiquated.
> The states are timid and ineffective.
> The states are not willing to face their problems.
> The states are not responsive.
> The states are not interested in cities.
> These half-dozen charges are true about all of the states some of the time and some of the states all of the time. On the other hand, at points in history, most of these charges have been applicable to both the national and local governments. (Sanford 1967, 1)

Although it would be difficult to view this quotation by Sanford, the former governor of North Carolina, as a spirited defense of state governments, it is important to remember that it followed decades of attacks on the states. In the same year that Governor Sanford's book defending the states appeared, the president of the American Political Science Association gave an address to the association entitled "The City in the

Future of Democracy," in which he characterized state governments as not being meaningful or important actors in the American system. Dahl (1967, 968) provides a vision of neutered state governments that in the future will be no more than "intermediate instruments of coordination and control." More important, he contends that states do not matter to the average citizen.

> Yet in the perspective I am suggesting the states do not stand out as important institutions of democratic self-government. They are too big to allow for much in the way of civic participation—think of California and New York, each about as large in population as Canada or Yugoslavia and each larger than 80 percent of the countries of the world. Yet an American state is infinitely less important to citizens of that state than any democratic nation-state to its citizens. Consequently the average American is bound to be much less concerned about the affairs of his state than of his city or country. Too remote to stimulate much participation by their citizens, and too big to make extensive participation possible anyway, these units intermediate between city and nation are probably destined for a kind of limbo of quasi-democracy. They will be pretty much controlled by the full-time professionals, whether elected or appointed. Moreover, many of the problems that states have to deal with will not fit within state boundaries. It cannot even be said that the states, on the whole, can tap any strong sentiments of loyalty or likemindedness among their citizens. Doubtless we shall continue to use the states as important intermediate instruments of coordination and control—if for no other reason than the fact that they are going institutions.

Despite the lack of evidence for many of Dahl's assertions, his negative perspective continued a tradition of state government naysayers and doomsayers. A notable critic of state governments in the Great Depression/New Deal period was the eminent public administrationist Luther Gulick. After compiling a long and impressive list of the functions performed by the forty-eight states, Gulick (1933, 421) wrote, "The American state is finished. I do not predict that the states will go, but affirm that they have gone." He reasons that the states, despite their many responsibilities under our constitutional system, "were unable to deal even inefficiently with the imperative, the life and death tasks of the new national economy." This inability to act decisively was due primarily to competition for business and jobs in the increasingly integrated national economy of the 1930s. This theme or explanation for state impotence endures in studies of American federalism and state government.

Others writing in this period agreed with Gulick's assessment. Although some believed the corrupt and ineffective states lacked the will to act, most based their criticisms on the inability of individual states to respond to the economic crisis of that period. It was assumed that solving the massive economic crisis required national means of command and control. "All essential powers affecting economic planning and control must be taken from the states and given to the Nation" (Gulick 1933, 421). If this takeover occurred, what responsibilities would remain for the states? Gulick contends they would perform the tasks of "creating and maintaining the organs of local government and service."

In some contrast to these criticisms of the states and strong nationalist sentiments in the 1930s, U.S. Supreme Court Justice Brandeis, writing in 1931, characterized a major role of state governments as experimentation. In *New State Ice Co. v. Ernest A. Leibman,* Brandeis argued in his dissenting opinion that the massive economic and social problems of the Great Depression might be solved by legitimate state experimentation. The states could serve as laboratories for social change. "It is one of the happy incidents of the federal system that a single courageous state may, if its citizens choose, serve as a laboratory, and try novel social and economic experiments without risk to the rest of the country" (Pollack 1956, 161).

Although some states experimented and developed innovative policies and programs in the decades following Brandeis's dissent, the forces of nationalization and centralization continued. Unfortunately for the states and the advocates of the Brandeis viewpoint of American federalism, the most visible example of state autonomy and activism continued to be segregation and states' rights, especially in the 1950s and 1960s. The complex issue of state discretion and autonomy in the federal system became simplified and stereotyped as a question of segregation and racism. As a practical matter, how could one advocate a strong, active role for the states without also supporting racial segregation? Riker (1964, 155) equated the federal principle in the United States with racism. "Thus, if in the United States one approves of Southern white racists, then one should approve of American federalism."

Many of the later criticisms of the states were somewhat more theoretical or analytic than those of Gulick and others from the 1930s. Landau (1969) based his analysis of state governments on two competing images of federalism—the classic mechanistic model, which focuses on the maintenance of a relatively fixed balance and equilibrium between state and nation, and the instrumental model, which views federalism as an evolving system for social change and problem-solving. From this evolutionary perspective, Landau (p. 135) saw the result of a "long, uneven, but inexorable process of transfer" of authority to the central government as what he called the crisis of the states. "They have had to yield to a 'system dominated by the pervasiveness of federal power.' They have lost status, prestige, and power. They have lost so much, Leonard White stated, 'that competent observers at home and abroad have declared that American federalism is approaching its end.' Roscoe Drummond put it more directly: 'our federal system no longer exists.'"

Landau believed the system to be so out of balance by the 1960s that "it simply does not possess federal characteristics," and therefore the mechanistic view of a fixed balance of power was no longer appropriate or meaningful. His answer was to use the evolutionary or biological model to explain the development of American federalism. "From a collection of loose, uncentralized or decentralized units, the United States, as we are prone to speak, has evolved into a highly centralized, integrated community which exhibits symbiotic relationships. It no longer possesses federal characteristics. The history (evolution) of the last century is a striking story of vast changes in the structure of society and the needs it generated. That nation concealed under federalism finally emerged. The United States has been for a long time now becoming the United State" (p. 137).

Landau's vision is one of a system moving continuously toward centralized power and control. He described the 1930s and 1960s as periods of intense centralization, with the balance tipping significantly to the national government in those periods and by implication not returning at other times to more state power and authority. He viewed this phenomenon as part of the "voyage to nationhood," which conflicts with federalism. "The more we become an integrated nation, the less the need for federalism" (p. 140). The empirical question is to what degree we have become an "integrated nation," and whether government, or the "state," has developed concurrent with this social and economic integration. The normative question is whether more centralized and powerful government or a "strong state" is desirable.

Bell (1989, 49) moves to a level of abstraction beyond federalism or intergovernmental relations and argues there is no American State in the Hegelian sense. Because of individual self-interest and "passion for liberty," this nation has no unified, rational will expressed in a political order. Rather than a state, there is a government. The U.S. government is a political marketplace of contending ideas and interests based on constitutional protection of individual rights and economic liberty. Stillman (1991, 39) sees the American "stateless" nation formed in 1787 as making governance somewhat indeterminant and the administrative state impossible to define. "It is always open to change and revision. Clear, swift action that would benefit the majority and offer long-term payoffs to future generations is often infrequent and hard to come by because the system is so diffuse and open, without any well-designed, stable administrative system."

Although not disagreeing with the contention that American government has become more centralized over time, Bell contends that this change was unplanned and ideologically inconsistent and that it occurred primarily during times of crisis. Although centralization of government has occurred, he does not foresee the development of a strong state in America, primarily because of a balance between centralization and factionalism. In Bell's view, this balance is based on a distinct American political culture which attempts to avoid the "centrifugal dangers of faction and the centripetal hazards of centralized powers" (p. 51). Huntington (1981) focuses more on the potential hazards of centralized power with his contention that a fundamental component of the American Creed is fear of and opposition to power, especially that of big government. Conflicting interpretations of the nationalization thesis and the role of the states in our federal system will be discussed in more detail below and in subsequent chapters.

States as Meaningful Territorial Entities

Because of nationalization of the economy, population growth and movement, and advances in transportation and mass communications, the United States is alleged by some analysts to have become a national, highly centralized government and society. By implication, states and localities hardly matter any more (Landau 1969; Sundquist with Davis 1969). A pro-centralization argument mixing normative and empirical components can be constructed from the following points:

Most problems facing the nation are national in scope. States cannot deal effectively or efficiently with interstate problems, and in modern, industrial nations most social and economic problems cross state or regional political boundaries.

The unequal distribution of wealth and resources among the states creates huge and undesirable inequities in costs and benefits of state government policies.

There is more conflict than cooperation between states; therefore, a conflict mediator is necessary, and the only viable mediator is the federal government. There are numerous current examples of these interstate conflicts—solid waste transport, the savings and loans and banking crises, energy production and consumption, and the like.

It is easier for narrow, special interests to escape effective regulation at the state level than at the federal level. States lack the fiscal/economic tools and administrative/regulatory infrastructure to control industries under the pressures of increasingly mobile capital.

State and local governments are not closer to citizens than the national government; therefore, these subnational governments often escape citizen and media scrutiny. Small community size and resulting homogeneity of outlook are often closely related to inequalities of power.

Lack of citizen and media scrutiny and pressure not to overburden or overregulate existing businesses for fear of losing mobile capital lead to state and local government ineffectiveness and corruption.

The federal government raises considerable amounts of revenue and returns much of it to the states; therefore, it should control allocation and use of these funds. Without such control, state and local governments have few incentives to use these funds from the federal government effectively and efficiently. If states and localities do not have to be responsible for raising the revenue, they will be profligate in spending.

State and local officials continually seek additional federal dollars; therefore, they are relatively satisfied with the current system. Under this system, they do not have to make painful taxing decisions but still are able to spend revenue raised by another source.

State political institutions are weak, underdeveloped, and less capable than the federal government is of democratic policy-making. States have antiquated constitutions and inequitable, inefficient tax systems. They have understaffed, amateurish legislatures and weak governors and executive institutions. These incapacities have led to necessary expansion of federal action to meet needs and demands for solving social and economic problems.

Since it is the somewhat invisible, middle tier of the federal system, citizens tend not to identify with or display any loyalty to state governments and do not participate in public affairs at the state level.

States have neglected or abandoned their urban areas, requiring strong federal action to deal with the serious economic and social problems of these areas.

Finally, as we have seen, William Riker (1964) argues that American federalism, or "states' rights," equals racism.

If the evidence for nationalization is persuasive and these arguments for centralization are valid, then the answer to the question whether "the states of the United States matter (or are they of no political consequence)" (Erikson, McIver, and Wright 1987, 798) is self-evident. If states are of no political, economic, or social consequence, there would be little justification for examining public opinion and the institutions and policies of the American states. There would be no reason to expect that the public would display much knowledge of or concern with state government affairs. Before examining in detail public opinion and state government in subsequent chapters, the remainder of this chapter questions the centralization arguments and presents evidence that states are indeed meaningful and important units of government that have expanded their roles and responsibilities over the past two decades.

The following sections review theories and research findings relating to the components of this nationalization argument and to the issue of whether the American states are important and consequential actors in our federal system, or whether they are weak, placid, reactive components of a highly centralized governmental system. Certain sections also address the issue of whether the public identifies with or displays loyalties toward this middle level of our intergovernmental system. The evidence in each section is meant to be illustrative rather than complete and definitive. It is hoped that the cumulative effect of the evidence in these sections is to demonstrate that the American states are consequential politically, as well as socially and economically, and that the arguments for nationalization are incomplete and sometimes erroneous.

Constitutional Perspectives and Federalism

There are many theoretical, normative, and empirical justifications for examining state publics or electorates. Perhaps the most fundamental justification is based on historical and constitutional origins of the peculiar American system of mutual governmental influence, which Beer (1978) calls representational federalism. According to Beer, "Governing himself through two different governments, the voter views the political world through two perspectives, one shaped by the social pluralism of the general government, the other shaped by the territorial pluralism of state government. In his political life, as a member of one nation, he does not separate from one another the two perspectives and the interests each elicits in him. His state perspective affects his choices and decisions in federal politics as his federal perspective affects his choices and decisions in state politics" (p. 15).

Although Beer does not present a precise distinction between the two perspectives, he does provide a political, or representational, view of federalism. In Beer's view, the rationale for the states is representational, not administrative, economic, or cultural. He does not argue for a states' rights interpretation of the constitution, nor does he believe that dual federalism is relevant for the present stage of political and economic development in this nation. He does contend, however, that the framers intended one people and one nation with a division of powers between a general government and smaller, territorial governments. The key to this system of mutual influence (not balance) comes from Hamilton in Federalist 28. "Power being almost always the rival of power, the general government will at all times stand ready to check the usurpations of the state governments, and these will have the same disposition towards the general government. The people, by throwing themselves into either scale, will infallibly make it preponderate. If their rights are invaded by either, they can make use of the other as the instrument of redress" (Hamilton, Jay, and Madison 1937, 174).

Hamilton's view is of a rational, active electorate presumably supporting one or the other level of government on the basis of political or policy issues. Since each level of government will have some distinct powers as well as shared powers, people will gravitate to one or the other level, depending on the issues and circumstances.

Another example of historical assertions of state identifications comes from Madison, who states in Federalist 46: "Many considerations . . . seem to place it beyond doubt that the first and most natural attachment of the people will be to the governments of their respective States" (p. 305). It should be noted that Madison as the "defender of the national principle" (Diamond 1961, 33) was arguing in Federalist 46 that this attachment to the states would make it more difficult for a strong central government to prevail and that therefore the proponents of the federal principle should have little to fear from a national government.

Although not arguing for dual federalism, Beer suggests there is a "dual electorate" or some sense of identifiable and separate sets of attitudes and beliefs about government based on distinctions between the national and state governments. When viewed historically, there is considerable doubt about Madison's assertion of a "first attachment." However, if the idea is expanded to consider comparative attachments to levels or territorial units of government, several testable hypotheses emerge. Since the notion of a dual electorate is not discussed in any detail in Beer's analysis, many questions remain concerning attachments of people to one or another level of government.

Political Culture and a Dual Electorate

In a strong defense of the role of the states in the U.S. federal system, Elazar (1972) does not address directly the issue of a dual electorate or a state electorate in analyzing American federalism. He argues, however, for the states as "civil societies," a concept which could accommodate easily the notion of a dual electorate. Similar to Beer, Elazar in his noncentralized "partnership" model of federal democracy argues that the states and the general government must negotiate cooperative arrangements, with the states acting as equal partners with the national government.

In this arrangement, "proper use of the systemic aspects of a state's civil society enhances the possibility for the people and interests dominating the state's political system to speak in the name of their state" (Elazar 1972, 11). The states are "polities" governing within their territorial jurisdictions. The key term here is "govern," which implies authoritative choices. The state does more than manage or implement programs established by the national government on the basis of national goals and priorities, which is the concept of administrative federalism as suggested by Dahl (1967) and Sundquist with Davis (1969).

This conception of civil societies or polities is developed in much detail by Elazar in discussions of three distinct political cultures that are intermixed in each state. These varying cultural patterns play a major role in determining basic beliefs and attitudes of the inhabitants of the states. Examining settlement patterns and the dispersion of social and religious groups throughout the emerging United States, Elazar (1972, chap. 4) describes the varying spatial location or development of three political cultures. The Traditionalist Culture is elitist, maintains the status quo, and is highly personalized and paternalistic; the Moralistic Culture is highly participative, public spirited, nonpartisan, and oriented to community service; and the Individualistic Culture is utilitarian, personalistic, and businesslike.

The American states are characterized by varying combinations of these three related political cultures, with one tending to predominate in each state. One implication of Elazar's theory is that states differ significantly in their political/governmental systems, depending on the mix of political cultures in each state. In addition, the distinct state culture somehow both determines and is determined by public attitudes and beliefs. Many researchers have focused on Elazar's conceptualization and found political cultures to be an attractive but elusive way of characterizing differences between the states, regions, and localities (Sharkansky 1969; Lowery and Sigelman 1982; Nardulli 1990). Still, Elazar's conception of political cultures calls attention to differences in public values, attitudes, and beliefs across state boundaries, suggesting the existence of distinct state electorates.

Political Representation

Related to historical/constitutional arguments for state vitality and autonomy are perspectives on political representation and popular control of government. Are states viable sources, guardians, or protectors of democracy? Reichley (1964, 261) argued that political legitimacy was the most fundamental problem facing the states in the 1960s and asked, "Do the states, after all, have any real basis for continued existence? Do they inspire loyalty and respect in the hearts of their citizens?" As discussed above, Dahl (1967), in analyzing optimal units for popular control of government, concluded they do not. The alternative hypothesis that citizens identify with or are loyal to state governments (or as Madison claimed in Federalist 46, they form a "first and most natural attachment" to state governments) will be examined throughout the remaining chapters.

Although Riker (1964, 104) characterizes the American system as one of "centralized federalism," he asserts that not only are state governments independent of central institutions because of a direct relationship with the electorate (the key institution being a widely decentralized party system) but more fundamental to this separation or independence is a "sense of national and state identification." Despite the presumed existence of this dual identification (Riker uses the term "dual citizen loyalties" on p. 136), he suggests that identification with states has declined since the eighteenth century and that the decline has accelerated in this century. He believes a "gradual transfer of patriotism from state to nation" has occurred (p. 105). The hypothesized causes of this increased nationalism are mobility of labor and leaders, the existence of a common culture (which includes nationalized markets and communications), and military and quasi-military inculcation of patriotism.

In addition to the arguments advanced by Riker for the increased nationalization of mass identification with government, what other factors might inhibit the formation of separate, identifiable electorates forming around state issues and interests? In asserting that private or special interests exercise strong and disproportionate power and control in the states, which diminishes the role of the public, McConnell (1966) argues that states are not the appropriate units for popular control. If there is a strong interest-group system or a traditional political culture or a weak party system (or dominant one-party system), it is less likely that ordinary citizens will be aware of and concerned with state issues and institutions. Consequently, the public is less likely to participate in the relatively closed state polity, other things being equal. If McConnell's view of state government and politics is correct, it is not likely that the public will identify with, have knowledge of, or participate in state government affairs. As we shall see, however, evidence from state electoral and party systems tends to undermine some of the arguments of Riker and McConnell.

Nationalization of Elections and the Electorate

Related directly to questions of political representation and the existence of state electorates is the question of whether the states are becoming nationalized or homogenized politically. The evidence suggests that they are not, at least in terms of electoral and party systems.

One important structural change in state electoral systems has been the "decoupling" of federal and state elections. Only twelve states now hold gubernatorial elections in presidential election years, compared with thirty-four in 1932 (Salmore and Salmore 1989, 184). More candidate-centered contests for governor and increased money from political action committees are additional (and some would argue undesirable) indicators of changes in state electoral politics. The party system or systems in this country are related to these decentralizing trends in elections.

Although Ladd and Hadley (1978) contend that a two-tiered system of party politics exists, with differential effects of national and state forces, Jewell and Olson (1982, chap. 8) raise several issues concerning the future of state political parties, including the rise of independent voting, declines in party organizations, and the opening up of primary elections. Despite these concerns, they see signs of strength and revitalization in state party systems. On the basis of assessments of staffing, budgeting, fund-raising, polling, and other services, Bibby and his colleagues (1983) report wide variation in the organizational strengths of state and local party organizations. Although Republicans have increased in strength and Democrats have declined since 1960, "both parties were organizationally stronger at the state level in 1980 than they were in the 1960s" (p. 83). Despite the increase in Republican party organizational strength, in terms of party competition, states have become more Democratic and somewhat less competitive over time (p. 67).

Chubb (1988, 133) sees state governments as developing politically or becoming more institutionalized. "Its institutions have been growing in size, competence, and legitimacy while control of them has become the object of increasing competition." Elections are a key part of this developmental process, and Chubb believes that "insulation from powerful political shocks and surges is a virtual prerequisite for institutional stability and development." Chubb examines state election results in the period 1940–82 to assess the extent to which "major periodic forces— coattails, turnout, and economic conditions" affect outcomes and finds that institutionalization has insulated state legislative elections against these shocks and surges. Related to Chubb's finding of some insulation of state legislative races from national forces are conclusions drawn by Vertz, Frendreis, and Gibson (1987). Using election results in the period 1962–84 with a variance components model, these authors find that although presidential races are highly nationalized, Senate and gubernatorial races have a large state-level component to them.

The implication of these findings is that at least electorally, states are becoming more independent or autonomous, with the potential for the development of state electorates that can be distinguished from a national electorate.

Public Choice and Political Representation

Analysts in the public choice school, or advocates of a "theory of competitive federalism" (Dye 1990), contend that the existence of state and local governments competing with one another helps to ensure that citizens will obtain the "best array of public services at the lowest costs" (p. xv). By implication, this increased satisfaction of citizen preferences by more responsive public officials not only is more desirable from a utility maximizing perspective but also is more democratic.

In order for this theory to be viable or to work in practice, states must be meaningful or consequential units of government or territorial jurisdictions that can make authoritative allocations of values (goods and services). Also, voter-taxpayers must have information and participate in state governance (or move to another jurisdiction if they become sufficiently dissatisfied with the mix of policies being offered locally). "Competitive federalism requires that voter-taxpayers within the states bear the burdens, as well as the benefits, of their own choices" (Dye 1990, xvi). One implication of this model is that people identify with, have some knowledge of, and participate in the public affairs of the states in which they reside. If these behaviors occur, one could hypothesize that state electorates will form.

Peterson (1981) also takes a public choice perspective in relating types of policies to the three levels of government in our federal system.

> There are structured differences in the expenditure policies of the three levels of government as well. Allocation is the function that local governments can perform more effectively than central governments, because decentralization allows for a closer match between the supply of public services and their variable demand. Citizens migrate to those communities where the allocation best matches their demand curve. Redistribution on the other hand, is a national function. The more a local community engages in redistribution, the more the marginal benefit/tax ratio for the average taxpayer declines, and the more the local economy suffers. The state can be expected to have policy responsibilities midway between. Finally, developmental policies will be the shared responsibility of all levels of government. (p. 77)

On the basis of several assumptions, the public choice model argues that competition among states and localities for mobile capital and economic growth without excessive taxation for the median voter allows citizens to influence state and local policy choices through the ballot box and other political action (i.e., by "voice") or through moving from one jurisdiction to another (i.e., "exit"). The remaining alternatives for the citizen (loyalty or neglect) appear to have little relevance to the rational public choice perspective. Loyalty and neglect imply more affect or emotion than rational choice. Some might argue, however, that loyalty or neglect can be quite rational and self-interested responses to certain political or personal circumstances. In addition to questions of the extent to which the types of political behaviors are rational or emotional, there is some question whether the four categories are mutually exclusive.

Although both exit and voice might help strengthen democracy or promote more congruence between voter preferences and government policies (assuming relatively autonomous government jurisdictions), the concept of voice appears more compatible with the notion of a separate public identification with state government. Or perhaps it is more reasonable to suggest that citizens who move from one state to another to escape undesirable state policies or to find more desirable mixes of policies elsewhere may be less likely to identify strongly with the level of state government and thereby less likely to become part of a hypothesized state electorate, at least on more than a sporadic, self-interested, issue-specific basis. This hypothesis (as well as the entire framework of public choice) is based on the assumption of rationality, which contrasts with the conception of identification with state government as primarily an emotional attachment or symbolic predisposition (loyalty).

Public choice models concentrate on political and economic competition between the states. In their desire to attract jobs and capital (or prevent the loss of these desired goods), state officials will attempt to offer the public and certain state interest groups a mix of tax and spending packages that simultaneously encourages business growth and provides needed public services—obviously a delicate balance. In this competition, to what extent are states constrained by external political and economic forces, thereby leading to less autonomy?

The States and Economic Competition

Because of competition for resources that have become increasingly mobile, states are thought to be highly constrained in policy-making and regulatory behavior. Peterson (1981) argues that state and local governments are constrained politically because in competing for mobile capital and business investments, they are unable to withstand the pressures of business constituents. Neither public sentiment nor any evidence that policies often fail to achieve stated goals has much effect on these pressures. Because of these political and economic constraints, certain policies will be enacted regardless of whether they are in the public interest. This competitive pressure is believed to reduce state autonomy substantially.

Related to interstate competition for jobs and business growth is the question of whether the existence of a nationalized economy precludes effective state autonomy. As states compete for mobile capital and other resources, are state economies becoming more similar and national? Brace (1989) finds that although state economies have become more autonomous since the late 1960s, they are still very dependent on external forces, primarily the national economy. Despite this overall dependence, states continue to vary in the extent to which they are independent of external forces, and there is some evidence that these differences may be meaningful to the public. Chubb (1988, 140) examines changes in state per capita income over time and suggests that "there would appear to be sufficient differences in state economic conditions for voters to react to them." He also finds, however, that variation in state growth rates has declined steadily over time, suggesting increased nationalization of state economies.

Chubb uses aggregate economic and electoral data to examine the relationship between economic conditions and gubernatorial and state legislative races. He finds that in the period 1940–82 the electoral fortunes of state legislators and governors were much less affected by state economic conditions than by changes in the national economy. This finding that state elections are not much affected by the performance of state economies raises questions about models of interstate competition proposed by Peterson and others. If voters hold the president and the president's party primarily responsible for economic conditions, and if elected state officials realize this, why would these officials feel pressured to enact suboptimal, counterproductive, or undesirable policies?

One obvious answer is that they would do so because of pressures from elites and special interest groups rather than from voters (McConnell 1966). Ambrosius (1989b, 64) argues that certain occupational interests in the states use political power to have policies enacted that will enlarge their share of state benefits, regardless of the impact of the policy on overall economic growth (and by implication, regardless of the preferences of the citizens of the state). With this interpretation, the key demander of government policies and services supplied by politicians may be, not the median voter, but the "median special interest group."

Economic competition and "public choice" no doubt affect state policy-making. These models, however, are based on rather stringent assumptions concerning the rationality of voters and public officials and on the attentiveness of the public to state policy issues and the attentiveness of policy-makers to the public. Regardless of the extent to which the public choice model is based on rational voters and policy-makers, there is much evidence of meaningful differences across states in economic performance.

Nationalization and State Policy-Making

Do states play a significant or consequential role in the domestic public policy process, or are they mere administrative arms of the federal government? If, as Peterson (1981) contends, the national government will be most likely to enact redistributive policies, and if the states have lost autonomy and authority to the central government, one would expect policy and spending differences across the states to have declined over time. This would be the case especially after the surge of federal government activism and centralization in the 1960s. Are states becoming similar in policies, or do important variations in policies exist across state boundaries?

Hofferbert and Sharkansky (1971) examine cross-sectional state and local expenditure data over the period 1890–1962 and find significant decreases in variation over time. This is due to states with lower levels of policy activity increasing their spending at a faster rate than states with higher levels of spending. Although federal aid is recognized as contributing to this policy "nationalization," they suggest that emulation or diffusion of policies across states may be the most appealing explanation (p. 472). Despite evidence for the states' becoming more alike in terms of spending patterns, they do not believe that "the states are becoming amorphous units in a mass system"; rather, "plenty of diversity remains in the American states" (p. 474).

Using a later period, but with an approach similar to Hofferbert and Sharkansky, Kemp (1978) examines variance across states in four policy areas—state/local expenditures in education, health, welfare, and highways—and finds no significant decrease in relative variation in the period 1958–74. She concludes that there is little evidence to support a nationalization thesis. "Relative variation has remained fairly stable over the past 17 years; absolute variation has increased in all four policy areas" (p. 243). Dye (1990, 42) also finds little or no change in variance in spending across states over the past three decades.

Instead of expenditure differences, Peterson and Rom (1989, 714–15) examine average monthly payments of the Aid to Families with Dependent Children program as one indicator of state welfare policy and find that "as much variability in benefit policies existed in 1985 as in 1940." These inequalities across the states in AFDC benefit levels as well as the overall decline in real dollars of the benefits are mitigated somewhat by the federally controlled food stamp program, which gives higher benefits to those in states with lower cash benefits.

In addition to research using state/local spending variance over time, which attempts to trace systematically the extent to which policy-making has become centralized, it is reasonable to ask a basic descriptive question: What is the role of the states in formulating and implementing domestic policy in this country? Domestic policy-making, program implementation, and service delivery increasingly have become characterized by intergovernmental complexity involving three levels of government and numerous public, nonprofit, and even private organizations.

Despite the stereotype of a top-down governmental system, with the national government enacting laws and state and local government units implementing federal mandates, subnational governments maintain substantial autonomy in designing policies and programs within their own borders, and they also exert much influence on the formulation and adoption of federal policies. Although not extensive or conclusive, some previous research shows that states have significant responsibilities and influence in the implementation of intergovernmental policies (Goggin et al. 1990).

One important indicator of the autonomy of state and local governments relative to the federal government is the ability to acquire support and resources from taxpayers. In a study of the "crisis and anticrisis dynamic" in fiscal federalism, Kee and Shannon (1992) compare "own-source general revenues" for the federal and state and local governments in the period 1940–90. They find that since the "super crisis" of World War II, which gave Washington an enormous revenue-raising advantage, "the comparative general revenue-raising advantage has decisively shifted back to the state-local sector, and the great revenue imbalance that had long favored Washington has now virtually disappeared" (p. 322). From 1944 to 1990, own-source general revenue as a percentage of GNP declined from 23.5 to 13.7 percent for the federal government and increased from 4.9 to 13.2 percent for state and local governments.

Another factor in maintaining autonomy in public policy-making is institutional capability. In the face of complex socioeconomic and political pressures, state institutions have adapted and reformed. Bowman and Kearney (1986) document four waves of state executive branch reform, including the professionalization of the state bureaucracy (chap. 2) and reform of state legislatures (chap. 3). They conclude that both branches have been "reformed and rejuvenated" through better-trained and better-paid staff, improved management capabilities, streamlined procedures, greater accountability, more effective leadership, and the like.

The effects of these reforms on state policies and programs are not always clear or documented systematically, although some research, including case-studies as well as comparative and quantitative approaches, shows some positive impacts (Dye 1969; Grumm 1971; Karnig and Sigelman 1975; Roeder 1979; Herzik and Brown 1991). Bowman and Kearney (1986, 11–31) argue that institutional reform has been a major factor in the greatly expanded "scope of state operations," including innovations and expansions in productivity improvement, capital formation, energy planning and conservation, and criminal justice and public education reform. Not only are the states expanding and intensifying their operations, but "in some cases they are capturing policy fields from the federal government" (p. 27).

To support these somewhat general assertions of the role of the American states in public policy-making, we might ask more specifically what state governments actually do. Although state and local government spending as a percentage of the GNP has leveled off at about 13 percent since the 1970s (compared with the growth of federal spending in this period from about 18 to 22 percent of the GNP), state and local governments continue to have major policy responsibilities in education, health, welfare, highways, and public safety (Dye 1990, 35–40). The federal government contributes only small percentages of overall spending for education and public safety, with larger percentages for health and welfare. Even in the areas with larger proportions of federal dollars, state and local governments have much discretion in the implementation and administration of programs. States have significant responsibilities for criminal justice policies and programs and regulation of utilities, insurance, and other commercial enterprises within their jurisdictions. More detailed descriptions of state policy activities and responsibilities in certain of these areas will be provided in later chapters dealing with substantive policy issues.

In contrast to these findings of an important state role in domestic policy-making, Rose (1973) questions the viability of the states. Using a partitioning-of-variance approach to state policy-making, he questions the impact of the state in certain areas. He contends that states are not viable political systems but components of a national system dominated by national norms and policy goals. Using analysis of variance to compare the impact of the state on individual behaviors such as incidence of rape, divorce, infant mortality, selective service exam failures, auto registrations, aid to blind recipients, disabled recipients, and the like, he finds that states did not account for any meaningful variance in these behaviors. The flaws in this approach have been discussed by several subsequent researchers (Lyons and Morgan 1976; Wanat and Roeder 1976).

Overall, previous research finds little evidence that state policy-making has become nationalized. Even in those areas where some evidence exists for states' adopting similar policies and programs, it is difficult to sort out the effects of federal mandates with their incentives and penalties from the effects of interstate emulation or adoption of innovations (Walker 1969; Gray 1973; Welch and Thompson 1980).

Closely related to state policy-making, program autonomy, and spending patterns are questions of state administration. Have state governments somehow become administrative arms of the federal government, or are state bureaucracies relatively independent of federal control, with meaningful variations in organization structure and performance?

States as Intermediate Administrative Units

As discussed previously, Dahl (1967, 968) characterized the states as becoming "intermediate instruments of coordination and control," existing in a "limbo of quasi-democracy" led or "controlled by the full-time professionals." Others have viewed states as intermediaries or gatekeepers in the federal system. If accurate, Dahl's vision—the popular conception of the model bureaucratic state—would seem to be either the dream or the nightmare of many. Presumably Dahl believes that a cadre of professional state officials (elected and appointed?) will administer national policies, with the public participating meaningfully only in national and perhaps local politics.

In a related approach, Sundquist argues that in the 1960s the states became mere middle managers in the federal system, useful primarily for carrying out policies of the federal government, using large portions of revenue raised at the national level (Sundquist with Davis 1969). Although he frames the issue as one of administrative coordination of the complex system of grants-in-aid, the key is "close federal supervision and control to assure that the national purposes are served" (p. 3). Since the national government would contribute 50 percent and more to finance new and expanded domestic programs, Sundquist believes that states and communities would have little stake in the programs and therefore that "the expenditures must be closely supervised by the federal government from the standpoint of economy as well as substance" (p. 5).

Sundquist also proposes a model for how social problems become recognized by the public and become part of an intergovernmental policy agenda. This model has implications for the concept of a dual or state electorate.

> As a major internal problem develops—or comes to public attention—public attitudes appear to pass through three phases. As the problem begins to be recognized, it is seen as local in character, outside the national concern. Then, as it persists and it becomes clear that the states and communities are unable to solve it unaided (partly because the same political groups that oppose federal action are wont to oppose state and local action too), the activists propose federal aid, but on the basis of helping the states and communities cope with what is still seen as their problem. Finally, the locus of basic responsibility shifts: the problem is recognized as in fact not local at all but as a national problem requiring a national solution that states and communities are mandated, by one means or another, to carry out—usually by inducements strong enough to

produce a voluntary response but sometimes by more direct, coercive means. (p. 11)

Although providing no evidence or examples of problems and policies as they might pass through these phases or this process of opinion/ problem development, Sundquist contends that "in matters relating to the fundamental nature of society," the nation is well into the final phase. In effect, Sundquist is turning the adage "all politics is local" to "all problems become national."

Despite the almost exclusive emphasis on central control, Sundquist appears to recognize the difficulty of coercive measures as "limited in their applicability." He sees the basic dilemma of the Great Society as "how to achieve goals and objectives that are established by the national government, through the action of other governments, state and local, that are legally independent and politically may be even hostile" (p. 12). Although bargaining among national and state and local officials is the primary means of maintaining and operating the federal system, in his view the national government continues to be responsible for making policy, setting goals, and managing this new system. Apparently the bargaining and negotiation is between one very strong actor and fifty or more ineffectual subnational actors. Such a conceptualization of the intergovernmental system seems to render somewhat meaningless the term "negotiation." Again, this vision of Sundquist is what many believe is the ideal of a top-down system of policy-making and implementation.

Sundquist (p. 27) becomes even more prescriptive, arguing that with national government assistance the states somehow must become more competent and effective participants in the federal system. Rather than a legal perspective, with negotiations collectively between states and the federal government, the federal government decides how much each state can be relied upon or trusted and then confers on that individual state the appropriate amount of administrative responsibility for federal programs. The implication of this model is that under federal pressure, state administrative systems will become more alike. Despite Sundquist's advocacy of centralized federalism, just as the political cultures or public policies of the states might vary substantially, so state administrative structures may differ from state to state.

There is very little comparative, empirical research on state administrative structures and processes that might answer some of the claims
advanced by Sundquist. Not only are difficulties faced in judging
bureaucratic performance relative to efficiency, effectiveness, accountability, integrity, and the like, but comparing the administrative structures of different levels of government is even more problematic. Elling
(1983, 267) discusses the even more complex issue of the impact of state
bureaucracies in the policy-making process and the lack of systematic,
quantitative studies in this important area. The role of state bureaucracies in policy formulation and adoption goes far beyond the
narrow role specified by Sundquist. Little systematic research exists,
however, to document this policy-making role.

One of the few comparative studies of state bureaucracies finds variation in the quality of administration at this level (Sigelman 1976). Examination of seven standards of quality finds correlations among indicators
of "professional" and "political" standards, but not between them. The
quality of administration is higher in more affluent, industrialized, urban states. Although these standards are not applied to federal bureaucracies, the variation found by Sigelman suggests that states are not
homogenized administrative arms of the federal government. Also,
there is no evidence that the states are somehow inferior to the federal
government in these areas, despite Sundquist's argument for central
control and national standards.

In addition to variation in overall administrative performance, analysts find meaningful interstate differences in specific policy areas. In
addition to the research discussed in the previous section on policy-
making, Derthick (1987, 68) examines state administrative activities in
welfare policies (Supplemental Security Income and Aid to Families
with Dependent Children) and concludes: "Despite fears of some par-
tisans of the states that they were being turned into mere administrative
agents of an overbearing central government, federalism lives. It is
manifest in the persistence of interstate differences in program characteristics and in the ineffectiveness of much federal oversight of state
administration."

This assessment of arguments derived from theories of democracy,
federalism, intergovernmental relations, and public choice finds little
unambiguous evidence for increased nationalization of public policy-
making and policy implementation or for the view that the United States

has become a highly centralized political system. Disagreement persists over the precise distribution of the relative power of federal and state governments in domestic policy-making. There is much evidence, however, for the vitality and activism of state governments within the intergovernmental system. The next chapter examines relationships between public opinion and public policy, especially at the level of the American state, and, using data from national public opinion surveys, develops a composite measure of level of government identification.

3
Public Opinion and Levels of Government

Because of major social and economic transformations, continued demands for government services and regulations, and the apparently diminished role of the federal government in numerous policy areas, state governments have assumed greater responsibilities over the past two decades. There is some dispute over the extent to which these new or increased responsibilities result from federal government mandates (funded and unfunded), which the states follow reluctantly, or result from policy decisions initiated, implemented, and funded primarily by state governments (in which view the states are heroic or entrepreneurial). There is also a question whether recent changes are only a pause in the continuing ascendancy of the national government, or whether there is some periodicity in the surge and decline of national government power. Regardless of the answers to these questions, there is considerable evidence that during this period, state institutions have grown in visibility and capability and that these institutions have adopted and implemented numerous innovative policies. This chapter asks what role, if any, the public has played in these changes.

After discussing the role of public opinion in American democracy and assessing previous research on state public opinion and public policy, this chapter examines the extent to which citizens recognize and support an increased or larger role for states in the federal system—specifically, the extent to which state governments are viewed positively in terms of responsiveness, effectiveness, policy leadership, and other aspects of government performance. In addition, a composite measure of level of government identification is developed and analyzed. This measure will be used in this and later chapters as a potential explanation for political attitudes and policy preferences of the public.

In previous chapters, evidence for the existence of a state electorate was considered. This chapter will assess the assertions by Dahl (1967, 968) that the states do not "tap any strong sentiments of loyalty or likemindedness among their citizens" and by Riker (1964, 136) and others that people have "dual loyalties" to the national and state governments.

Public Opinion and Democracy

The role of public opinion on state policies and programs has not been addressed adequately. Even recent assessments viewing states as intergovernmental leaders focus primarily on government innovation and elite problem-solving, with little or no discussion of public involvement in these efforts. For example, an influential book by Osborne (1988) focuses almost exclusively on the role of elites (primarily governors) in state attempts to stimulate or promote economic growth. The book is subtitled *A New Breed of Governor Creates Models for National Growth*.

Van Horn's assessment of the state of the states (1989) focuses primarily on governors, legislatures, courts, political parties, and bureaucracies. The term "public opinion" is not found in the index of the book. The book by Bowman and Kearney (1986) on the resurgence of the states contains a chapter entitled "Citizen Participation in State Politics" which addresses several issues such as voter turnout, volunteerism, and institutional matters such as political party activities and interest groups. Except for a brief discussion on the lack of public confidence in the federal government, there is little focus on public opinion and its possible relationship to institutions and policies at the state level. The neglect of public opinion in these two excellent overviews of contemporary state government reflects primarily the lack of research on state government and federalism by public opinion and political behavior researchers, and the lack of research on public opinion and mass politics by researchers in comparative state politics and policy.

Although a basic question in a democracy is how citizens relate to their government, this deceptively simple question becomes even more complex when more than one level of government is involved. In the United States the middle-level, or state, government has often been the forgotten piece of the puzzle. At other times, it has been the most maligned level of government. Most political experts believe that if the public knows or cares anything about the public agencies or officials that affect them, it is the national level (dealing with "large issues" such as war and peace, the economy, and major domestic programs) or the local level (addressing immediate concerns of public safety, garbage collection, streets, and the like) that command disproportionate shares of citizen identification, knowledge, or loyalty. The predominant view is that state governments have been the invisible level of government, at least in regard to public opinion. Before discussing public opinion and levels of government, a more basic question is what role public opinion plays in a democracy.

Not surprisingly, much research indicates that executives, legislatures, and other governmental and nongovernmental elites are crucial to adoption of policies by governments. There is mixed evidence of the extent to which the public plays a role in the formulation of government policies in this country. Despite the view of some that the electorate acts as a "rational god of vengeance and reward," research dealing with representation and relationships between public policies and citizen preferences is not that conclusive. Disentangling the complex web of cause and effect is difficult, even when congruence between public opinion and policy is found.

Dye argues that there is little direct evidence that public opinion has much influence on policy. Not only do surveys reveal that the masses have little knowledge of or interest in policy questions, but the opinions of the public on governmental issues are unstable and inconsistent (1987, 326). Despite the lack of direct public influence, following the work of V. O. Key, Dye contends that elections, political parties, and interest groups ("that thin stratum of persons referred to variously as the political elite, the political activists, the leadership echelons, or the influentials") help translate citizen concerns into public policies (pp. 328–29).

In examining the gap between the expectations of democratic theory for an active, informed citizenry and the reality of public lack of knowledge and participation in the political process ("the paradox of mass politics"), Neuman (1986) argues that the key to the paradox is stratification. His "theory of three publics," based on political knowledge and sophistication as well as the costs of processing political information, is a version of the political elite argument of Key and others. Neuman (pp. 170–71) contends that the bulk of the mass public (perhaps 75 percent) are "marginally attentive to politics and mildly cynical about the behavior of politicians, but they accept the duty to vote, and they do so with fair regularity." In contrast, the apolitical strata (about 20 percent) do not share the norms of keeping informed or voting. The activist strata (about 5 percent) exhibit relatively high levels of political sophistication and "uniquely high levels of political involvement." The relative success of this stratified, democratic political system depends on the balance between "the specialized knowledge of the elite and the generalized common sense of the mass polity" (p. 189).

The above theories focus on relationships or flows of communication between elites and masses. What can be said about mass influence on public policies? Page and Shapiro (1983) examine hundreds of national surveys containing policy items from three different polling organizations in the period 1935–79. Using these policy-related survey items, they examine significant changes over time in opinion and relate these opinion changes to policy changes and find "substantial congruence between opinion and policy (especially when opinion changes are large and sustained, and issues are salient)." But "congruence" is far from causality, and the flows of communication or directions of influence between elite policy-makers and masses are not well understood. Only recently have researchers begun to assess systematically and empirically the values and attitudes of the elite, and in some cases to compare these attitudes to those of the masses of citizens (McCloskey and Zaller 1984; Verba and Orren 1985).

Although there is little evidence for the direct influence of the public on policy-making at any level in our democratic system, most analysts believe that citizens are not masses of ignorant, ill-informed nonparticipants and that public opinion has at least indirect impacts on policy-making. Neuman (1986, 184) argues that "most citizens do have carefully developed opinions on some issues and partial or vague opinions on most issues." Burstein (1981, 295) concludes that government does "what the people want in those instances where the public cares enough about an issue to make its wishes known."

In a quite different interpretation, Ginsberg (1986) argues that public opinion has been tamed or "domesticated" by modern Western governments to benefit the state. "Expansion of the role of mass opinion in political life opened the way for expansion of the size and power of the state" (p. 28). His analysis suggests little more than a relatively quiet, reactive, nonevaluative role for the public in modern Western democracies.

State Public Opinion and Public Policy

Although empirical research on state public opinion is not abundant, some support for the existence of state identifications or state electorates does exist.[1] An early analysis of public opinion and levels of government using national survey data seems to contradict Dahl's view of the "limbo of quasi-democracy" occupied by the American states. The concept of salience maps "arranged according to geopolitical units" developed by Jennings and Zeigler (1970) refers to an individual's relative interest in or identification with certain levels of government.

Using national survey data from the 1968 American National Election Study (NES), Jennings and Zeigler analyze the attentive public for state affairs, on the basis of how closely followed state government affairs are, compared with those on other levels. Using a question asking respondents to rank-order the kinds of public affairs they follow most closely, and combining first and second ranks, they find state and local levels approximately equal in rankings ahead of international affairs but behind national affairs. They contend that "while the states may not be uppermost in the political thoughts of their residents, they do occupy a secure niche" (p. 525). In addition, they find significant differences in several political attitudes and behaviors based on the extent to which respondents attend to state politics. For example, people who pay more attention to state politics are less trusting of the world about them, feel that what Washington does makes less difference in their personal lives, and think that the federal government is playing too powerful a role in society (p. 528). They conclude, "The states still loom large in the perspectives of the American public" (p. 535). It is important to note that these opinion data are from the years following a period of major domestic policy activity by the federal government, namely, the Great Society of President Lyndon Johnson.

In contrast to Jennings and Zeigler's focus on public opinion regarding levels of government at the level of the individual, other research in this area examines relationships between aggregated state opinion and

various state policies. Most research that examines the relationship between public opinion and public policies in the American states uses
national public opinion surveys and assesses the impact of state opinion
on policy, using simulations or dummy variables to obtain state opinion
estimates. One of the earliest attempts to assess empirically the impact
of public opinion on state policy-making uses computer simulations to
measure state opinion (Weber and Shaffer 1972). National survey data
on such policy issues as gun control, support for teachers' unions, and
right-to-work laws are converted into state-by-state estimates of public
opinion based on relationships between the demographic characteristics
of the national sample and the respective demographic characteristics
of the population of each state. Using multivariate models to predict
policies, Weber and Shaffer find that certain state statutes are related
to simulated state opinion, controlling for other characteristics of the
states.

Erikson (1976) examines state opinion and policy, using an approach
different from the simulation methodology, but finds similar results.
Using Gallup survey data from the 1930s which had samples of sufficient size to provide estimates of individual state opinion, he finds
strong correlations between state opinion and state policy for the issues
of capital punishment, child labor, and female jurors. Recognizing the
high visibility and salience of these issues at the time, Erikson (p. 35)
concludes that "state legislators are rather responsive to public opinion—at least on certain issues."

Almost two decades after the Jennings and Zeigler analysis, Erikson,
McIver, and Wright (1987, 801) examine the question of empirical
support for the concept of state electorates and find that state of residence does affect significantly individuals' partisanship and political
ideology, independent of demographic characteristics. Using a survey
data-set with over 50,000 respondents from the period 1976–82, they
find that living in one state or another has roughly the same effect on
respondent ideology and partisanship as having a high rather than a low
income, being black or white, or being Jewish or Protestant. "Knowing
a person's state, therefore, does add to our ability to forecast a person's
partisanship or ideology beyond what we know from the person's demographic characteristics alone or even beyond what we know from the
person's demographics and region together" (p. 799).

After finding significant state differences, they turn to the question of the extent to which these differences are due to the different demographic characteristics of state residents or to "unique state cultures." Through a process of partitioning variances, they conclude that "most of the variance in state partisanship and state ideology is due to state-to-state differences that cannot be accounted for by demographic variables measured here" (p. 804). The residual explanation appears to be "the unique political context within each state" (p. 805). They do not find support, however, for a regional explanation, or for a "social-context" effect, or for Elazar's conceptualization of political culture, especially when the southern states are removed from the analysis. They conclude, "One's state of residence contributes somewhat to one's political attitudes, but it is not clear why this is so" (p. 812).

After demonstrating significant differences between state electorates in liberal or conservative ideological identification, these researchers next focus on relationships between state opinion (ideological identification) and state policy (composite measure of policy liberalism). Using the same survey data-set, they find significant relationships between state ideological identification and policy liberalism, controlling for median family income, percent high school graduates, and percent urban (Wright, Erikson, and McIver 1987, 990–93). "The longterm inclination of the state to enact a certain mix of liberal and conservative policies is largely determined, in a variety of ways, by state public opinion" (p. 998).

Lowery, Gray, and Hager (1989) reexamine the same data, using a longitudinal model, and find even stronger relationships between opinion and policy than Wright and his colleagues. Focusing on tax progressivity and education spending rather than the composite of liberal policy used by the latter, they find that states moved toward greater opinion-policy congruence between 1977 and 1982 for tax policy but less so for education policy. Despite these differences in policy areas, they conclude that opinion does influence policy.

In some contrast to the ambiguity of the opinion-policy relationship based on national issues and data, the very limited state-level research is relatively positive and consistent in asserting relationships between state publics and policy-makers. Such findings, although limited in scope, suggest the importance of this territorial entity called the American state and the need for further investigation of this important issue.

Comparing and Evaluating Government Institutions

In recent years numerous political commentators and pollsters have asserted that public confidence and trust in political institutions has declined. These claims are usually made in very broad terms or are linked to national institutions such as Congress and the executive branch. Available data do not support these assertions consistently. Using NES data, Lipset and Schneider (1987, 17) demonstrate that although confidence in government or trust in government declined steadily from 1958 through 1980, it actually increased from 1980 to 1984.

The items and data leading to the conclusion of declining confidence usually refer to government leaders and public officials. When Lipset and Schneider examine other items dealing with the "political system" rather than its officials or leaders, they suggest that the confidence of the American public has not declined. "It appears that the trend of declining trust in government is focused on the behavior of public officials, and not on the system itself or the institutions and norms associated with it" (pp. 27–29).

If we examine public confidence in institutions rather than in the leaders of those institutions, there is additional evidence of lack of recent decline. For example, although Gallup survey data show a steady decline in confidence in Congress from the early 1970s to the early 1980s (a drop from 42 to 28 percent of those expressing a great deal or quite a lot of confidence), the proportion increases from 28 to 41 percent from 1983 to 1986 (Gilbert 1988, 18). Despite the increase in this later period, a majority of the public still demonstrate only some or very little confidence in this national institution. Data from the General Social Surveys–National Opinion Research Center (GSS-NORC) show patterns similar to the Gallup data. Those in the GSS expressing a great deal of confidence in Congress decrease from 24 percent in 1973 to 13 percent in 1982 but increase slightly to 16 percent in 1987. The figures for the same years for the "executive branch of the federal government" are 29 to 19 to 18 percent (Niemi, Mueller, and Smith 1989, 97–99). As a comparison, the percentages expressing a great deal of confidence in the U.S. Supreme Court remain roughly in the low to mid-30s from 1973 through 1988.

Despite periods of surge and decline, a majority of Americans do not have much confidence in the U.S. Congress and the executive branch. Lipset and Schneider (1987, 61) examine Gallup data as well as data from Harris, the National Opinion Research Center, and the Opinion Research Corporation and conclude that the findings for the presidency and other major institutions of government suggest "a continuing low level of confidence from the mid-1970s to the early 1980s." They also find that institutional confidence is correlated closely with economic conditions (e.g., rates of unemployment and inflation).

In summary, public confidence in American national government varies depending on whether public officials or institutions are being evaluated, and depending on which institutions or officials are being assessed in which time period. Although confidence in general is not high, there is no clear evidence that confidence has declined since the 1970s. In fact, there is some evidence of increased confidence in American government during the Reagan administration.

In earlier periods such as the 1930s and 1960s, the claims of lack of confidence in government institutions often were made about state governments (Gulick 1933; Landau 1969). Data from the Harris Survey show somewhat less fluctuation in the period 1973–86 for public confidence in state and local governments compared with that in Congress and the national executive (Gilbert 1988, 19). The proportions expressing a great deal of confidence in state and local governments (teens and low twenties) are comparable to those for the Congress and national executive in the early to mid 1980s. This suggests relatively equal confidence (or lack of confidence) in the three levels of government in this period.

Although research discussed in the previous chapters suggests that the states were both invisible and maligned in earlier periods of our history, few researchers attempted to ascertain whether the public recognized these developments or supported increased federal government control of and responsibility for domestic government functions in these periods. Analysts did not focus on whether the public felt the United States had become a nationalized society—as Landau suggested, the United State. While it is difficult to find questions in previous studies identical to these used in the SSP to help answer the question of changes over time, there are some similar questions from other surveys.

In their study of public attitudes toward big government, Bennet and

Bennet (1990, 21–23) suggest, on the basis of surveys from the newly formed Gallup organization in the late 1930s and early 1940s, that the public favored the growth of power in the central government. Despite their conclusion, the data presented suggest ambiguity regarding federal and state power. In 1937, when asked if they favored "concentration of power in the federal government" or in the state government, people favored the federal government by a margin of approximately 4 to 3. In the same survey, however, when asked whether state governments "should transfer more of their powers to the federal government," people disapproved by a margin of 2 to 1.

In 1968, the Comparative State Elections Project (CSEP) asked respondents in which level of government they had the most confidence. Most (44 percent) named the national government, 18 percent the state, and 17 percent the localities, with 20 percent unsure (Black, Kovenock, and Reynolds 1974, 188). Similarly, the 1972 National Election Study (NES) found that almost half of the respondents had more faith and confidence in the national government than in state or local government; state government ranked in the middle, and local government last. When the same question was asked in the 1976 National Election Study, local government was ranked first by 39 percent, national government by 33 percent, and state government by 28 percent of the sample. In the 1968 CSEP survey, about one-fourth of the respondents felt that the national government "pays a lot of attention to what people think," while 33 percent gave that response for state government. Very high proportions thought the national government (85 percent) and state government (68 percent) wasted a lot of money.

The U.S. Advisory Commission on Intergovernmental Relations (ACIR) has been assessing public opinion on certain political and policy issues on a yearly basis since 1972. One question that has been asked continuously during this period is which level of government people feel they "get the most for their money?" From 1972 through 1989, respondents to the national survey consistently ranked state government (ranging from 18 to 27 percent) behind both the federal and local levels. The only exception is 1984, when state ranked ahead of the federal government by a margin of 27 to 24 percent. In 1988, although state government again ranked last, the three levels were within three percentage points of each other.

The federal government consistently ranked ahead of local government by margins of 1 to 13 percentage points until 1979. From 1979 to 1989, local government tended to finish ahead of the federal government quite often but by a large margin only in 1984 (11 percent). In this period the federal government finished ahead of local government in 1989, 1985, 1982, and 1980 (ACIR 1989, 3). It is important to note that many of these differences between levels are within the margin of error for the samples.

Although it is difficult to draw any strong conclusions from these varied data from the ACIR, the NES, and the CSEP, it appears that preference for, identification with, or confidence in both local and state governments has been growing or at least not declining since the late 1960s and early 1970s. In some contrast, confidence in the national government appears to have declined somewhat from the 1960s to the early 1980s.

SSP Survey Items Evaluating Levels of Government

Conventional wisdom concerning lack of public confidence in government, combined with survey data that are somewhat ambiguous concerning different levels of government, suggests the need for additional comparisons of public attitudes toward government at the national, state, and local levels. In the State Survey Project, several questions are asked requiring respondents to compare the three levels of government in the federal system:

> Which do you believe is most responsive to the needs and desires of the public?
> Which is most efficient when it comes to providing public services?
> Which do you believe has the most honest public officials?
> Which do you believe is the most likely to provide the leadership needed to solve the complex problems facing our society?

As responses to these items demonstrate (table 3-1), the public in 1988 ranked state government behind local government but ahead of the federal government in responsiveness, efficiency, and honesty. For the leadership item, the federal government ranked first and state govern-

Table 3-1. Level of Government Identification, 1988

Evaluation	Federal (%)	State (%)	Local (%)	N
Most responsive	19	28	53	1,114
Most efficient	18	32	51	1,105
Most honest	18	27	56	871
Most leadership	53	29	18	1,079

ment again ranked second. State government was consistently ranked in the middle, with local government and the federal government exchanging positions at opposite ends of the ranking in the area of leadership to solve problems.[2]

There are several issues to consider in these data. First, although the items were asked together in the questionnaire, respondents were not very consistent in their judgments about levels of government. There appears to be little or no "positivity bias." This is demonstrated by the major shift in preference for the federal government regarding the elusive concept of leadership ("to solve the complex problems facing our society"), and by the more than 200 respondents who answered "don't know" or "refused" to the item on honesty of public officials. Also, the high ranking of the federal government on the leadership item may be due to the reference to problems "facing our society."

A clue to the complexity of public opinion dealing with the honesty of public officials might be found in survey data provided by the ACIR. In the 1989 ACIR survey when asked "On the whole, who do you think are the most honest—federal officials, state officials, or local officials?" 25 percent volunteered the response that none of them were, and 5 percent volunteered that all were most honest (p. 5). It could be assumed that the large number of don't know or refused responses to the honesty item in the SSP survey would be distributed in a manner similar to the ACIR item if voluntary responses had been coded. This assumption would lead to similarity in responses to the two items.

Although these findings are not easy to interpret, they do suggest that respondents were making meaningful distinctions between evaluative concepts or subjects (honesty, leadership, efficiency, and responsiveness) and between levels of government. Also, the patterns appear to be somewhat understandable or explainable, suggesting that there may be some underlying logic or pattern to the perceptions. People were much less willing or able to judge which level of government had more honest public officials than which level was more responsive, efficient, or provided leadership. In addition, respondents preferred the federal government only for leadership and problem-solving and viewed it generally as more remote, inefficient, and unresponsive to citizens' preferences and needs than were state and local governments. State government was viewed consistently in the middle on the four dimensions of evaluation.

Correlations among SSP Items on Levels of Government

Responses to the SSP items on choosing levels of government can be explored further through examination of relationships between items. Table 3-2 presents the intercorrelations among the four items discussed above. As might be expected on the basis of the frequency distributions, the first three items are moderately related. The item dealing with leadership and problem-solving is less closely related to the other three items.

As a partial validity check, respondents were asked later in the survey to assess state government power. In 1988, a majority (58 percent) stated that state governments had the right amount of power. Although 31 percent believed they should have more power, only 11 percent felt they had too much power. The chi-square statistics for this state government

Table 3-2. Level of Government Identification: Inter-Item Correlations, 1988

	Efficiency	Honesty	Leadership
Responsive to public	.26	.23	.04
Efficient public services		.28	.10
Honest public officials			.11

Note: Coefficients are tau-b's. Except for the leadership and responsiveness items, all are significant at least at the .01 level.

power item and the four government identification items are all significant at least at the .01 level. Respondents choosing state government for the four preference items believed state government either had the right amount of power or should have more power. By margins of more than 5 to 1 for three items and more than 4 to 1 for the other level of government identification item, those choosing state government believed that state governments should have more power rather than that they had too much power.

The patterns of relationships indicate that the items are tapping related but somewhat different aspects of respondent identifications with levels of government. People had consistent and similar views concerning responsiveness, efficiency, and honesty of these levels but were less clear and consistent in their beliefs about the distribution of power among levels and which level provided more leadership. Although it is impossible to tell whether people saw power as a limited-sum or zero-sum game, they distinguished between levels of government and tended to prefer state over federal government power.

Composite Measure of Level of Government Identification

After analyzing separately the four survey items asking respondents to choose among levels of government, the next task is to construct a scale to categorize or differentiate persons who consistently choose one level over the others from persons who demonstrate a mix of identifications or preferences. After differentiating these categories of respondents, relationships between state, federal, and local government identifiers and their demographic characteristics, and opinions and preferences regarding government institutions and political leaders will be analyzed.

Several combinations of items and methods were examined to find a meaningful and functional scale of level of government identification. After developing a scale using the four items and examining patterns and interrelationships, it was decided to omit the item dealing with honest public officials. The primary reason for this is missing data. When the honesty item is combined with the other items, approximately 400 of the original 1,100 subjects are unavailable for analysis. The two versions of the scale (with and without the honesty item) are highly correlated; because of missing data, however, the scale based on three items results in 994 respondents available for analysis versus 774 for the four-item scale.

The first step in constructing the composite measure is to add the three items for each case using the values of 3 for federal, 2 for state, and 1 for local government responses. Summing these values results in a possible score for individuals ranging from 3 (respondent chooses local government for all three items) to 9 (respondent chooses federal for all three items). The difficulty with a simple additive scale is interpreting scores between the two extremes. For example, a respondent could have a total score of 6 by choosing state government for each of the three items or by responding one federal, one local, and one state for each item. The scores would be identical, but the interpretations would differ. To clarify and properly differentiate all the possible mid-range scores, summed scores for the three items are classified as in table 3-3.

Although only one in five respondents chose the same level of government for each of the three items (4.4 percent chose federal for all three items, 6.2 percent chose state, and 9.3 percent chose local), an addi-

Table 3-3. Classification of Level of Government Identification

Total Score	Classification	Frequency N	%
9 (3 + 3 + 3)	Federal	44	4.4
8 (3 + 3 + 2)	Federal/state	59	5.9
7 (3 + 3 + 1)	Federal/local	92	9.3
7 (3 + 2 + 2)	State/federal	100	10.1
6 (2 + 2 + 2)	State	62	6.2
6 (3 + 2 + 1)	Mixed	162	16.3
5 (1 + 2 + 2)	State/local	85	8.6
5 (1 + 1 + 3)	Local/federal	190	19.1
4 (1 + 1 + 2)	Local/state	108	10.9
3 (1 + 1 + 1)	Local	92	9.3
	Total:	994	

tional two-thirds of the sample chose the same level for two of the three items. Only 16 percent of the sample were "inconsistent" or "mixed" and preferred a different level for each item. More than 8 of 10 respondents were relatively consistent in identifying with one level of government over the other two.

The composite scale also indicates which level was chosen most often. Approximately 20 percent of respondents are in the three federal dominant categories, 25 percent in the state, and 39 percent in the local. The local/federal category is the largest single group (19 percent), followed closely by the mixed category (16 percent), with local/state and state/federal categories next with between 10 and 11 percent each.

As expected, examination of relationships between the composite measure and the items used to form the scale finds moderately close relationships between the single items and the composite. The correlations between the composite and the single items of responsiveness, efficiency, and leadership are .53, .59, and .46, respectively (all are significant tau-b's at least at the .001 level).

Socioeconomic Characteristics of Government Identifiers

After constructing the composite measure, certain characteristics of state, local, and federal identifiers are examined. On the basis of previous political and policy analyses contending that the states are either innovative, liberal heroes or conservative, do-nothing villains in our intergovernmental system, one could pose competing hypotheses of state identifiers either being more ideologically conservative, older, less educated, and more rural; or more liberal, educated, younger, and urban. Again, both these hypotheses assume congruence between mass preferences and the policy-making elites in the states. The assumption is that the institutions and policies of state government to some extent reflect the interests and preferences of its citizens and vice versa.

Examination of selected social and demographic characteristics finds that age, gender, and years lived in the state are not related to level of government identification, while education, race, and income are only moderately related to the composite measure. For example, as table 3-4 indicates, those who were most consistent in preferring the federal

Table 3-4. Characteristics of Level of Government Identifiers

| | Government Identifiers[a] | | |
Characteristic	Federal (%)	State (%)	Local (%)
Age			
< 31	29	16	23
31–60	52	68	58
61 +	19	16	19
Education			
< High school	25	10	11
High school graduate	57	55	65
College graduate +	18	35	24
Income			
< $15,000	45	19	25
$15,000–$40,000	37	65	46
$41,000 +	18	16	29
Years lived in state			
< 10	11	15	10
10–25	30	26	32
All	59	60	59
Gender (male)	39	40	45
Race (nonwhite)	24	21	20
Party identification (Democratic)	38	47	39
Presidential choice (Bush, over Dukakis)	51	41	58
Rating of Reagan (positive)	61	52	54

[a]The categories include respondents who consistently chose one level of government for each item in the scale.

government were less educated and had lower incomes than those consistently preferring either state or local government. Of the federal identifiers, 45 percent were in the lowest income category, compared with 19 percent for state and 25 percent for local government. Twenty-five percent of federal identifiers had less than a high school education, which is more than twice as high as those identifying with state or local governments. By small margins, nonwhites preferred federal over state and local governments. Although correlations (tau-b's) between the composite measure of government identification and respondent education, race, and income are significant at least at the .01 level, the modest relationships suggest that the extent to which people preferred or identified with one or another level of government was not highly class-based, at least not as "social class" is measured here.

There is not much previous research to compare these findings about level of government identification and social class. Bennet and Bennet (1990, 39–50) examine characteristics of those who think government is too big and those who do not. This issue is not the same as level of government identification; the item they use, however, does focus on government size and power. Initially, they state that Gallup data from 1964 examined by Free and Cantril (1968) show that opinion on power in Washington varies by socioeconomic class with lower classes (less educated, lower income, and blue-collar workers) more favorable to an expansive central government. Bennet and Bennet's examination of NES data from 1964 through 1988 provides more complex findings for this purported relationship.

One major complicating factor using the NES item on fear of power in Washington which includes a "filter" is the tendency of lower classes to claim they are uninterested, have no opinion, or do not know what their opinion is about Washington's power ("nonsubstantive responses"). In the late 1970s and thereafter as many as 40 to 55 percent of lower SES individuals expressed such responses, compared with 25 to 33 percent of upper SES individuals (Bennet and Bennet 1990, 42). Also, class differences regarding the Washington power item have narrowed over time.

Another question about the "big government" item relates to the meaning for the public of the power of the government in Washington. Does the item tap economic or noneconomic issues or both? The interpretation of the item and the question of economic and noneconomic liberalism relate to issues of race. Bennet and Bennet (1990, 43–44) find that even during the peak of the racial crisis and civil rights movement in the mid-1960s, about 40 percent of blacks expressed nonsubstantive responses, but "very few blacks believed the central government had become too powerful." After this period there was an increase in nonsubstantive responses by blacks to the 55–64 percent range, but also a decrease in the belief that government had not gotten too big. Bennet and Bennet conclude that "SES and race have been important determinants of opinions about big government, but they are not the only factors behind differing views about Washington's power" (p. 46). These other factors include partisanship and ideology.

Although not exactly comparable, these findings on the socioeconomic determinants of public opinion on government size lend some support to these SSP data, or at least are not contradictory. Race, education, and income are related modestly to whether people identify with state, local, or the federal governments.

Political Predispositions and Level of Government Identification

With the SSP data, examination of the political predispositions of each group of consistent level of government identifiers suggests no significant differences (table 3-4). Consistent state identifiers were slightly more Democratic in their identifications, and somewhat less likely to vote for President Bush or to rate Reagan positively than were federal or local identifiers. For example, the Democrat/Republican percentages for consistent local identifiers are 39 to 26, for state identifiers 47 to 17, and for federal identifiers 38 to 21. These are not percentages that might be expected, given the history and politics of federalism in this nation, as well as the stated conservative ideology and desires for decentralization of Republicans and Reagan in the 1980s.

Despite the overall lack of a significant relationship between party identification and level of government identification, it is interesting to note that those who chose a different level of government for each item (the category of "mixed"), by a margin of 41 to 29 percent are more likely to identify themselves as strong or weak Democrats rather than strong or weak Republicans. Democratic identifiers are more likely than Republican identifiers to be inconsistent in their identification with a level of government.

To explore party identification and levels of government further, the concept of state party identification is examined. In the 1987 SSP, respondents were asked separately about national and state party identification. The data show that people did not distinguish between a national and a state party identification. When the seven category measures for each type of identification are compared, the correlation is quite strong (tau-b = .82 and r = .89). Of the 137 respondents (14 percent) who identify themselves as strong Republicans at the national level, only 9 see themselves as strong or weak Democrats at the state level, while one person classifies himself or herself as an independent at that level. Of the 195 (20 percent) strong Democrats at the national level, none classify themselves as either weak or strong Republicans at the state level, and only two classify themselves as independent or leaning toward the Republicans. On the basis of these data, individuals do not distinguish between a state or national party identification, and neither measure of party identification is related significantly to level of government identification.

As a comparison to this finding of no relationship between party identification and level of government identification using SSP data, the measure of salience of levels of public affairs as presented by Jennings and Zeigler (1970, 528) also is not related to the NES measure of party identification. As a further comparison (Bennet and Bennet 1990), when examined over time, the relationship between party identification and government power is more complex than the nonrelationship found in the cross-sectional SSP data from 1988 and the Jennings and Zeigler analysis of 1968 NES data.

Bennet and Bennet's historical examination of the NES item on big government finds that Republicans tend "to fear concentration of power in Washington," especially when a Democrat occupies the White House. The pattern is more complex, however, for Democrats. Bennet and Bennet suggest that in the 1930s and 1960s, Democrat identifiers did not oppose power in Washington; however, "from 1972 on, Democrats were more likely to think that government was too big than it was not, even when Carter was President" (p. 50). In some support of the SSP finding of no relationship in 1988, they conclude that partisanship in 1984 and 1988 did not relate to views about big government. These findings based on NES data are compatible with the SSP data in the late 1980s showing no relationship between party identification and level of government identification.

The next symbolic construct to be examined is political ideology. Previous research finds that party identification and political ideology share considerable meaning (Levitin and Miller 1979; Conover and

Feldman 1981), and this meaning "centers around the symbol of capitalism" (Conover and Feldman 1981, 643). How does level of government identification relate to political ideology as they are conceptualized and measured in the State Survey Project? What are the interrelationships among these symbolic predispositions?

The ideology item used in the 1987 SSP survey is, "In politics today, do you think of yourself as a liberal, a conservative, or middle-of-the-road, or don't you think of yourself in those terms?" If respondents answered conservative or liberal, they were asked whether this was strong or not so strong; if they responded middle-of-the-road, they were asked whether they were closer to liberals or conservatives. The percentage responses are:

Strong liberal	7.0
Not so strong liberal	7.7
Closer to liberals	10.3
Middle of the road	6.9
Closer to conservatives	13.9
Not so strong conservative	11.1
Strong conservative	13.0
Not accept terms	30.1

Note the many individuals who take advantage of the filter in the item and state that they do not think of themselves in these ideological categories. If these respondents are omitted, one has the widely used, one-dimensional measure of ideological identification ranging from extremes of strong liberal to strong conservative; 30 percent of the sample, however, is unavailable for analysis (342 respondents in 1987).

If respondents who do not accept the common ideological labels ranging from liberal to conservative are omitted, there is a moderately strong relationship between party identification and political ideology in the expected direction. The tau-b of .30 and Pearson r of .38 for these two variables in the 1987 survey confirm a significant relationship. By margins of more than 3 to 1, strong liberals are more likely to be Democrats than Republicans, and strong conservatives are more likely to be Republicans than Democrats. Those who identify themselves as "middle-of-the-road" ideologically, however, are no more likely to identify themselves as "independents" than as Republicans or Democrats.

Just as with party identification, level of government identification does not relate to political ideology. Those who identify with a level of government are not more likely to identify with a political ideology, as table 3-5 indicates. Although the relationship between the composite measure of level of government identification and the ideology scale is not significant statistically, table 3-5 shows that consistent federal identifiers are more likely than state and local identifiers to classify themselves as strong liberals. Also, state identifiers are more likely than federal and local identifiers not to accept these ideological terms.

As with party identification, the category of "mixed" for level of government identification relative to ideology is interesting. Those who choose a different level of government for each item of the scale are much more likely not to accept the ideological terms than to identify themselves as a liberal or conservative. Of the mixed category, 31 percent do not accept the ideological terms, versus 15 percent who say they are strong conservatives, 6 percent who are middle-of-the-road, and 4 percent who are strong liberals.[3]

In some contrast to their finding no relationship between party identification and views on big government in the late 1980s, Bennet and Bennet (1990, 61) suggest that ideology is related to central government power, "but the details differ depending upon whom one consults."

Table 3-5. Ideological Identification of Consistent Level of Government Identifiers, 1987

| | Government Identifiers | | |
Ideological Identification	Federal (%)	State (%)	Local (%)
Strong liberal	16	5	8
Not strong liberal	8	9	8
Closer to liberal	8	9	9
Middle of the road	6	5	8
Closer to conservative	12	9	18
Not strong conservative	8	15	6
Strong conservative	14	12	16
Reject terms	26	35	29

Their conclusion is based on a long and complex argument using many sets of data and interpretations. One consistent finding, however, is that the relationship varies over time. The tau-c between the two NES measures of ideology and support for big government is .17 in 1984 and .14 in 1988, with, as expected, conservatives more likely than liberals to say that the federal government was too powerful, "but the differences were far smaller than in any year save 1972" (p. 67). They go on to argue that the key to this relationship is party identification, which as has been shown is related to political ideology. In terms of the relationship between ideology, party identification, and perceptions of big government, the important year was 1972. "The most notable aspect of the period from 1972 on is that majorities of liberals, moderates, and conservatives, whether Democrats, independents, or Republicans, consistently believed too much power was concentrated in the federal establishment" (p. 73).

Dimensions of Identifications

Finding so many individuals who reject the common ideological terms, who are not consistent in choosing levels of government, and who are "independents" regarding party identification leads to questions of the "dimensionality" of these concepts. The issue of dimensionality has become prominent regarding party identification (Weisberg 1983; Knight 1984; Alvarez 1990) and political ideology (Conover and Feldman 1981).

Dimensionality assumes that if one is closer to the Democrats or liberals, one is further from the Republicans or conservatives and vice versa. Also, for party identification, some analysts contend the independent category is not a single, neutral category in the middle of a continuum. Instead, it is argued that Democrat, Republican, and independent are separate and not necessarily orthogonal categories or dimensions (Weisberg 1983). Using feeling thermometer items and other items, Weisberg shows that people have multiple and separate identifications with American parties. Conover and Feldman (1981, 630) examine the issue of dimensionality for political ideology and find that evaluations of liberals and conservatives based on feeling thermometers have only a weak relationship with one another, suggesting that rather than a bipolar dimension, "evaluations of ideological symbols are relatively independent."

As with party identification and political ideology, the middle category also may be problematic for level of government identification. Where should those who are in the mixed category be placed on the continuum, or should there be more than one dimension of level of government identification? Should federal, state, and local as well as mixed identifiers be considered as separate and related dimensions? For all three symbolic identifications, if the middle groups are included in the measure, there are questions of where to place them on the scale and then how to interpret the scale. If these groups are omitted, many respondents are not available for analysis, and information about the symbolic identifications of many respondents is lost. This issue becomes crucial for multivariate analysis.

A partial answer to these questions is that the composite level of government identification developed here using SSP data is viewed as one-dimensional. Although the choices for each individual item composing the composite measure are orthogonal, the composite measure is not. Identification with one or another level does not preclude identification with the others. A positive evaluation of state government does not predict a negative evaluation of the other levels; instead, the composite scale is a continuum of identification ranging from federal to local. The composite can be thought of as a centralization of government scale ranging from complete decentralization (consistent local) to complete centralization (consistent federal), with many gradations between the two extremes.

To summarize relationships between these three symbolic dispositions, although there is overlap between party identification and political ideology among the SSP samples, neither measure is related to the composite measure of level of government identification. Level of government identification as conceptualized and measured here is a relatively distinct symbolic political predisposition, but does it relate to other political attitudes or evaluations?

Conclusions

These 1988 SSP survey data show that the public has positive views of state governments when compared with other levels. On several dimensions, the public views state government as being "in the middle" of the three levels. There is also a belief, however, that this level of government should have more power, especially compared with that of the federal government.

Analysis of attitudes toward levels of government finds that individuals can be classified according to the consistency of their views regarding federal, state, and local government. Approximately 85 percent can be classified as relatively consistent level of government identifiers, with 39 percent choosing local, 25 percent choosing state, and 20 percent choosing the federal level. Only 16 percent are mixed or not consistent in their choice of a level of government.

There are modest relationships between level of government identification and "social class," with individuals with lower levels of education and income as well as racial minorities somewhat more likely to identify with the federal government. Neither party identification nor political ideology is related to respondent identification with a level of government.

Although these data indicate the existence of a small but identifiable group of citizens who consistently choose state government over federal and local governments for efficiency, leadership, and responsiveness, it is not clear that these individuals necessarily form a "state electorate." It is possible that these state identifiers have the potential to behave in a cohesive manner when questions of conflict between levels of government arise, but these data do not address this issue.

Individuals display loyalties and identifications with the three levels of government. In contradiction to Dahl, states do matter to some people, and there is at least a potential state electorate—that is, a group of individuals who consistently identify with and prefer state government on several dimensions of policy and politics. It remains to be seen whether level of government identification remains influential in a multivariate model of political and policy attitudes. That is the subject of the following chapters.

Notes

1. The expense of conducting identical surveys in more than one state and the overall lack of interest in this issue by public opinion researchers are two important reasons for the lack of comparative state public opinion research. One of the difficulties in assessing the impact of state public opinion is the lack of consistent, comparable surveys of public opinion on states and intergovernmental relations. Despite the relatively recent phenomenon of extensive public opinion polling on virtually every aspect of American social, economic, and political life, little is known about public perceptions and attitudes toward state government.

Although few would dispute the importance of assessing public preferences and attitudes toward government (to which the spectacular growth of the polling industry attests), most public opinion polls dealing with political issues and governmental institutions are carried out at the national level, and most focus on national institutions and issues. Why is this major component of the complex relationship between the leaders and the led (public opinion on state institutions and issues) in our federal system so often ignored? One answer may be a perception that few people care about state government issues. If this is the case, however, what explains the tremendous number of single-state surveys conducted over the years?

A more likely answer is that it is costly and complicated to conduct the same survey in fifty separate locations, or even in ten locations. Most surveys dealing with state government issues are conducted in single states rather than nationally, often with question wording, question ordering, and other methods of survey design and implementation that are not comparable across states and over time. Because of these weaknesses or gaps, we know little about whether citizens recognize the changing roles of state government, what roles they expect state government to play, what policies they think it should give priority to, and how they assess the performance of state institutions. Most important, we do not know what factors may influence people's opinions and beliefs concerning these questions and how these attitudes may vary over time.

2. As the percentages in table 3-6 demonstrate, responses to these items in the 1988 survey are virtually identical to the 1987 and 1989 responses. This stability suggests that these items are tapping stable predispositions (similar to party identification or political ideology) rather than less stable perceptions of self-interest that might vary over time because of short-term circumstances and political and economic events or nonattitudes that might vary randomly. Despite this apparent stability, it should be emphasized that these are not panel data, and therefore reliability of measures and stability at the individual level over time

Table 3-6. Level of Government Evaluations, 1987–89

Evaluation	Federal (%)	State (%)	Local (%)	N
Most responsive				
1989	20	27	54	957
1988	19	28	53	1,114
1987	17	30	53	1,152
Most efficient				
1989	19	33	48	932
1988	18	32	51	1,105
1987	17	38	44	1,111
Most honest				
1989	18	24	58	714
1988	18	27	56	871
1987	17	29	55	931
Most leadership				
1989	51	28	21	911
1988	53	29	18	1,079
1987	53	29	18	1,097

cannot be assured. Because of the varying survey subjects and items used in different years, the 1988 data are used for most of the analyses in this chapter. Exceptions to using 1988 data are noted in the text. The distribution of the level of government identification composite in 1987 also is very similar to that in 1988 and 1989. This variable is discussed in the next section. In addition, relationships between level of government identification and socioeconomic characteristics and political attitudes (discussed below) display similar patterns in all three years.

3. The measure of ideology (excluding those who reject the terms) is related to several public attitudes and other characteristics. As would be hypothesized, conservatives are significantly more likely than liberals to rate President Reagan highly (tau-b = .26). Also, elderly whites with higher incomes are more conservative than liberal, but the relationships for these measures of social position are not as strong as for the political attitudes of support for Reagan and party identification.

Another series of items in the 1987 survey also could be hypothesized as tapping a liberal/conservative dimension. Respondents were asked the extent of their support for a guaranteed payment for poor families, for requiring employers to provide health insurance, and for the federal government creating public service jobs. Each is related significantly to political ideology, with more conservative persons opposing these policy positions (tau-b's range from .17 to .21). These items are discussed in more detail in chapters 8 and 10.

Another item relating to federalism and "liberalism" asks whether people favor the federal government using grant money to redistribute from rich to poor states. This item is related weakly to political ideology, with conservatives opposing redistribution through federal grants (tau-b = .08, p < .002). These same items also are related significantly to the political ideology measure when those who reject the ideological terms are included. For example, the chi square for the expanded or complete measure of ideology and support for a minimum family payment is 74.1 (p < .0001), and for required employer health insurance it is 59.7 (p < .0001).

4

A Model of State Policy and Political Attitudes

Previous research suggests that public opinion varies across the American states and that relationships exist between state public opinion and state public policies. An important question is, What determines these state public opinions? More broadly, What determines the political and policy attitudes of the public? What are competing or complementary theories or hypotheses about the determinants of political and policy attitudes? The discussion to this point has focused on developing plausible arguments for considering the role of the American state in determining public attitudes toward politics and public policies. The argument includes two components: individual identification with state government, and the contextual effect of the American state, that is, the extent to which one's state of residence somehow shapes or affects policy and political attitudes independent of individual social and economic characteristics. What are plausible alternatives to these hypotheses concerning state contexts and state identifications as determinants of public attitudes?

Although many factors have been advanced as explanations of human behaviors and attitudes, the alternatives derive from either rational, self-interest assumptions or broader assumptions such as altruism, ideology, the public interest, or symbolic politics. At one extreme (or two opposite extremes), both Marxists and market advocates argue that self-interest is the dominant motivating force for human behavior. They see little or no role for larger or broader motivations such as values, beliefs, or ideologies. As Adam Smith has stated, "Every man feels his own pleasures and his own pains more sensibly than those of other people."

Others disagree with both the Marxist and market perspectives on self-interest but still frame the issue in broad philosophical or economic terms. In discussing "rational fools" and the many assumptions of modern economic theory, Sen (1977, 34) argues for the importance of "commitment" and concludes: "I have argued against viewing behavior in terms of the traditional dichotomy between egoism and universalized moral systems (such as utilitarianism). Groups intermediate between oneself and all such as class and community, provide the focus of many actions involving commitment. The rejection of egoism as description of motivation does not, therefore, imply the acceptance of some universalized morality as the basis of actual behavior. Nor does it make human behavior excessively noble. Nor, of course, does the use of reasoning imply remarkable wisdom."

Some analysts see the issue as public- versus private-regardingness, with certain classes of voters or subcultures defined along ethnic and economic lines "more disposed than others to rest their choices on some conception of 'public interest' or the 'welfare of the community'" (Wilson and Banfield 1964, 876). Orren (1988, 14) argues that "widely held ideas, broadly shared values, and intensely felt opinions are the most powerful forces in political life." People are motivated by "values, purposes, ideas, goals, and commitments that transcend self-interest or group interest" (p. 13). In some contrast to both the self-interest and public-interest approaches, other researchers are concerned with the lack of interest, knowledge, and sophistication of the masses regarding politics and government and how this affects political choices in our democratic system (Neuman 1986). If people are uninterested, ignorant, and unsophisticated about public affairs, the issue of whether individuals are motivated more by self-interest versus some type of broader interest would appear to be irrelevant.

Given findings about the lack of clear and consistent political attitudes, knowledge, and participation of the masses, several public opinion researchers have begun analyzing elite attitudes and behaviors and how they might relate to public opinion (Verba and Orren 1985; McCloskey and Zaller 1984). For example, McCloskey and Zaller (1984, 234) contend that public attitudes toward capitalism and democracy "are, to a great extent, shaped by the traditional ideologies and values of the political culture, as articulated by its opinion leaders."

In assessing the idea of equality in America, Verba and Orren (1985, 248) contend that values matter, ideas have consequences, and self-interest may not be a reliable or useful guide to understanding public opinion.

One of the most compelling and counterintuitive discoveries of social science research over the last 30 years is that the influence of self-interest on most political thought and action is tenuous. Values do not merely rationalize action in accordance with self-interest. Often they arise quite independently of an individual's life experiences and in turn play an independent role in molding political behavior. Such behavior reflects people's group attachments and antipathies, and concern for larger purposes that transcend their own immediate situation. Thus, politics often resembles more closely the world of religion than the world of economics.

Exploration of some previous research on political and policy attitudes in the worlds of economics, politics, and perhaps religion will begin with "economic voting."

Economic Conditions and Rational Models

Extensive investigation has found economic conditions to be important determinants of individual political and policy attitudes. Perhaps the most basic statement summarizing the role of economic conditions on political and policy attitudes of the public is that people "vote their pocketbooks." Researchers have examined this pocketbook thesis and its many variants, using two broad approaches. One approach examines the extent to which aggregate economic conditions affect electoral outcomes over time. Other studies assess individual perceptions of economic conditions and their relationships to vote choice and other political behaviors.

Both the aggregate and the individual approaches are based on rational models that assume that individual behavior reflects self-interest, usually economic or financial self-interest. Although it is assumed that political behavior is determined by economic conditions (perceived and actual), researchers dispute the extent to which personal economic circumstances or the economic conditions of a collectivity (usually the national economy) are more influential determinants of behaviors such as vote choice (Kinder and Kiewet 1979).

In a variation of this approach, Weatherford (1983a, 159) argues that both self-interest and collective referents are used by voters in making political choices, with personal conditions more important for individuals vulnerable to economic dislocations. Lower-class individuals and blue-collar workers as well as women and minorities are more likely to have perceptions of their personal economic circumstances condition their political attitudes than other socioeconomic groups, especially in periods of economic dislocations.

Much of the earliest work assessing relationships between economics and elections analyzes aggregate data to assess changes in the national economy and support for parties or candidates (Tufte 1978; Kramer 1971; Arcelus and Meltzer 1975; Bloom and Price 1975). Although there are exceptions, these aggregate, over-time studies tend to find that as the economy improves, support for incumbent parties and candidates increases. Although most work in this area focuses on presidential and congressional elections, Kenney (1983) examines aggregate data for fourteen states from 1946 to 1980 and finds that adverse state economic conditions do not harm incumbents. Chubb (1988) examines aggregate economic and electoral data and finds gubernatorial and legislative races less affected by state than national economic conditions.

Although the primary focus of this research is the use of survey data to assess relationships between individual perceptions of economic conditions and political and policy attitudes, a variation of the aggregate approach to the question of economic effects on public attitudes toward politics and policies will also be examined. Aggregate conditions of state economies will be assessed as possible contextual determinants of individual attitudes.

Symbolic Politics Models

In contrast to the focus on rational models and self-interest, some researchers find symbolic attitudes such as ideology or party identification to be major determinants of voter attitudes for several issue areas (Sears et al. 1980). In this symbolic politics perspective, in preadult years people acquire "stable affective preferences" such as party identification, liberal or conservative ideology, nationalism, or racial prejudice. These long-standing predispositions or values are hypothesized as determining later political attitudes.

Understandably, political scientists have invested heavily in this area of research. Two of the most prominent psychological constructs in political behavior research have been party identification and political ideology. Although there is a long history of interest and research in American political parties and ideology, the most comprehensive, empirical investigation of these two areas of mass belief systems began with the University of Michigan Survey Research Center in the late 1950s (Campbell et al. 1964). This early research found that the public was not very ideological in its attitudes and beliefs, at least not as ideological as a more sophisticated political elite. The authors conclude, "The concepts important to ideological analysis are useful only for that small segment of the population that is equipped to approach political decisions at a rarefied level" (p. 144).

Converse (1964) continued this assessment of mass belief systems, focusing on attitude "constraint," or the interrelatedness among political ideas. Using panel survey data for 1956, 1958, and 1960, he found little consistency in people's attitudes over time, with only about 20 percent of respondents having stable, consistent opinions and the remainder displaying responses over time that were "statistically random" (p. 74). The finding of relatively nonideological thinking or organizing of attitudes among the masses is usually related to the contention that the United States is a relatively nonideological nation and the major political parties are not organized ideologically.

As would be expected, the SRC research model has been subject to extensive criticism, both methodological and substantive. Critics of the Michigan SRC approach contend that individuals are relatively ideological in their thinking about political objects (Nie with Anderson 1974; Nie, Verba, and Petrocik 1979). Much of the differences center on the time period when people were surveyed, with the SRC research findings in the late 1950s criticized as time-bound because of the political quiescence of that period. In contrast to the placid 1950s, in the late 1960s and early 1970s, when there were new, more controversial political issues and new voters, the electorate allegedly became more attentive to politics, more knowledgeable, and more ideological in their thinking. The broader research questions dealing with ideological thinking among the masses also became intermixed with complex methodological disputes regarding question wording, "filtering" of samples, measurement error, and the like.

Although the terms "liberal" and "conservative" are common in political debate and discourse, the extent to which the concept of political ideology and related ideological labels are significant to the ordinary citizen is not clear-cut. Previous research suggests that although many individuals "lack a complete understanding of such ideological terms as traditionally conceptualized, these labels and related self-identifications nonetheless have considerable impact on political perceptions and behavior" (Conover and Feldman 1981, 618). Although these ideological labels and identifications are significant politically, Conover and Feldman question the unidimensionality and issue content of political ideology. Using 1976 NES data, they find that "the meaning of ideological labels is largely symbolic in content and nondimensional in structure" (p. 636). An extensive review of findings in this area led Kinder and Sears (1985) to conclude that the American public does not much think about issues in ideological terms; almost everyone, however, is aware of and opinionated about some political issues.

Another psychological construct—party identification—has become the weapon of choice for many political behaviorists. Hardly any research on the political behavior of the masses ignores party identification. This concept shares considerable meaning with political ideology. Although party identification has been subject to numerous conceptual and methodological disputes, there is less disagreement among researchers about party identification than political ideology as an organizing political construct for mass attitudes. This psychological identification or attachment to a political party functions as an important cue for individuals to organize and evaluate complex political information and issues. Partisan attachments or loyalties tend to be relatively stable over time, and "few factors are of greater importance for our national elections than the lasting attachment of tens of millions of Americans to one of the parties" (Campbell et al. 1964, 67). The SRC researchers also conclude that "party identification has a profound impact on behavior" (p. 79).

How do these symbolic predispositions perform relative to self-interest as determinants of public attitudes? Using 1976 NES survey data, Sears et al. (1980) find "self-interest to have little effect on voters' policy preferences, while symbolic attitudes had major effects" (p. 673). Citrin (1979, 126–27) analyzes national survey data (the 1977 NORC survey) and California data (the 1978 California Poll) using a multivariate model and finds significant effects for liberalism and Democratic party identification. These two variables "independently dilute the tendency to demand a reduction of public spending in all social groups." In examining the impact of group economic interests on political evaluations, Conover's (1985, 153) regression models show that although group interests have significant effects, party identification is also a significant predictor of all four measures of evaluations of Reagan's performance as president and evaluations of the government's handling of the economy. Much evidence exists for the impact of these political predispositions "beyond self-interest" on public attitudes toward political objects.

Dependent Variables in Models of Political Attitudes

In attempting to explain or predict political and policy attitudes, previous research has concentrated on variables such as preferences for political candidates (Feldman 1982; Fiorina 1978; Kinder and Kiewet 1979; Kinder, Adams, and Gronke 1989; Kuklinski and West 1981; Sigelman and Tsai 1981; Sears et al. 1980) and support for government spending (Sears and Citrin 1982; Citrin 1979; Sanders 1988; and Welch 1985). Both these types of attitudinal variables will be examined in this research, using SSP data.

VOTE CHOICE AND CANDIDATE EVALUATION

A major area of interest of public opinion researchers is choice of political candidates. For voting decisions and the role of economic conditions in these choices, the major variations in approach and method are whether the economic conditions being examined are personal, group based, or national; whether the economic conditions are in the present or the past; and whether the election is presidential or congressional. Regardless of the conditions examined, research at the individual level finds that perceptions of personal economic conditions have little effect on political attitudes. Sigelman and Tsai (1981, 373) summarize previous research by stating, "There is at best a modest relationship between personal economic circumstances and voting decisions."

Rosenstone, Hansen, and Kinder (1986) approach the purported relationship between personal economic well-being and political preferences by focusing on measurement issues. They question whether the validity and reliability of measures of personal economic well-being would be improved by multiple measures and concern for the time frame being considered. Although they find that using a five-category response set rather than the traditional three-category set increases significantly the predictive power of personal economic well-being on political attitudes, use of a six-month or twelve-month retrospective makes no difference.

Within this rational framework, Kuklinski and West (1981, 437) argue that many previous studies (primarily those using aggregate data, but also some using individual-level data) are mistaken in relying on indicators of past economic conditions. They contend that the rational model assumes that individuals seek to maximize their expected utility and therefore that voters are future oriented. Using 1978 NES data, they find that economic voting exists in Senate but not House elections and argue that the differing contexts account for this difference. For House elections, party identification and region (South/non-South) are the major determinants of vote choice (Kuklinski and West 1981, 442). At least partially, political predispositions are important determinants of voter preferences for candidates for political office.

In another variation in this research area, some researchers have examined how individuals assess the economic conditions of groups, compared with personal and national assessments (Kinder, Adams, and Gronke 1989; Conover 1985). In addition to or instead of assessments of personal economic well-being or of the national economy, individuals may make political judgments based on the economic well-being of relevant social groups. The competing theoretical frameworks are "social cohesion" and "social identification" (Conover 1985, 141–43). Because of shared interests, cohesion, and interaction, the social cohesion model sees group interests as a proxy for self-interest. The social identification model focuses more on emotional attachment to the group. "The group's interests take on a symbolic value for the individual that is unrelated to his or her material self-interest" (p. 143). Conover finds that people do distinguish group economic interests from personal and national economic interests and suggests that group influence is based on symbolic attachments rather than material self-interest.

With the SSP survey data used in this research, individual perceptions of the economy of their state, rather than those of a group, will be assessed. Although this level or domain has mostly been ignored as a possible source of identification for individuals in the relationship between economic conditions and political attitudes, there is some justification for its use. Just as Conover (1985, 140) sees social groups as falling in a middle ground between the "broad spectre of national economic well-being and the narrow range of personal self-interest," it is reasonable to assume (and the SSP data in the previous chapter suggest) that identification with state government would fall between national and personal economic interests. This possible intermediate position in the governmental system also relates to the concept of representation and territorial democracy. For example, in the research dealing with relationships between economic conditions and vote choice, the economic performance of the state and its effects on voter assessments of state officials have been considered and assessed, with mixed results (Chubb 1988; Kenney 1983).

Despite theories (Peterson 1981; McConnell 1966) that states and localities are highly constrained in their policy-making and regulatory behavior because of economic competition and consequent inability to control mobile capital and labor and because of the strength of narrow business interests, a common-sense hypothesis is that state political incumbents behave as if they feared voter punishment for poor economic performance in the state. Chubb (1988, 134) contends there is reason to believe that state election outcomes are affected by economic conditions. "State politicians must be concerned about the condition of their economies not only now that state responsibilities for social welfare and economic development have increased but because economic conditions affect the ability of states to attract and retain businesses and taxpayers."

Regardless of this possibility, when using aggregate data in assessing the effects of the national economy and state economies on state legislative elections, Chubb (pp. 140–42) finds little support for state economic effects and concludes, "State legislative elections appear to turn on factors that are substantially national." Although he finds that national economic rather than state economic factors determine state legislative elections, Chubb (p. 149) also finds that "state economic conditions, and the assumption of gubernatorial responsibility for them, have a significant impact on gubernatorial election outcomes." The effects are still smaller, however, than those for national economic conditions.

In related research, Stein (1990) examines an extensive set of exit poll data for 1982 senatorial and gubernatorial elections and finds that voters hold the national government responsible for economic conditions, although state officials are accorded some responsibility for conditions in their state. "The findings reported in this study suggest that voters recognize that their personal financial condition is more closely tied to federal policies and actions than to the state's, and vote accordingly. The same voters, however, clearly make an evaluation of incumbent governors' efforts to protect the state and its citizens from the impact of national and subnational economic conditions" (p. 51).

These two studies, one using aggregate data (Chubb) and one using individual-level data (Stein), provide mixed support for the impact of state economies on electoral choices. It is plausible that individual perceptions of state as well as national economic conditions be considered as determinants of vote choice and ratings of the performance of state and national public officials and governmental institutions. These hypotheses will be tested in subsequent chapters.

GOVERNMENT SPENDING PREFERENCES

Another area of concern for public opinion researchers is public support or preference for government spending. The major issue is the degree to which the public is rationally self-interested. If one basic question in political attitude research is the extent to which pocketbook voting exists among the public, the follow-up question might be, Whose pocketbook? Does the public want "something for nothing"—that is, more spending in many policy areas, but lower taxes (self-interested, but irrational)—or does the public want to spend more only on programs that benefit them personally (self-interested, but "too rational") (Sanders 1988, 315)?

Sanders examines 1982 and 1984 NES data on public preferences for government spending in certain program areas and finds limited effects of self-interest. Although people are more likely to "support programs which are of potential benefit to them or those like them," the extent to which program clients or beneficiaries are perceived as legitimate is also a major factor in these public perceptions (p. 322). In a related approach using different data, Welch (1985, 315) finds that although public support is high for increased government spending, the presumed irrationality of wanting more services and less spending characterizes "only a minority" of citizens. "Most citizens are willing to raise additional revenue to pay for these services, or at least to reallocate from less desired to more desired services" (pp. 315–16).

The SSP research will assess public attitudes toward state government spending for many policy areas. In what policy areas do people want their state governments to spend more (or less) money? What determines these preferences or priorities? In addition, the research will examine public attitudes toward government regulation in such areas as education, health care, and "moral" issues such as pornography.

Contextual Analysis

The research discussed above suggests the many individual-level factors that have been investigated as possible determinants of public attitudes toward politics and public policies. Similar to previous research, the dependent variables of the model proposed in this research are political and policy attitudes such as public policy preferences, program spending priorities, ratings of government institutions and officeholders, and preferred policy responsibilities for levels of governments. The specific survey items will be discussed in subsequent chapters.

In addition to identifications at the level of the individual, this research also focuses on contextual determinants of public attitudes and preferences. As Books and Prysby (1988, 213) note, "Contextual analysis assumes that social interactions, social structures, and even factors like local institutional arrangements affect individuals." Some researchers have found certain mediating structures operating between the individual level and the national level. The mediating structures have included social groups (Conover 1985), local market areas (Weatherford 1983b), and American states (Erikson, McIver, and Wright 1987). The research by Conover and by Erikson and his colleagues which finds significant independent effects of groups and states on individual opinions has been discussed above.

Weatherford (1983b, 870) uses an information processing framework to assess contextual effects on opinion formation. He argues that information about personal and national economic conditions represents poles on a "continuum in which economic information is aggregated successively from the individual, through several geographical clusters centered on the individual, to the national level." In addition to the characteristics of the individual, the social environment in which the individual is located affects individual political opinions. The fundamental issue in contextual analysis is defining the appropriate context. Because of concern with "identifiably distinct economic activity and policy impacts," Weatherford uses Local Market Areas (as the Department of Labor has defined these) as the context in a multivariate model of opinion formation and finds some contextual effects.

In this research using SSP data, three basic types of contextual variables will be examined as possible determinants of individual evaluations of political leaders and government institutions, as well as policy preferences. First, the economy of the state will be examined. Analysis at the individual level shows that perceptions of the state economy have significant independent effects on evaluations of governors as well as other government institutions. To what extent are these perceptions of the state economy relatively accurate? Do individuals who have positive perceptions of the economy of their state reside in states with stronger, more rapidly growing economies? Regardless of this relationship, does the aggregate economy of the state display any independent effects on political and policy attitudes?

Another type of contextual variable analogous to individual-level measures of political predispositions is the political condition of the state. What type of political culture characterizes the state, and does this factor relate to individual political attitudes? Three measures of state political context are considered. These are political culture as conceptualized by Elazar (1972) in the 1960s and quantified by Sharkansky (1969), the "general policy liberalism" of the states as measured by Klingman and Lammers (1984), and the extent of state political conservatism as measured by Holbrook-Provow and Poe (1987) using congressional roll-call votes.

The third type of contextual factor is variations in policies across the states. In the areas of economic development, health, education, and welfare, states vary in policies and programs enacted. Do these policy differences at the state level influence individual attitudes concerning issues in these areas? For example, are people who reside in states with higher levels of spending for public education more likely to support education reforms? Are individuals residing in states with higher rates of people living in poverty more likely to support welfare reforms?

Conclusions

As demonstrated in previous research, attempting to explain public attitudes and preferences towards politics and policy is a complex undertaking. Explanations other than an individual's level of government identification and state context must be considered in the model. These alternatives include the social and economic characteristics of individuals (social location, or "class") and perceptions of economic performance. A major hypothesis from the rational perspective is that people vote their pocketbook, but the focus of this rational self-interest may vary depending on whether the federal government or state government is the object of concern. This distinction will be considered in the model.

Another potential explanatory factor includes individual political predispositions. In this perspective, people will vote their ideology or their political party preference rather than their pocketbook. In this research using SSP data, identification with a level of government is hypothesized as another basic political predisposition similar to party identification. On the basis of the competing explanations from previous research of self-interest or symbolic politics as determinants of political attitudes, preference for or identification with a particular level of government is viewed as a psychological attachment or long-standing identification rather than a rational attempt to maximize self-interest on particular issues. The idea of an "attachment" or "loyalty" implies emotion rather than calculation, a viewpoint that may depend on the issues or policies being considered.

In summary, four categories of predictor variables will be assessed in multivariate models of political and policy attitudes. These four categories are political predispositions, level of government identification, economic perceptions, and state economic and political contexts. It is assumed that the predictor variables are separate and unrelated; this assumption, however, will be tested for various indicators of the predictor variables. It is assumed also that none of the predictor variables is causally dependent on any of the other predictors. The following chapter describes the survey items on public evaluations of government institutions and policy leadership and the measures of the various predictor variables and then tests the basic model using those measures.

5
Political Attitudes and Evaluations

This chapter specifies in more detail the basic model introduced in the previous chapter, which will be used to explain public attitudes toward presidents, governors, state legislatures, the Congress, and local governments. One proposed determinant of these political evaluations—level of government identification—was developed in chapter 3. It is hypothesized that federal identifiers will be more favorable to national institutions and political leaders, state identifiers to state institutions and leaders, and local identifiers to local institutions, controlling for other factors. Furthermore, these relationships will hold when tested in the multivariate model.

Rating the Governor and the Legislature

A majority of people surveyed in the 1988 SSP had favorable views of both their governor and their state legislature. When asked to rate the job that each is doing, 72 percent of the respondents gave the governor an excellent or good rating, and 64 percent rated the state legislature's performance as excellent or good. In late 1988, governors had higher approval ratings than President Reagan (72 percent excellent or good versus 63 percent), one of our most popular presidents serving in his last year of office, and state legislatures rated higher than Congress (64 percent excellent or good versus 52 percent). However, when asked in a single item to choose which one of several political institutions (or individuals) is doing the best job, most respondents chose the president (34 percent), followed by local government (25 percent) and governors (20 percent), with Congress (11 percent) and state legislatures (9 percent) at the bottom of the forced choice.

How can these ratings of governors and state legislatures be interpreted? One way of answering is to provide some historical perspective. The 1968 Comparative State Elections Project (CSEP) includes both a national sample and separate samples in thirteen states. For the national sample, 55 percent agreed that their governor had "done an excellent job in office." The proportions agreeing with that statement in the thirteen state samples range from 32 to 79 percent (Black, Kovenock, and Reynolds 1974, 185). In the median of nine separate state surveys conducted in 1980, 54 percent of respondents rated the governor's performance as excellent or good, with the favorable ratings for the nine governors ranging from 23 to 69 percent (Cohen 1983, 224). In a national poll conducted in 1979 by Louis Harris, 46 percent of respondents ranked governors excellent or pretty good.

In the 1968 CSEP, the proportion of respondents rating the legislature as excellent or good was 41 percent in the national sample (42 percent fair or poor, and 18 percent unsure). In the thirteen-state survey the proportion ranged from 29 to 56 percent and was 46 percent in the median state (p. 186). In 1980, similar surveys in ten states produced excellent or good legislative ratings from 33 percent of respondents in the median state. A 1979 Louis Harris poll found that 34 percent rated their state legislature excellent or pretty good.

The 72 percent favorable rating for governors and 64 percent favorable rating for legislatures in the 1988 State Survey Project are both much higher than those achieved when similar questions about governors and legislatures were asked in earlier polls. The public in the late 1980s appeared to be more satisfied than in the past with the job being done by state governors and legislatures. [1]

State Identifiers and Political Leadership

Do state identifiers have higher opinions of governors and state legislatures than do federal and local identifiers? Do local and federal identifiers have higher opinions of those levels of government than do the other groups? Table 5-1 provides answers to these questions.

For single-item job ratings in table 5-1, consistent state identifiers by a wide margin rate their governor more favorably (excellent and good) than the other groups (95 percent versus 64 for consistent federal identi-

Table 5-1. Level of Government Identifiers and Ratings of Government Officeholders and Institutions

Government Officeholder/Institution Rated	Government Identifiers[a]		
	Federal (%)	State (%)	Local (%)
President Reagan	61	52	54
Congress	67	53	39
Governor	64	95	67
State legislature	43	83	60
Local government	47	59	72

[a]The categories include respondents who consistently chose one level of government for each item in the scale. Figures show the percentage of each group rating the job performance of the respective officeholder/institution as excellent or good.

fiers and 67 for consistent local identifiers). Federal identifiers rate the Congress more favorably than do the other groups (67 percent versus 53 and 39 for state and local identifiers respectively), and local identifiers rate local governments more favorably than do the other two groups.

When respondents were asked to choose the one individual or institution doing the best job, the differences between levels of government identifiers are also significant (chi-sq = 137.1, p < .001) and in the expected direction, in that higher proportions of local identifiers chose local government (52 versus 12 percent for both federal and state identifiers); state identifiers have higher proportions for the governor (52 percent versus 16 for federal and 9 for local) and state legislatures (15 percent versus 7 for federal and 8 for local); and federal identifiers were highest for the president (42 percent versus 26 for local and 18 for state) and the Congress (23 percent versus 5 for local and 3 for state).

The results lend some validity to the composite measure of level of government identification. Additional hypothesized determinants of political attitudes must be examined, however, before ascribing much importance to the concept of level of government identification.[2]

Perceptions of Economic Conditions

Do economic conditions or perceptions of these conditions influence political attitudes, and to what extent do individuals distinguish between personal, state, and national economic conditions? The three SSP items used are, How would you describe the nation's economy these days? How would you describe the condition of your own personal finances? and How would you describe the economy of your state? The possible response categories are excellent, good, not so good, and poor. Table 5-2 indicates that in late 1988, people were somewhat dissatisfied with the national economy and more satisfied with their personal financial conditions, with perceptions of the economies of their states falling between the national economy and personal finances.

The results are similar for the perceived future of each area. The SSP item used was, During the next few years, do you think the national economy (the economy of your state, or your personal finances) will get better, get worse, or stay about the same? As evidence of optimism in this period, substantially more of the sample believed their personal finances would get better rather than worse, in contrast with a slight plurality believing the national economy would get worse rather than better. Perceptions concerning the future of their state economy fell in

Table 5-2. Perceptions of Economic Conditions, 1988

	National Economy (%)	State Economy (%)	Personal Finances (%)
Perception of the present			
Excellent	5	6	7
Good	42	56	57
Not so good	35	29	25
Poor	19	9	11
Perception of the future			
Get better	27	38	52
Get worse	31	17	8
Stay the same	42	45	40

the middle, but people still believed by a 2-to-1 margin that their state economy would get better rather than worse.

Correlations among the six variables demonstrate a moderately high level of consistency for perceptions of present conditions for all three levels and for future conditions for the three levels, but much less consistency between perceptions of present and future conditions. Respondents who evaluate their present personal finances favorably also evaluate their state economies and the national economy favorably, although these perceptions are certainly not identical. In contrast, those who evaluate present conditions favorably do not necessarily evaluate the future favorably.

Of those who perceived their present personal financial condition as not so good or poor, a rather surprising majority of 58 percent believed the future would get better, versus only 10 percent who felt it would get worse. Of those who perceived their present condition to be excellent or good, the same comparison for the future is 49 versus 7 percent. These percentages indicate a high degree of personal financial optimism but a weak relationship between perceptions of present and future personal financial conditions. Regardless of perceived present financial condition, most people are optimistic and believe their personal future will improve.

In contrast, of those who believed the present national economy was not so good or poor, only 23 percent believed it would get better, while 39 percent felt it would get worse. Of those perceiving the national economy to be excellent or good, 32 percent felt it would get better, while 22 percent felt it would get worse. Although dissatisfied with the national economy, respondents were moderately consistent in their perceptions of the present and future national economies.

These SSP data show no relationship between perceptions of present and future personal financial conditions (tau-b = $-.04$). In contrast, Kuklinski and West (1981, 440) find moderately strong relationships between perceptions of past and expected financial well-being, using 1978 NES data for House (tau-b = .39) and Senate (tau-b = .38) elections. Even with this relatively high level of association, they suggest that past and future perceptions are distinct conceptually and empirically. Also, they contend that perceptions of future conditions are more theoretically desirable measures of personal economic conditions when using rational models.

On the basis of these SSP survey items and findings, we can say that individual assessments of present versus future economic conditions are distinct conceptually and empirically.[3] Personal, state, and national domains are not as distinguishable. This contrasts somewhat with Kinder, Adams, and Gronke (1989, 512), who use the domain of "group" rather than the domain of "state" used here and who find empirical distinctions between the three types. The hypothesis that economic conditions determine political attitudes will be examined in the multivariate model.

Social Class and Economic Conditions

Weatherford's (1983a) argument (discussed in chapter 4) that perceptions of economic conditions and economic voting are likely to be class based and contextual leads to several hypotheses about perceptions of economic conditions. First, one would hypothesize that individuals who report higher personal incomes would also have more positive perceptions of their personal financial circumstances (as well as state and national economic conditions).[4] Table 5-3 indicates mixed support for this hypothesis. Reported personal income is correlated strongly with perceptions of present personal financial condition and is correlated moderately with perceptions of the national and state economies. Personal income, however, is not related to the measures of perceived future economic conditions. Individuals with lower incomes are not more likely than those with higher incomes to be pessimistic about their future personal financial conditions.

Because of intercorrelations between certain demographic items, some consistency in these correlations is expected. Education, gender, and race are similar to income in that they display mixed and moderate relationships with perceived present economic conditions. As hypothesized, based on the concept of "economic vulnerability," males, whites, and those with more formal education (as well as those with higher incomes) perceive present economic conditions more positively than do females, minorities, and those with less education.

In contrast to the other demographic characteristics, age is related significantly to perception of future personal finances, but not to perceptions of present conditions. The tau-b of $-.29$ indicates that older respondents are significantly more pessimistic about their future per-

Table 5-3. Correlates of Perceived Economic Conditions

	Present			Future		
Characteristic	National Economy	State Economy	Personal Finances	National Economy	State Economy	Personal Finances
Age	−.03	−.05	.01	.07	.06	−.29
Education	.11	.06	.18	.09	−.03	.04
Income	.17	.10	.31	−.01	−.01	.01
Gender	.10	.09	.09	−.04	.00	.06
Race	−.09	−.05	−.18	−.02	.01	.07
Party identification	.25	.09	.20	.12	.07	.03
Level of government identification	−.01	.03	.08	.02	−.05	−.03

Note: Coefficients are tau-b's. Those .07 and greater are significant at least at the .01 level.

sonal finances than are younger respondents. Race is related weakly to perceptions of future personal finances, with minorities somewhat more optimistic. Respondents with higher levels of education are more pessimistic about the future national economy than those with less education. Although 1988 would not seem to be a period of economic dislocation compared with other years, these data provide modest support for Weatherford's findings that perceptions of economic conditions are class based.[5]

Political Predispositions and Economic Conditions

Table 5-3 also indicates moderately strong relationships between party identification and perceptions of present economic conditions. Republican identifiers have more positive perceptions of present economic conditions at each level than do Democrats. Except for income, the party identification correlations are higher than those for the other socioeconomic measures. The relationships between party identification and perceptions of the future tend to be weaker than those for present conditions, but in the expected direction. The composite variable "level of government identification" is related significantly only to perceptions of present financial conditions, and that relationship is quite weak.

To summarize, although individuals distinguish between present and future economic conditions, they do not differentiate much between personal, state, and national levels for either present or future economic perceptions. Perceptions of the economy are related weakly to moderately to individual socioeconomic characteristics and to party identification in the expected directions. Level of government identification is related only to perceptions of present personal financial condition. None of these relationships is of a magnitude to suggest potential collinearity problems in multivariate models.

Financial Well-Being and Political Attitudes

One of the few relatively consistent findings from previous research is that there are only modest relationships between perceptions of personal financial well-being and vote choice. The items used to measure vote choice and related evaluations of individual political leaders are the following: "If the 1988 presidential election were being held today, for whom would you vote, George Bush or Michael Dukakis? Which of the two candidates—Michael Dukakis or George Bush—do you feel has a better understanding of the problems facing your state? How would you rate the job Ronald Reagan is doing as president? and How would you rate the job your governor is doing?" The choices for the last two items are excellent, good, not so good, or poor.

The data examined here appear to contradict previous findings of lack of relationships between perceived personal economic well-being and vote choice. Table 5-4 indicates significant relationships in the expected direction between perceptions of present personal financial conditions and three measures of political preference (evaluation of Reagan [tau-b = .19], vote for Bush/Dukakis [.20], and evaluation of Bush/Dukakis [.17]). No significant relationship is found, however, with the rating of the governor. Since the three significant relationships are for items dealing with national leadership, and the nonsignificant relationship is for state leadership, the impact of level of government on the relationship between financial well-being and vote choice should be considered.

Table 5-4. Political Evaluations and Perceived Economic Conditions

	Present			Future		
Evaluation/Choice	National Economy	State Economy	Personal Finances	National Economy	State Economy	Personal Finances
Pres. Choice (Bush)	.33	.11	.20	.20	.16	.07
Evaluation of Bush/Dukakis	.27	.07	.17	.22	.17	.03
Rating of Reagan	.42	.16	.19	.21	.12	.12
Rating of the governor	.09	.12	.00	.07	.10	.07
Rating of the state legislature	.06	.11	.04	.12	.15	.06
Rating of Congress	.02	.10	− .02	.10	.12	.11
Rating of local government	.13	.17	.12	.10	.15	.06

Note: Coefficients are tau-b's. Those .07 and greater are significant at least at the .01 level.

Despite significant correlations between perceptions of personal finances and three indicators of attitudes toward national political leaders, the first column of correlations in table 5-4 suggests that perceptions of the national economy rather than personal finances may be more important in explaining these attitudes toward national figures. Such a finding would support certain previous research. For example, Kinder, Adams, and Gronke (1989, 512) find that personal, group, and national domains "constitute distinct areas of economic assessment." They conclude further that "voters were moved primarily by their assessments of the nation's economic condition" in the 1984 presidential election. Although these SSP data suggest the same finding for the 1988 presidential election, additional indicators of political attitudes should be examined. Also, a test is needed of the relative influence of various predictors of these attitudes.

Chubb (1988) and Stein (1990) suggest that national economic conditions are more important determinants of vote choice than are state economic conditions, although they do find some support for the impact of state economies on evaluations of state officials. With these SSP data, respondent evaluations of the state economy are somewhat more closely related than evaluations of the national economy to ratings of the governor, which is the opposite of the ratings of national political leaders and 1988 presidential vote choice. This suggests that individuals to some extent may be holding the governor responsible for the performance of their state economy.

In contrast to ratings of individual political officeholders at the national level (Reagan and Bush), table 5-4 indicates that evaluations of the national economy are not related to evaluations of Congress. As with the rating of governors, however, ratings of state legislatures are more closely related to evaluations of present state economies than to personal finances or the national economy.

The item asking people to chose which among the president, Congress, their governor, the state legislature, and local government is doing the best job appears most closely related to evaluations of the national economy (the chi-square for this relationship is 138.9, p < .0001). As seen in table 5-5, almost half of those evaluating the performance of the national economy as excellent or good chose the president as the officeholder or institution doing the best job, with the next highest percentage choosing local government (21 percent). The proportions among those evaluating the national economy less favorably are more evenly balanced among the officeholder/institutional choices. Although not as strong, the relationship of this choice item to perception of the future national economy also is significant in the expected direction for the president, but not for Congress.

Party Identification

Regardless of the strength of relationships between perceptions of economic conditions and certain political attitudes, previous research finds consistently that party identification is a strong predictor of vote choice. Table 5-3 shows that party identification correlates moderately with perceptions of present economic conditions. As expected, the SSP data also demonstrate very strong bivariate relationships between party identification and 1988 presidential vote choice, evaluation of Bush/

Table 5-5. Perceptions of the Officeholder/Institution Doing the Best Job and Condition of the National Economy

	Condition of the National Economy	
The One Doing the Best Job	Excellent/Good (%)	Not So Good/Poor (%)
President Reagan	49	20
Congress	7	15
Governor	17	23
State legislature	7	12
Local government	21	30

Dukakis, and rating of President Reagan (tau-b's of .60, .55, and .42 respectively). Democrats prefer Dukakis and rate Reagan much less favorably than do Republicans and independents.

The next step is to attempt to sort out the relative effects of perceptions of economic conditions, party identification, socioeconomic position, and level of government identification on political attitudes of respondents. The approach assumes that party identification is a relatively stable predisposition and is the cumulation of past judgments of the economy and other issues and perceptions. The "normal vote" approach often is used to assess issue voting; that is, issue voting is viewed as a "deviation" from the vote that would occur ("normally") if nothing but party identification was used (Achen 1979, 24–25). Weatherford (1983c) contends that normal vote approaches which use party identification in models along with perceived economic conditions and social class measures as predictors of political preferences are misleading in that party identification overcontrols for both economic conditions and social status, thereby exaggerating the effects of party identification.

Weatherford's argument about including party identification along with economic perceptions and indicators of social class in vote choice models is persuasive. However, since the primary concern of this research is the extent to which the composite measure of identification with levels of government is a significant determinant of political attitudes, including party identification in the model will provide a very conservative test of the role of level of government identification on political attitudes.

In addition to the predisposition to identify with a political party, it is hypothesized that voters also consider present and future economic conditions (personal as well as state or national) in making their political choices. Finally, the social location of individuals and the extent to which persons identify with one or another level of government are also hypothesized as having independent effects on political attitudes and preferences. The primary method used to assess the independent effects of these many variables on attitudes toward national and state leaders and institutions is discriminant analysis. Excellent discussions and applications of discriminant analysis can be found in Aldrich and Cnudde 1975, Legge and Zeigler 1979, Martinez and Gant 1990, and Bennet and Bennet 1990.

Discriminant analysis is a technique designed to differentiate individuals based on certain known characteristics into mutually exclusive and exhaustive groups (Legge and Zeigler 1979, 28). In this case, for two variables—presidential choice and candidate evaluation—the two groups are those who chose either Bush or Dukakis. The remaining dependent variables are collapsed from four categories into positive/negative ratings of Reagan, the governor, Congress, the state legislature, and local government. Since membership of respondents in these categories is known, other discriminating variables are used to predict membership in the groups.

Just as in other multivariate techniques such as OLS regression or probit analysis, discriminant analysis provides information on the overall fit of the model and the relative strengths of relationships between the grouping (or dependent) variable and the discriminating (or predictor) variables. Standardized discriminant function coefficients provide information on the relative strength of predictor variables. These coefficients tell us which variables are significant in discriminating between categories or groups (i.e., those for Reagan versus those for Dukakis), controlling for the other variables in the model. Percentage of cases classified correctly and canonical correlations can be used to assess overall fit of the models. Additional tests of the overall fit of the models using OLS adjusted R^2 also are reported below.

Estimates of the Model

Discriminant models are estimated for two categories of dependent variables—evaluations of individual political officials and evaluations of political institutions. The category "ratings of individual political leaders" includes 1988 presidential vote choice, evaluation of Bush/ Dukakis, and ratings of President Reagan and the current governor. The other set of dependent variables includes the three single-item institutional ratings for Congress, state legislatures, and local governments.

The initial set of predictor, or discriminating, variables used includes respondent party identification, perceptions of personal financial well-being, perceptions of the state and national economies, three measures of perceptions of future economic conditions, five measures of socio-economic status or social class (age, education, income, gender, and race), and the composite measure of level of government identification.

The model to be estimated is:

$$Y = b_0 + b_1 \text{ persfin} + b_2 \text{ stecon} + b_3 \text{ natecon} + b_4 \text{ futperfin} + b_5 \text{ futstec} + b_6 \text{ futnatec} + b_7 \text{ PID} + b_8 \text{ age} + b_9 \text{ educ} + b_{10} \text{ inc} + b_{11} \text{ race} + b_{12} \text{ gender} + b_{13} \text{ LGID} + e$$

where Y = political attitude or evaluation
persfin = perception of personal financial condition
stecon = perception of state economy
natecon = perception of national economy
futperfin = future personal financial condition
futstec = future state economy
futnatec = future national economy
PID = party identification
age = age in years
educ = years of education
inc = reported income
race = white/nonwhite
gender = male/female
LGID = composite measure of level of government identification

It is hypothesized that after controlling for party identification, percep-tions of the state and national economies, perceptions of present and future personal financial condition, and social class or location, the composite measure of level of government identification will remain a significant predictor of public evaluations of political leaders and institutions.

The results in tables 5-6 and 5-7 provide some support for this hypothesis. Even with the other predictors in the model, the discriminant function coefficient for level of government identification is significant

Table 5-6. Ratings of Individual Political Leaders

	Dependent Variables			
	Presidential Choice (Bush)	*Evaluation of Bush/Dukakis*	*Rating of Reagan*	*Rating of Governor*
Predictors				
Present conditions				
National economy	.31	.24	.53	.22
State economy	−.09			
Personal finances				.71
Future conditions				
National economy	.14	.17	.22	
State economy	.15	.17		.23
Personal finances		−.11	.09	.20
Identification with				
Level of government		.09	.12	
Party	.85	.86	.64	
Demographic characteristics				
Age	−.09		−.20	
Education	−.13	−.23	−.15	
Income	.13	.10	.10	−.26
Gender	.24	.19	.19	−.52
Race	−.16	−.07	−.09	
Statistics				
Eigenvalue	.90	.64	.44	.06
Canonical correlation	.69	.63	.55	.24
OLS adjusted R^2	.47	.42	.29	.04
F	40.3	32.0	18.1	2.6
N	700	707	772	733
Percentage of grouped cases classified correctly	81	78	78	72

Table 5-7. Ratings of Political Institutions

	Dependent Variables		
	Rating of Congress	Rating of State Legislature	Rating of Local Govt.
Predictors			
Present conditions			
National economy			
State economy	−.43	.60	.64
Personal finances	−.14		.26
Future conditions			
National economy			
State economy	−.39	.58	.53
Personal finances			
Identification with			
Level of government	−.28		−.30
Party	.42		
Demographic characteristics			
Age	.51	−.47	
Education			
Income	.38	−.22	
Gender	.40	−.40	
Race			
Statistics			
Eigenvalue	.11	.09	.07
Canonical correlation	.32	.28	.26
OLS adjusted R^2	.08	.06	.05
F	4.5	3.9	3.1
N	750	731	761
Percentage of grouped cases classified correctly	63	66	67

for four of seven dependent variables: evaluation of Bush/Dukakis, and ratings of Reagan, Congress, and local government. The signs of the coefficients indicate that federal government identifiers are more positive than state and local identifiers about Bush and Reagan, but more negative in rating Congress and local governments (controlling for the other predictors). The level of government composite is not significant for either of the state-level evaluations (governor and state legislature).

Coefficients for perception of the present state economy are significant for two of the individual evaluations (presidential choice and rating of the governor) and all three of the institutional evaluations (ratings of Congress, state legislatures, and local governments). Those perceiving their state economy as strong have positive evaluations of their governor, state legislature, and local government but negative evaluations of Congress and Bush. Coefficients for perceptions of the future state economy are significant for all but the rating of Reagan. Those optimistic about their future state economy are also positive about political leaders and institutions, with the exception of Congress. Public perceptions of the national economy are significant predictors of the four ratings of individual political leaders (including the governor), but not the three institutional evaluations.

Also as hypothesized, discriminant function coefficients for party identification are significant for the three national political leaders and Congress, but not for the ratings of the governor, state legislatures, or local government. This suggests that party identification is more national than subnational in its effects on individual attitudes, a finding that is similar to Cohen's (1983) that partisanship plays a smaller role in evaluations of the governor than the president.[6] These findings based on SSP data tend to support Sears et al. (1980) that the "symbolic predisposition" of party identification is a much stronger predictor of political attitudes than perception of the national economy and personal finances, at least for national political leaders and institutions.

Tables 5-6 and 5-7 also indicate that several demographic variables are significant, even controlling for party identification. Income and gender are significant for all but the evaluation of local government (none of the demographic indicators is significant for evaluation of local government). Education and race are significant only for the three national ratings of political leaders. Those with more education and less income are less positive about Reagan and Bush. Males and whites are more positive than females and minorities about these two political leaders. In contrast to ratings of Bush and Reagan, those respondents more positive about their governors are female and report lower incomes. For the institutional ratings, older Republican males with higher incomes evaluate the Congress positively. Younger, lower-income females evaluate their state legislatures positively.

Overall, the most important discriminator of respondent evaluations of political leaders and institutions tends to be party identification. Several other variables, however, including perceptions of the national economy and present and future state economies, gender, and age, also are strong predictors of certain dependent variables. Level of government identification, although not consistently strong, performs as well as or better than several other variables thought to be important determinants of political attitudes.

Finally, several indicators of strength and significance of the overall fit of the models are presented in tables 5-6 and 5-7. OLS adjusted R^2s ranging from .29 to .47 and the percentage of grouped cases classified correctly ranging from 78 to 81 for the ratings of Bush and Reagan indicate relatively strong predictive power for the model. However, the lower figures for the ratings of governors, Congress, state legislatures, and local governments are less impressive and indicate that the overall model is much less successful for these dependent variables.

Economic and Political Contexts

Two basic types of contextual variables are examined as possible determinants of individual evaluations of political leaders and government institutions. First, the economy of the state will be examined. Analysis at the individual level shows that perceptions of the state economy have significant independent effects on evaluations of governors as well as other government institutions. To what extent are these perceptions of the state economy relatively accurate? Do individuals who have positive perceptions of the economy of their state reside in states with stronger, more rapidly growing economies? Regardless of this relationship, does the aggregate economy of the state display any independent effects on political attitudes?

The accuracy of individual perceptions of the condition of the economy of the individual's state can be assessed by combining aggregate data on the state economy with the individual measures. Substituting the values of changes in state per capita income, gross state product, and jobs added for the individual state of residence in the period from 1980 to 1986, correlational analysis finds moderately strong relationships between individual perceptions of the state economy and these aggregate measures. Individual perceptions of the present state economy are correlated significantly with the measure of change in state per capita income (tau-b = .31), change in gross state product (.31), and change in jobs added (.11). Individuals with more positive perceptions of their state economies reside in states with the largest increases or improvements in their economies, suggesting that people are making relatively accurate comparative assessments of aggregate economic conditions at the state level.

The other contextual variables examined are political. Three measures of state political context are considered. These are political culture as conceptualized by Elazar (1972) in the 1960s and quantified by Sharkansky (1969), the "general policy liberalism" of the states as measured by Klingman and Lammers (1984), and the extent of state political conservatism measured by Holbrook-Provow and Poe (1987) using congressional roll-call votes.

Since Holbrook-Provow and Poe find very strong correlations among these three variables at the state level and since the correlations among these three measures using the 1988 SSP survey data range from .73 to .84, it is assumed that they are tapping roughly the same dimension of the political context of the states. The measure of political conservatism developed by Holbrook-Provow and Poe will be used in the analysis. This contextual measure of the political culture or ideology of the state is related weakly to respondent party identification (r = .05, p < .04), choosing Bush over Dukakis (r = .08, p < .004), and evaluation of Reagan (r = .11, p < .0001). Republican identifiers who are positive about Bush and Reagan are somewhat more likely to reside in politically conservative states, but the relationships are not strong.[7]

To assess the independent effects of these contextual measures on political attitudes, the indicators of state economies and state political conservatism are entered into the discriminant models in tables 5-6 and 5-7. For the ratings of individual political leaders in table 5-6, several contextual variables are significant but have only modest impacts on goodness of fit or successful classification of cases. The percentage of cases classified correctly increases only 2 percent for the ratings of Bush and Reagan and does not increase for gubernatorial ratings. Also, entering the contextual variables in the discriminant models does not change the significance or direction of any of the individual-level measures found in table 5-6. The extent to which persons reside in politically conservative states is a significant predictor of the three national-level evaluations of Bush and Reagan, but not of governors. Measures of gross state product and jobs added are significant predictors of these four evaluations of political leaders.

For the institutional ratings, the contextual measures have minimal effects on the discriminant models. The equations for evaluations of state legislatures and local governments did not change with the addition of the contextual measures. None of the added variables were significant, and the percent classified correctly did not change. Two measures of the state economy were significant for ratings of Congress, but the percentage of cases classified correctly increased only 1 percent.

To summarize the contextual analysis, measures of the economy and the political conservatism of the individual's state of residence have very modest effects on evaluations of political leaders and virtually no impact on evaluations of political institutions at the national, state, and local levels.

Conclusions

Public evaluations of both the governorship and the legislature appear to be more positive than in the past. As state executives and legislatures have become more visible, with more resources and professional staffing, the public appears less critical than in the past. In addition, apparently the public has come to accept a more professional legislature playing at least an equal role with the governor in state policy-making.

A multivariate model using discriminant analysis provides mixed success in explaining political attitudes, as they are reflected in seven measures of evaluations of government institutions and political leaders. The predictor, or discriminating, variables include individual demographic characteristics, perceptions of economic conditions, and the two political predispositions of party identification and level of government identification. Although party identification tends to be the strongest and most consistent predictor and other variables perform well for certain political evaluations, the composite measure of level of government identification has independent effects on four of seven ratings of individuals and institutions. The extent to which individuals identify with a level of government has a significant impact on public attitudes toward political leaders and government institutions, controlling for other individual-level and contextual characteristics.

Also, with these survey data, some evidence of economic prospective voting is found, at least for the 1988 presidential election. The focus of this economic voting is perceptions of the national economy rather than personal finances. In contrast to perceptions of future personal finances and the future national economy, which do not have significant effects on institutional evaluations, perceptions of the future state economy are significant predictors of institutional ratings. The two strongest predictors of evaluation of the state legislature are perceptions of the present and future economy of the state. The strongest predictor of rating of the governor is perception of the present state economy. These perceptions display significant impacts, even after controlling for party identification and social class characteristics. Citizens appear to base their evaluations of state political leaders on the economic performance of the state, or the perceptions of that performance. Despite these relationships, it is important to note the poor overall fit of the models for rating the governor and state legislature.

Notes

1. Patterns of public support for political institutions and individuals are fairly consistent in the period 1987 through 1989. The percentages in table 5-8 from SSP surveys are those perceiving each institution or officeholder as doing an excellent or good job. Support for the president increased, while support for the Congress and governors and state legislatures declined somewhat over this three-year period.

Although governors were evaluated somewhat more favorably than state legislatures, when respondents were asked, "Which should take the lead in proposing policies in your state?" 60 percent said the legislature, and only 35 percent said the governor. An even more unexpected finding is that 81 percent of the respondents believed that state legislators should serve full-time rather than part-time. As state legislatures have become more professional, with more resources and staffing, the public apparently has begun to accept the concept of a more professional legislature playing at least an equal role with the governor in policy-making.

Table 5-8. Perceptions of the Performance of Government Officeholders and Institutions

Government Officeholder/ Institution	Job Performance Rated Excellent or Good			The One Officeholder/ Institution Doing Best		
	1987 (%)	1988 (%)	1989 (%)	1987 (%)	1988 (%)	1989 (%)
President[a]	57	63	76	31	34	40
Congress	56	52	49	11	11	8
Governor	76	72	66	22	20	20
State legislature	65	64	61	12	9	8
Local government	67	62	63	25	25	23

[a]Figures for 1987 and 1988 are for Reagan; those in 1989 are for Bush.

2. Although significant relationships are found between level of government identification and attitudes toward government institutions, the question of direction or causality is not answered. Whether identification with particular levels of government influences opinions about government leaders and institutions or whether individuals come to identify with levels of government after they develop opinions about various government institutions or political leaders is not tested directly in this research. Although either direction of causality may be plausible, in the 1988 survey instrument the items rating political leaders and institutions come before the items for identification with levels of government. The working assumption of this research is that level of government identification is a relatively stable symbolic predisposition similar to party identification or political ideology, while choice of candidates, rating of political leaders, and policy preferences tend to be more changeable or less stable.

3. Sigelman and Tsai (1981) note the possible interaction between perceived economic satisfaction and financial change and are critical of Weatherford's attempt to deal with this type of interaction. Their solution to the possible interaction of these two measures is to create a composite variable. A similar procedure is attempted here.

The six cells for the relationship between perceptions of present and future economies can be used to classify individuals and create an index based on degree of pessimism or optimism about the future and satisfaction/dissatisfaction with present conditions. (See the accompanying chart.) Perhaps the easier cells to categorize are the "consistent" extremes—satisfied optimists (upper left)

Attitude toward present conditions	Attitude toward the economic future:		
	Get better	Stay the same	Get worse
Satisfied	(1)	(3)	(5)
Dissatisfied	(2)	(4)	(6)

and dissatisfied pessimists (lower right). The remaining cells can be classified as dissatisfied optimists (lower left), satisfied neutrals (upper middle), dissatisfied neutrals (lower middle), and satisfied pessimists (upper right). In order to get a rank-ordered index, the categories were ordered as follows for personal financial conditions and perceptions of the state and national economies: (1) satisfied optimists, (2) dissatisfied optimists, (3) satisfied neutrals, (4) dissatisfied neutrals, (5) satisfied pessimists, and (6) dissatisfied pessimists.

The relationships between the three indices for personal finances and state and national economies are moderately strong (tau-b's range from .23 to .43). The relationships with the components of the indices measuring present conditions are also moderately strong (tau-b's ranging from .27 to .30). Also as would be expected, on the basis of the way the scale was constructed, there are very strong relationships between the indices and the other component used to construct them, namely, future perceptions. The tau-b's for these relationships range from .86 to .89. Given the high correlation between the indices measuring interaction and the individual items measuring perceptions of future economic conditions, it was decided for the sake of simplicity to use the individual items in the remaining analyses.

4. Another question related to the "pocketbook thesis" is whether people correctly or accurately perceive economic conditions for the state or nation. (It is assumed that individuals perceive their personal financial circumstances accurately or correctly.) Some analysts attempt to assess the validity of these survey items by relating them to other survey items. These items include whether the person is employed or whether certain actions have been taken over some past period such as borrowing money, putting off medical treatment, or looking for a second job (Rosenstone, Hansen, and Kinder 1986). For these economic perceptions, here I can only relate perceived present financial conditions to income reported by individuals. Table 5-3 shows that the two measures are moderately related (tau-b = .31), indicating that individuals reporting higher incomes also tend to be more positive about their present financial condition.

5. Although the term "social class" is used in this research, it is recognized that the term has somewhat different meanings when used by other researchers. Weatherford (1983c) has an extensive discussion of the relationship of class to political attitudes and proposes an elaborate measurement strategy for the con-

cept, using occupational data. Here, the term refers more to the location of the individual in the social and economic structure rather than the more complex idea of occupation and identification with a particular class based on this occupation.

6. Recall from the previous chapter that, on the basis of 1987 SSP data, people do not appear to be distinguishing between a national and a state party identification.

7. The measure of political context used here also is related to certain indicators of state economic conditions. For example, the product-moment correlation of state conservatism and per capita income is $-.60$, and with jobs added as a percentage, the correlation is .30. In contrast, the correlation of conservatism and gross state product in manufacturing is only $-.07$; the correlation of conservatism and change in gross state product is .06; and the correlation of conservatism and overall gross state product is $-.20$.

6

Program Responsibilities and Spending Priorities

The analysis to this point provides evidence that the public has positive perceptions of state government and its institutions. The SSP data in chapter 3 show that the public perceives state government "in the middle" of the intergovernmental system. People rank state government behind local government but ahead of the federal government in responsiveness, efficiency, and honesty. For leadership, the federal government is ranked first, with state government again in the middle, ahead of local government. Despite this middle position, preference for or confidence in state government has increased or at least has not declined since the late 1960s and early 1970s.

The previous chapter examined relationships between level of government identification and assessments of political leaders and government institutions. The next question for this research is whether individuals who identify more with state government than federal or local government are more supportive of state policies and programs. Are state identifiers more likely than local and federal identifiers to choose state government when asked which level of government should be responsible for specific policy or program areas? How does the public rate the job being done by their state government in selected policy areas? To what extent does the public support increased spending for certain state programs? Are those who identify with state government more likely to rate state government highly and support increased spending for state programs?

It is hypothesized that individuals who identify with or prefer state government also want that level to be responsible for regulating and controlling certain areas of domestic policy. The relationships will be the same for those who identify with the federal government or with local governments. In contrast, although it is expected that the public will rate state programs highly and prefer to increase or at least not to cut the budgets of these programs, it is hypothesized that public evaluations of state programs and spending preferences will not be related to the composite measure of level of government identification. The primary reason for this is that individuals will react more to the substantive policy area being queried than to the level of government being referred to in the items. For the state program evaluation items and the spending items, the response categories are not levels of government; rather, they are positive/negative or increase/decrease categories. These expectations will be tested in this chapter.

Levels of Government and Policy Preferences

Table 6-1 shows respondent preferences for the level of government which was believed to be best for dealing with selected policy areas. Majorities believed state government was best for education and the federal government was best for economic development. By narrow margins, pluralities believed the federal government was best for public health care and pollution control, with state government the next preferred. By a somewhat wider margin, a plurality believed local government was best for crime prevention (with state government the next level preferred), while respondents were virtually evenly divided over preferring state or local government for aiding the homeless.

Do those who identify with state government also prefer state/local control or regulation rather than federal control of these programs? The composite measure of level of government identification developed in chapter 3 is used to assess the relationship between this variable and respondent preference for which level of government should be responsible for these specific policy areas.

The correlation coefficients in the last column of table 6-1 show that level of government identification is related significantly to the single-item preference measures for level of government in each policy area. Those identifying with one or another level of government preferred those same levels for each of the policy areas, with the weakest relationships for economic development, pollution control, and public health care (tau-b's = .10), and the strongest for education (tau-b = .19). In addition to using the composite measure of level of government

Table 6-1. Level of Government Preferred for Policy Areas, 1988

Policy Area	Level of Government Preferred			Correlation with Composite[a]
	Federal (%)	State (%)	Local (%)	
Education	19	58	22	.19
Public health	46	42	13	.10
Pollution	44	42	14	.10
Homeless	26	38	37	.17
Crime	19	37	44	.15
Economic development	61	31	9	.10

[a]N's range from 945 to 963, and tau-b's are significant at least at the .001 level.

identification, these single items for preference in policy areas will also be used in later chapters dealing with health, education, and economic development.

Table 6-2 provides policy preference data for consistent state identifiers only and shows differences between these state identifiers and all respondents. As expected, by small to moderately large margins, state identifiers, when compared with the total of all identifiers, believed state government was best for all policy areas. For example, although only 31 percent of all respondents believed state government was best for economic development, 60 percent of state identifiers preferred state government for this function. Although a majority of the total sample of identifiers chose state government for public education (58 percent), state identifiers chose state government for this policy area by an even larger margin of 67 percent.

Levels of Government and Program Responsibilities

One series of items in the State Survey Project is introduced by the statement: "It has been proposed that the Federal Government turn over control of a number of programs to state and local governments." Re-

Table 6-2. State Identifiers and Policy Areas, 1988

Policy Area	Level of Government Preferred[a]		
	Federal (%)	State (%)	Local (%)
Education	17	67	16
Public health	29	64	7
Pollution	27	59	14
Homeless	22	52	26
Crime	20	51	29
Economic development	38	60	2

[a]The categories include respondents who chose consistently one level of government for each item in the scale. The N's range from 54 to 60.

spondents are then asked their opinion on eight programs, using a four-point scale from strongly favor to strongly oppose. Table 6-3 shows that in 1987, while relatively few respondents had strong opinions for or against, at least 60 percent of the respondents favored turning over control of each program to state and local governments.

Approximately three-quarters of the respondents favored state and local control of public schools, day care and social services, school lunch programs, and public service jobs. Approximately two-thirds favored state and local control of highways and mass transit and hospitals, while 62 percent preferred state and local control of welfare programs. As might be expected for a series of preference questions asked in order, the items are moderately to closely related. The inter-item correlations range from .26 to .51, all of which are tau-b's significant at least at the .001 level in the expected positive direction.

As a comparison, a 1981 ACIR survey asked a national sample which functions the federal government should turn back to state and local governments. The ACIR item states that this would "get the federal government completely out of the financing and administration of such programs" and then asks from which functions respondents would like to "see the federal government withdraw." The proportions in 1981 wanting to see the federal government withdraw range from 15 to 30

Table 6-3. Preferred Control of Program Areas, 1987

Program Area	Respondent Preference for State/Local Control				Correlation with Composite[a]
	Strongly Favor (%)	Favor (%)	Oppose (%)	Strongly Oppose (%)	
Day care services	19	59	19	3	−.08
Public schools	26	51	18	5	−.06
Public service jobs	12	64	21	3	−.07
School lunch	15	60	21	4	−.08
Mass transportation	14	55	25	6	−.05
Hospital/health care	16	52	26	6	−.03
Highways	16	51	18	5	−.10
Welfare	16	46	29	10	−.13

[a]Figures are tau-b's for the level of government composite and preference for state/local control. Correlations of .06 and higher are significant at least at the .01 level.

percent. Respondents were least likely to favor federal withdrawal from public hospitals and health (15 percent), welfare-AFDC (15), and highways (18); they were more likely to favor withdrawal from mass transportation (30), day care and other social services (29), public schools (26), public service jobs (26), and school lunch programs (25).

Although the question wording and response categories are not identical, comparing these ACIR percentages with those in table 6-3 for respondents strongly favoring returning the function to state/local control finds almost identical percentages for welfare, highways, public hospitals, and public schools in the 1981 and 1987 surveys. The remaining functional areas (day care, public service jobs, school lunch, and mass transportation) are at least 10 percent smaller in the 1987 SSP survey than in the 1981 ACIR survey, suggesting some softening in public desires to return these functions to state/local control.

Public preferences to return certain programs to state and local control are related to level of government identification. When examined separately, the single indicators of preference for returning control to state and local governments are related to level of government identification in the expected direction. Federal identifiers are less willing to return the programs to state and local control. All coefficients except mass transportation and public hospitals are significant at least at the .01 level. The remaining six correlations range from $-.06$ to $-.13$. A composite measure of preferred state and local control constructed by summing responses to the eight policy items is also related significantly to the composite level of government identification (Pearson r = .14).

Levels of Government and Regulation

Respondents in the SSP also were asked which level of government should set laws or standards for regulating certain policy/program areas. The responses to these questions provide interesting contrasts in attitudes toward federalism across policy areas (table 6-4). The strongest support for national regulation was in the area of hazardous waste disposal, where 60 percent favored federal control, 29 percent state control, and 11 percent local. Although 49 percent of respondents favored a national standard for the legal drinking age (compared with 42 percent favoring state standards), only 40 percent preferred the federal government setting speed limits for major highways (53 percent believed that speed limits should be set by state governments). These two issues may be perceived by the public as so-called states' rights issues, or perhaps the public believes there are more risks on the highway if some states let persons drink at an earlier age than if some states raise speed limits.

As most previous research shows, respondents favored state control, or state and local control, of education. Although most favored state or local certification of teachers, a somewhat surprising 27 percent favored national certification. Most favored state or local selection of public school texts; 25 percent, however, would have the federal government choose textbooks. The fact that about one in four Americans prefers that the federal government choose textbooks and certify teachers should give pause to advocates of local control of education. Given the long and relatively stable history of state/local control of schools, why would such a large minority of citizens prefer national control in these two crucial areas of public education? These and additional issues will be examined further in chapter 9. In other areas of regulation, more persons favored national licensing of physicians (49 percent) than favored state licensing (43 percent), and a slight plurality believed the federal govern-

Table 6-4. Level of Government Preferred for Regulation of Program Activities, 1987

Program Activity	Respondent Preference[a]			Correlation with Composite[b]
	Federal (%)	State (%)	Local (%)	
Teacher certification/ training	27	57	16	.07
Highway speed limits	40	53	7	.08
Public school texts	25	47	26	.14
Physician licensing	49	43	8	.04
Legal drinking age	49	42	9	.07
Indigent patient care	41	38	18	.12
Pornography	36	32	29	.12
Hazardous waste disposal	60	29	11	.07
Public school prayer	31	27	30	.08

[a]The percentage of respondents volunteering none of the levels or no regulation preferred is 1 percent or less, except for indigent patient care, with 3 percent; pornography, with 4 percent; and school prayer, with 12 percent.

[b]Figures are tau-b's for the level of government composite and preferred level to regulate the program area. Correlations of .06 and higher are significant at least at the .01 level.

ment rather than the states should set standards for hospital care for indigents (41 to 38 percent).

There is no public consensus about what level of government should establish and enforce standards of morality. A slight plurality (36 percent) favored national regulation of pornography, compared with 32 percent for state control, 29 percent for local control, and 4 percent for no control. Respondents were nearly evenly divided over which level of government should regulate prayer in the public schools, while 12 percent were opposed to government regulation in this area. The nine policy items are moderately to highly correlated, with tau-b's ranging from .15 to .45 in the expected directions.

This same survey item asking which level should regulate certain activities was used in 1989 with most of the same program areas from 1987, but also with some differences. For the program areas used in both 1987 and 1989, there is little change in responses for the two years. Two issues were added in 1989: capital punishment and abortion. Although the public preferred that the federal government regulate both the death penalty (56 percent) and the availability of abortion (45 percent), substantial minorities preferred state regulation of capital punishment (37 percent) and abortion (32 percent).

The patterns for the items asking respondents which level should regulate certain activities are similar to the state/local control items. As the last column in table 6-4 indicates, only one of nine items from the 1987 survey is not related significantly to level of government identification. Except for licensing physicians, those who identify with federal, state, or local governments preferred that same level to regulate the other policy areas. Again, a summed composite for these nine public policy areas is related significantly to level of government identification (Pearson r = .19).

The data demonstrate that the public believes state government, or state and local governments, should have more responsibility for several domestic policy areas, and the national government should have less. People are more closely divided over which of the three levels of government should be responsible for regulation of certain morality issues. The data also indicate that aggregate public preferences for which level should regulate program activities were relatively stable from 1987 to 1989. Finally, level of government identification is related significantly to public preferences for assigning policy and program responsibilities.

Policy and Program Evaluations

Surveys of citizens are often used to evaluate the job being done by their state, federal, or local governments. How does the public rate the job being done by their state government in selected program areas? The performance of state governments in senior citizens programs was rated as excellent or good by 70 percent of respondents in 1988 but declined slightly to 66 percent in 1989 (table 6-5). This highest rated program is followed by programs to provide health care for children in the first year of life, with 66 percent in 1988 and 63 percent in 1989 rating their state as excellent or good.

Table 6-5. Ratings of State Programs

	Ratings							
	Excellent		Good		Not So Good		Poor	
Program Area	1988 (%)	1989 (%)	1988 (%)	1989 (%)	1988 (%)	1989 (%)	1988 (%)	1989 (%)
Day care for children	6	4	46	49	31	32	17	15
Infant health care	9	7	57	56	23	27	11	10
Child abuse prevention	6	5	46	43	34	36	14	16
Reduce illiteracy	7	5	56	48	28	34	10	12
Senior citizens	12	9	58	57	30	25	0	8

Positive evaluations of programs to reduce illiteracy declined from 63 to 53 percent in this one-year period, while child abuse prevention and treatment decreased from 52 to 48 percent in 1989. Day care services for children increased 1 percent to 53 percent in 1989. Except for programs to reduce illiteracy, which showed a decline in support of 10 percent, the programs changed little in public support from 1988 to 1989. Except for senior citizens programs and infant health care, the public was evenly divided in evaluations of the other three programs. These evaluations of state programs in 1988 are correlated moderately, with tau-b's ranging from .18 to .47. Evaluations of senior citizens programs are less strongly related to the other program evaluations.

In contrast to the single items and composites for state control of policy and program areas and regulation of activities in 1987, level of government identification is not related significantly to any of the five single items rating state government programs in 1988. When the five program area responses are added for individuals to create a program rating composite, the correlation with level of government identification also is not significant (Pearson r $= -.05$).

Evaluations of state programs do not relate to identifications with levels of government. Individuals identifying with state government were no more likely than those identifying with the federal or local levels to have positive evaluations of state programs. It seems likely that individuals were evaluating programs without reference to the level of government used in the item. Since the item does not refer to other levels and the response set does not include choices among levels, people are probably judging the overall policy area rather than comparing levels. It is likely that these evaluations would be quite similar, regardless of which level of government is referred to in the item. A later section will explore other factors that might relate to these program evaluations.

State Spending Priorities

The above items directly asked respondents to evaluate state government programs. Another way of assessing opinion about government programs is to ask whether the public favors spending more or less government dollars on certain programs. After being asked to make out the budget for state government in the coming year based upon the assumption of a fixed amount of money to spend, respondents were asked whether they would increase, decrease, or keep the same spending in fourteen program areas. Table 6-6 summarizes the responses from the 1988 and 1989 SSP surveys.

The first conclusion from these data is that a majority wanted to increase or maintain spending for all of these programs. As previous research demonstrates (Sanders 1988; Welch 1985), people are not eager to cut government programs. Even the least popular programs in this group—tourism, highways and transportation, state parks, and corrections and prisons—had 18 percent or fewer respondents wanting to decrease spending. In contrast, a majority of respondents favored increased spending for eight of thirteen program areas in 1988 and ten of fourteen in 1989.

Despite the relative consistency in support for the programs, public policy priorities can be seen in these program comparisons. Education, drug abuse prevention, day care for children, health care for the poor, and child abuse prevention are the top priorities, while highways and transportation, corrections and prisons, tourism, and state parks are the lowest priorities of the fourteen program areas. Despite these compari-

Table 6-6. State Spending Priorities

State Program	Increase 1988 (%)	1989 (%)	Decrease 1988 (%)	1989 (%)	Same 1988 (%)	1989 (%)
Education improvements	81	84	2	1	17	14
Drug abuse prevention	72	80	4	3	24	18
Child abuse prevention	72	77	1	1	27	22
Day care for children	67	71	2	3	31	26
Reduce illiteracy	66	69	3	2	32	29
Environmental protection	64	68	3	2	33	31
Infant health care	55	62	2	1	42	37
Senior citizens programs	52	55	1	2	47	43
Low-income housing	49	57	10	9	41	35
Corrections/prisons	43	46	11	14	46	40
Highways/transportation	38	40	9	10	53	50
Tourism	24	19	16	18	60	63
State parks	23	20	10	12	67	69
Health care for the poor[a]	—	80	—	2	—	18

[a]This item appeared only on the 1989 survey.

sons, even the bottom four programs have majorities preferring at least to maintain present levels of spending.

Examination of intercorrelations among these items finds few insignificant relationships. Preference for spending on senior citizens programs is not related to spending for education improvements or for highways. Spending for day care is not related to highway or tourism spending, and spending for education improvements is not related to highways or tourism spending. Also there are no significant relationships between preferences for environmental protection and tourism spending, or between spending on drug abuse prevention and parks/recreation. It is difficult to discern patterns in the data on the basis of an examination of bivariate relationships; it is likely, however, that some "positivity bias" is present.

Because of the number of program areas and the overall support for maintaining or increasing spending, a principal components analysis is used to explore patterns in the responses. One would expect the items dealing with children and the elderly to vary together, as well as the drug abuse and prisons items, and the traditional state government activities of parks, tourism, and highways. The factor analysis results in table 6-7 provide support for this proposed grouping. Funding for senior citizens programs, child abuse prevention, infant health care, day care, and low-income housing vary together or load highly on factor 1. Low-income housing appears not to fit with the other items dealing with helping children and elderly or vulnerable populations. As a low-income program, however, an argument can be made that it is designed for many of these same more vulnerable populations and that the public tends to view it this way.

Also as expected, the traditional state programs of parks, tourism, and highway spending vary together in factor 2. The third factor contains the policy areas of drug abuse, prisons, illiteracy, and environmental protection. The latter item seems out of place on this dimension, which is crime related. For example, in Hofferbert's factor analysis of policy data for the fifty states, spending for natural resources loads

Table 6-7. Factor Analysis of Spending Priority Items

Program Budget Item	Factor 1	Factor 2	Factor 3	Factor 4
Senior citizens programs	.72			
Child abuse prevention	.60			
Infant health care	.59			
Day care for children	.52			
Low-income housing	.42			
State parks		.74		
Tourism		.70		
Highways/transportation		.67		
Drug abuse prevention			.71	
Corrections/prisons			.57	
Reduce illiteracy			.54	
Environmental protection			.41	
Education improvements				.81

highly on a dimension termed "Highways-Natural Resources" (Hofferbert 1974, 216). Although it was expected that environmental protection
would relate more closely to the dimension of parks, tourism, and
highway spending, this is not the case with these survey data. Finally,
education is the only item loading on factor 4. The four factors account
for 50 percent of the variance in the items.

Since education is the only item loading on factor 4, and since environmental protection does not seem to fit with the other items in factor
3, the principal components model was run again without these two
variables. The results are a three-factor solution accounting for 47 percent of the variance, with the same variables loading on the same first
three factors, with roughly the same loadings. These results are used to
construct composite measures of budgetary support for vulnerable
populations, support for highways and tourism, and support for prisons
and control of crime. It was decided to use the single items for environmental protection and education spending separately and individually.

Determinants of Spending Preferences

There has been much research in the area of public spending preferences for government programs (Citrin 1979; Sears and Citrin 1982;
Sanders 1988; Welch 1985). Although previous research shows that the
public consistently favors expanding public services, the findings do not
show that the public wants "something for nothing"—that is, more
spending (or at least no less spending) with lower taxes, or spending
only for programs perceived to benefit them personally. Some research
finds support for programs believed to benefit many people (fighting
crime and drugs, education, health care, and the environment), with less
support for programs appearing to benefit small groups of individuals,
especially unpopular groups such as welfare recipients (Sears and Citrin
1982).

Sanders (1988) also shows there is some balance between public
desires for spending cuts or increases. For example, although 32 percent
want to cut more programs than increase, 50 percent want to increase
more programs than are cut. Welch finds that very few people appear to
want a "free lunch." Although some individuals support more spending
without increased taxes, many are "willing to shift the burden of gov-

ernment to a higher level with consequent increased taxes there, or reallocate in a meaningful way, or assess more user charges" (Welch 1985, 314). Less than one-fourth of the sample in the Welch study are in the categories where spending is desired, "but means to pay for it are not very concrete." Although the SSP data do not allow testing of these same hypotheses, several related hypotheses concerning support for state spending will be examined.

Multivariate Models of Program Preferences and Evaluations

The multivariate model developed and analyzed in the previous two chapters is estimated for the indicators of state program evaluation and preferred program control, regulation, and budgeting. It is hypothesized that level of government identification will be related significantly to attitudes toward state program control and regulation but not to program evaluations and spending preferences, when controlling for social class, political predispositions, and contextual measures of state economies and political systems.

The major reason for this distinction is that the latter items do not contain a comparative or intergovernmental referent. For the program spending and evaluation items, respondents are asked to judge or choose on the basis of the policy subject and its implied recipients or beneficiaries, without any reference to whether that area is more the responsibility of one or another level of government. Although not tested in these data, it is hypothesized that if the spending items and the evaluation items were related to the various levels of government having more or less responsibility or authority in that area, level of government identification would relate significantly to those items.

The first sets of state policy variables to be examined are the composite measures of preferences for program evaluations, state/local control, and preferred level of government regulation. Table 6-8 presents results of regression models for three composite dependent variables. Although all three equations are significant, the explained variance is low, with adjusted R^2s ranging from .04 to .10. As hypothesized, level of government identification is significant for two of three dependent variables when controlling for the other predictors. The extent to which

Table 6-8. Determinants of Program Regulation and Evaluation

| | Program Composites[a] | | |
	Program Evaluation	State/Local Control	Government Regulation
Predictors			
Level of government identification	−.16	.25	
Rating of the governor	.14		
Rating of Reagan		.16	
Politically conservative state	−.19		
Increase in jobs created	.19		
Education			.13
Race			−.12
Income	−.12		
Statistics			
Adjusted R²	.06	.04	.10
F	2.89	2.57	5.24
N	543	517	517

[a]Figures given are standardized regression coefficients that are at least twice as large as their standard errors, indicating significance at least at the .05 level. All three dependent variables are summed composites, with the Program Evaluation model for 1988, and the State/Local Control and Government Regulation models for 1987.

individuals identify with a level of government is related positively to the preferred level for regulating certain activities and related negatively to the desire to return control of certain programs to state/local governments. (Federal identifiers do not favor state/local control.)

Except for level of government identification, the significant predictors differ for each composite dependent variable. For evaluation of programs, those who were more positive were lower-income supporters of their governor who resided in more politically liberal states that had larger increases in jobs created from 1980 to 1986. Recalling that the programs being evaluated are oriented to human service or vulnerable populations (more "liberal" in orientation?), these findings make some sense. The findings support both a self-interested perspective as well as a symbolic or ideological perspective.

For the composite measuring the extent to which individuals prefer state/local control of certain program areas, those identifying more with state and local governments and rating Reagan more positively preferred state/local control. Those who identified with the federal government and were whites with higher levels of education preferred federal regulation of certain activities. These results provide support for the ideological or symbolic perspective on public attitudes toward government programs, although it is not clear why whites with more education would prefer federal control. There does not appear to be an obvious self-interest explanation for this finding.

Political Ideology

Chapter 3 discusses the relationship of political ideology to level of government identification as well as other variables. Of the policy composites based on 1987 data used in this chapter, preference for state/local control is related modestly to the political ideology scale, omitting individuals who do not accept the ideological terms (tau-b = .08, p < .01), while level of government preferred for regulating certain activities is not related (tau-b = − .04). When this ideology scale is entered in the regression equations for these two policy composites (table 6-8), the adjusted R^2s for the equations increase slightly. The measure of ideology is not significant in either equation, and the significant predictors from the original equations change only slightly in magnitude but not direction. Adding ideology to the equations results in a decrease in the N's from approximately 500 to less than 400. Because of missing data, almost two-thirds of the original sample have been lost for the analysis. With the other variables in the model, political ideology has no independent effect on preference for state/local control or regulation of certain activities.

Budgetary Preferences

For spending priorities, three composites and two single items are used as dependent variables in regression models (table 6-9). The previous factor analysis of respondent budgetary priorities finds the human services programs for vulnerable populations varying together. On the basis of that analysis, individual responses for senior citizens programs, child abuse prevention, infant health care, day care, and low-income housing are summed to provide a human services composite measure. The regression model for this composite demonstrates that as hypothesized, more vulnerable groups such as nonwhites and females, as well

Table 6-9. Determinants of State Budget Preferences

	Program Area[a]				
	Education	Envir. Protection	Human Services	Tourism/ Highways	Crime
Predictors					
Rating of Reagan	−.10		−.12		
Pres. choice (Bush)			−.17		
Rating of the governor			.09		.13
Increase in gross state product	.18	.13			
State per capita income	−.17				
Age	−.12			.12	
Education	.09			−.16	
Gender			−.10		
Race			.10	.09	.09
Statistics					
Adjusted R[2]	.04	.02	.15	.05	.04
F	2.6	1.7	8.1	3.3	2.5
N	712	712	637	637	637

[a]Figures given are standardized regression coefficients that are at least twice as large as their standard errors, indicating significance at least at the .05 level.

as those more likely to be "liberal" (i.e., those who rate Reagan negatively and choose Dukakis over Bush), favored increased spending for these programs. The only possible divergence from this pattern is that those who rated their governor highly were more likely to support increased funding for these program areas. This may indicate broad support or attachment to the current state political system or support for the individual political leader perceived as responsible for these programs. Of the five models for budgetary preferences, this equation has the highest adjusted R^2 of .15.

Another factor or group of budgetary responses varying together is tourism and highways. The responses to items dealing with spending for parks, tourism, and highways are summed to form this composite. Table 6-9 indicates that older nonwhites with lower levels of education were more supportive of increased spending for highways and tourism. The third composite sums responses to the items for drug abuse control, prisons, and illiteracy. Minorities who rated their governor highly were more supportive of spending for this area. For the three spending composites, the one consistent explanatory factor is race. Minorities more than whites were supportive of state spending in these three policy areas. Support for the governor was related significantly to spending for human services and crime-related policy areas, but not to highways and tourism.

On the basis of the earlier factor analysis, the items for spending in education and environmental protection are analyzed singly and separately. Table 6-9 shows that younger respondents with more education who rate Reagan negatively and reside in states with lower per capita incomes but larger increases in gross state product were more supportive of increased spending for education. The only variable significant for spending for environmental protection is increase in gross state product. Individuals residing in states with growing economies preferred increased spending for this area. As hypothesized, level of government identification has no significant impact on these spending preference measures.[1]

Contextual Analysis

The measures of state context presented and discussed in the previous chapter are entered in the regression models for the composites of program evaluations, state/local control and regulation, and spending priorities. For some equations, contextual variables are significant, controlling for individual-level variables. For program evaluation, individuals living in more conservative states were less positive in rating the state programs, while individuals residing in states with larger numbers of jobs created were more positive about these liberal state programs. The contextuals are not significant predictors of the composite either of state/local control or of the level of government regulation.

For the five regression models dealing with spending preferences, contextual variables are significant only for two dependent variables: education and environmental protection. Individuals residing in states with larger increases in gross state product but smaller state incomes were more favorable to increasing spending for state education programs. Those residing in states with larger increases in gross state product were more positive about spending for environmental protection. Contextual measures are not significant predictors for the composites for spending on human services, tourism/highways, or crime.

Conclusions

These data on program priorities and preferences for level of government control of programs should be viewed with some caution. Many Americans probably give little thought to the role that various levels of government should play or the effectiveness of their performance in various policy areas. Given how poorly the average American understands the complexities of the federal system, most probably do not know how much responsibility each level of government actually has in each policy area. Since many experts disagree over this complex issue, it would not be realistic to set too high a standard for citizen understanding of and judgments about intergovernmental policy responsibilities.

Because of the complexities of American federalism, it may not be surprising to find that approximately half the sample favored federal licensing of physicians and federal regulation of the legal drinking age. However, given the tradition in this nation of overall strong support for state and local control of education, it is somewhat surprising that approximately one-fourth of the sample favored federal regulation of public school teacher certification and selection of textbooks. Although these four policy areas historically have had virtually no federal involvement, people appear to want an increased national government role in these areas. Regardless of these somewhat unexpected findings, there is strong public support for the growing role that state governments have been assuming in many areas of public policy, and it is possible to identify a rather clear set of policy control priorities.

On the basis of differing sets of SSP items, the public prefers state or state and local control of education, crime, transportation, and certain social services such as day care or care of the homeless. Federal control or regulation is preferred for economic development and hazardous waste disposal. Other areas such as welfare, public health, and certain morality issues tend to be less clear in the public mind. Although it is probable that these attitudes and preferences are more emotional than rational, at the aggregate level there is reasonable consistency and stability in public preferences in these policy areas. With few exceptions, these measures of public preferences for control or regulation of certain policy or program areas are related significantly to the composite measure of level of government identification.

For spending priorities, SSP data show that most people do not want to cut spending in any policy area. This finding is consistent with previous research in this area. Respondents are most positive about spending for education, drug abuse prevention, day care for children, health care for the poor, and child abuse prevention. These same individuals are least supportive of increased spending for highways and transportation, prisons, tourism, and state parks.

A principal components analysis finds consistency in spending preferences. Spending preferences on programs for vulnerable populations vary together on one factor, while those for parks, tourism, and highways vary together on a separate factor. Spending preferences on prisons, drug abuse, and illiteracy also vary together. In contrast to the measures of preferred level to regulate or control certain programs, level of government identification does not relate to spending preferences.

Regression models on summed measures of state program control, regulation, evaluation, and budgeting show that level of government identification is related significantly to preferred state/local control and regulation of certain activities or policies, but not to either state program evaluations or spending preferences. Since the latter two areas of budgeting and program evaluation do not include comparisons of levels preferred in the response set, it was not expected that the composite measure of level of government identification would be a determinant.

Are people rationally self-interested, or are they more emotional about these policy preferences? These data do not answer this question unambiguously. Perhaps the clearest finding of economic self-interest is that potentially more vulnerable populations (nonwhite females) were significantly more likely to support increased spending in policy areas directed toward helping vulnerable populations (elderly, infant health care, day care, child abuse prevention, low-income housing). Despite this rational component, political ideology or affect is demonstrated by the support of those negative toward Reagan and supporters of Dukakis over Bush for increased spending in these same program areas. The data suggest that both self-interest and symbolic politics help to determine public attitudes toward spending preferences and preferences for which level of government should be responsible for certain policy areas.

Further evidence of both self-interest and political affect is found in evaluation of selected state programs. Since the programs evaluated are directed to vulnerable populations (infant health care, day care, child abuse, reduced illiteracy, and elderly programs), it is not surprising that lower-income respondents were positive about the programs. In addition, supporters of these programs were also significantly more likely to support their governor and reside in politically liberal states with higher rates of job creation. The model for preferred level to regulate certain activities also demonstrates both self-interest and symbolic perspectives, with lower-income minorities who identify with state/local governments opposing federal regulation of these policy areas.

Political affect with little or no evidence of self-interest is evidenced by the model for preferred level of control or regulation of certain policy areas. The composite measure of level of government identification (which is argued to be an emotional attachment rather than a rational choice) and support for Reagan are significant predictors of preference for state/local control.

Note

1. In the previous chapter, perceptions of present and future national and state economic conditions and personal finances were used in the multivariate analyses of political evaluations. In this chapter, these economic perception variables are not used for the analyses of preferred level for program control or regulation. One reason is that the economic perceptions items were not used in the 1987

survey. Also, it is difficult to see any connection between economic perceptions and preferences for control and regulation of programs or functions by a particular level of government.

In contrast, it could be argued that individual perceptions of economic conditions would relate to preferences for spending on state programs. One might hypothesize that those who are pessimistic about present or future economic conditions would be less likely to prefer increased spending for certain state programs. None of these six indicators of economic perceptions are significant, however, when entered in the regression models from table 6-9. For the two single items and three composite measures of program budget preferences, regression coefficients for economic perceptions tend not to be significant, and the adjusted R^2s do not increase when these variables are entered in the five equations. The only exception is that perception of the future state economy is significant for the composite summarizing responses for spending for prisons, drug abuse, and illiteracy. Despite this added significant variable, the adjusted R^2 declines slightly with this variable in the equation.

7
Economic Development and Competitiveness

Previous chapters have examined relationships between state economic conditions and public opinion on political institutions and policy and program preferences. The role of economic conditions (both real and perceived) in affecting political choices and policy outputs nationally and at the level of the state has been studied in much detail in previous research. Primarily because of economic factors, Peterson (1981) argues that different levels of government will emphasize different types of public policies. Because of competition for mobile capital, the states will be highly constrained in the types of policies they will enact. This economic competition is alleged to be a brake on the ability and the desire of state governments to attempt redistributive policies, regardless of public preferences. According to the public choice perspective, mobile capital, information, and workers and other human resources will locate in jurisdictions that offer the most benefits and least costs of living and working. This interstate competition not only will increase the rate of economic growth but will improve democracy as politicians respond to increasingly mobile and knowledgeable constituents.

Although states have been competing for business growth, jobs, and investments since the nation's founding, state economic and political elites increasingly have been promoting competitiveness as a cure for the nation's economic ills. In this economic and political struggle, there is evidence that some state governments might be far ahead of the federal government in seeking ways to make their states more competitive in creating or generating jobs and investments. On the basis of the increased level and intensity of economic development activities of most states over the past decade or more, governors and other state officials apparently perceive opportunities to improve the business climate of their states and promote economic growth, and they act on these perceptions. Although the tactics and goals of the participants in this struggle have evolved over time, the basic question for state decision-makers remains relatively simple. How can they encourage or create business growth sufficient to provide jobs and improve the standard of living in their state?

The question for this chapter is, If state officials succeed in creating a business climate that facilitates successful competition with other states and leads to economic growth, does the public recognize and support such efforts and activities? How does the public assess the economy of their state, its receptivity to business growth, and its ability to compete in this economic struggle? To what extent does the public support specific state economic development activities and programs? What factors help explain public attitudes and preferences toward state growth policies and economic performance?

State Business Climates and Competitiveness

Evaluating state economies and business climates, and assessing state efforts to stimulate their economies, is a complex and controversial undertaking. In examining what he calls a "new progressive era," Osborne (1988) provides a detailed analysis of recent economic development efforts by certain states. Focusing primarily on six states and their governors since the late 1970s, Osborne explores in detail initiatives and innovations designed to create economic development. His concern is documenting problems and assessing programs and innovations designed to create economic growth rather than providing a scorecard of state efforts or suggesting who are the winners and losers in this economic struggle. In Osborne's wide-ranging and detailed account of domestic and global competitiveness, with its questions about the role of government in economic development, discussion of the role of the public is virtually absent.

Despite Osborne's cautions about the "scorecard" approach to state economic development efforts, numerous experts provide such assessments. In contrast to the case-study approach of Osborne, the accounting firm GrantThornton (1987) rates states according to their "manufacturing climates" (energy costs, labor costs, taxes, quality of life, etc.). In 1986 it found the top states to be North Dakota, Nebraska,

South Dakota, Virginia, and Colorado. The Corporation for Enterprise Development (CfED) criticizes the methods used by GrantThornton as overemphasizing low taxes, low wages, and no unions. The CfED (1987, 2–8) uses numerous measures to derive state performance, business vitality, capacity, and policies indices and provides a "Development Report Card" for the states. As examples, the top states in the Performance Index are Massachusetts, Connecticut, New Hampshire, and Minnesota; the top states in their Business Vitality Index are Alaska, Arizona, California, and Texas.

AmeriTrust/SRI (1986, 5) also criticizes the GrantThornton approach, saying that "states can score high on the GrantThornton index if they spend little on education, resulting in low taxes but also in an unskilled workforce that can command only the lowest wages." The AmeriTrust/SRI approach is to measure "economic capacity," which includes quality of science and engineering faculty, research and development in universities, industry research and development, capital availability, quality of labor, and the like.

As debate over state competitiveness and economic capacity continues, some question the desirability of the states' becoming involved in a zero-sum competition for business development, especially if the contest is over which state can provide the lowest wages and lowest taxes. The result could be development efforts for many states based on a definition of "favorable business climate" that equates with low wages, low taxes, no unions, and little government regulation. Another outcome of this competition could be some few states winning, with most others losing in a no-holds-barred competition. In contrast to these more critical assessments, public choice advocates see this competition in much more positive terms. In this policy debate, one question that has received some attention is the extent to which state policies affect economic growth.

Public Policies and Economic Growth

Brace (1989) suggests that any relationship between state policies and economic growth depends on the extent to which state economies are independent of external forces, especially the national economy. He finds that although still dependent on external forces, state economies have become more autonomous since the late 1960s. State economies also vary considerably in the extent to which they are independent of external forces.

Despite Brace's caution about the dependence of state economies on the national economy, several analysts examine the relationships of state policies to state economic growth (Ambrosius 1989a; Dye 1980; Jones 1990; Rubin and Zorn 1985). In the period from 1964 through 1984, Jones (1990, 229) finds that state welfare spending tended to detract from economic growth, while education and highway spending added to economic growth in some periods and detracted in others. After noting that many presumed determinants of state economic growth may be exogenous and not easily manipulated by state governments, Dye (1980, 1101) uses regression models to predict changes in state economic indicators (growth in personal income, employment, and value added by manufacturing), finding that transportation investments by state governments are influential predictors of economic growth in the period 1972–76. State tax policies, right-to-work laws, and spending for health, education, and welfare tend not to be related to economic growth in the states in this period.

Ambrosius (1989a, 296) examines economic time-series data for the states and fails to find any positive impact of selected state policies on state economic health. She suggests that rather than contributing to overall state economic growth, many of these economic development policies serve "narrower interests within the state." If the policies do not improve the overall rate of growth, why do officials continue to behave as if they do? Most explanations focus on elites.

Hill and Durand (1988, 742) survey local elites and find that local political leaders are closely tied to or are part of the "growth-machine" and are therefore unable or unwilling to control the pro-growth attitudes of business elites. These findings continue and expand an area of research that has focused on the economic power of business interests and on the limited ability of state and local public officials to control or regulate private interests or enact policies that might harm those interests in their state or locality (McConnell 1966; Peterson 1981).

Ambrosius (1989b, 64) contends that certain occupational interests use political action to have policies enacted that will enlarge their share of state benefits, regardless of the impact on overall state economic growth. She believes that "citizens and policymakers must ask whether the funds presently spent on state economic development policies could be more productively invested on other endeavors" (1989a, 296).

The assumption of Ambrosius that the public plays a role (at least a potential role) in state economic development policy-making leads to the primary focus of this chapter. Questions examined here that so far have been ignored in debates over economic competitiveness are whether the public is aware of the performance of the economy of their state, whether citizens of the states understand and support state economic development efforts, and whether this support influences state policy-makers.

There is little evidence that ordinary citizens are aware of or involved in the economic development activities and policies of state and local governments. One exception is a study of public opinion in Rhode Island regarding the "Greenhouse Compact." Using data from three separate statewide surveys, Hudson, Hyde, and Carroll (1987, 411–13) find widespread public support for an active role for government in stimulating the state's economy. However, those who did not feel they would benefit personally from the compact and "those who mistrusted state government and thought it benefited special interests" voted against the compact. This conclusion from Rhode Island survey data supports both the self-interest and the political-affect models of opinion formation.

Despite the scarcity of research on public opinion regarding economic development policies and activities, some analysts suggest that certain economic development policies are supported by the public. Beaumont and Hovey (1985, 329) describe the expansion of state and local policies toward reducing business costs as a development strategy supported by political leaders and suggest also that these policies "appear to enjoy the support of the electorate." This "electoral support" hypothesis is evaluated in this chapter. We assess public perceptions of state economies, business climates, and competitiveness, as well as attitudes toward state economic development programs such as offering tax incentives to businesses, advertising, development offices and trips overseas, and improving public education. Two composite variables—state economic optimism and support for state economic development programs—are created and analyzed. Characteristics of individuals who are economic optimists and support state policies to promote state economic development also will be assessed, using the basic multivariate model described in previous chapters.

Perceptions of State Competitiveness

The efforts of state officials to promote and encourage economic development are recognized and supported by the public. According to data from the first State Survey Project in 1987, the vast majority of respondents perceived that the leaders of their state were either "very active" (36 percent) or "active" (48 percent) in trying to attract new business into their state (Council of State Governments 1987). Not only did people recognize these efforts, but not surprisingly they viewed the activities very favorably, as indicated by 63 percent saying they "strongly favor" and 27 percent saying they "somewhat favor" efforts to attract new businesses to their state (p. 25).

The public has positive perceptions of the business climates and present and future economies of their state. When asked to characterize the business climate of their state, 83 percent said it was very favorable or favorable, while only 17 percent perceived it as unfavorable or very unfavorable. Respondents were confident their state would succeed in this economic competition (79 percent confident or very confident).

As noted above, this overall public optimism about state economies is not shared by many professional analysts who rate states according to the quality of their educational institutions, long-term investments in research, and the development of human resources thought to be important to businesses (such as the CfED or GrantThornton indices). Since there are few states considered to be at the forefront of policies thought to foster economic growth, and since the public generally rates their states very highly in this area, there appear to be contradictions between expert judgments and public perceptions of state economies and competitiveness.

It is also likely that the relatively positive responses of the public for certain items reflect "socially desirable" responses, or are based on a generalized "state pride" or identification rather than knowledge of comparative state economic conditions. The possible lack of congruence between public and expert evaluations of state business climates is complicated further by the variation in methods and data used by the experts and different rating organizations.

Perceptions of Economic Conditions

Public perceptions of state economies in 1988 are examined in chapter 5. It is reemphasized here that perceptions of state economies tended to fall between perceptions of the national economy and personal finances and that perceptions were relatively stable from 1988 to 1989 (table 7-1). Respondents perceived their personal finances slightly more favorably than the condition of their state's economy, with both perceived as healthier than the national economy.

The results are similar for the perceived future of each area. A large majority of the sample believed their personal finances would get better rather than worse, with a slight plurality believing the national economy would get worse rather than better. Perceptions concerning the future of their state economy fell in the middle, but people still believed by a

Table 7-1. Perceptions of Economic Conditions, 1988 and 1989

Evaluation	National Economy		State Economy		Personal Finances	
	1988 (%)	1989 (%)	1988 (%)	1989 (%)	1988 (%)	1989 (%)
Perception of the present						
Excellent	5	2	6	4	7	5
Good	42	36	56	50	57	55
Not so good	35	40	29	34	25	28
Poor	19	21	9	12	11	12
Perception of the future						
Get better	27	22	38	33	52	52
Get worse	31	31	17	20	8	8
Stay the same	42	46	45	47	40	40

2-to-1 margin that their state economy would get better rather than worse. Modest changes from 1988 to 1989 indicate declining optimism for both the national and state economies; perceptions about personal finances, however, do not change in this period.

Although there is a strong and positive relationship between people's perceptions of the present state economy and the "business climate" of their state (tau-b = .30), and confidence that their state will succeed in economic competition with other states (tau-b = .31), these relationships with perceptions of the future state economy are much weaker. In addition, the weak relationship between perceptions of the present and future economies of their state (tau-b = .06) suggests that individuals are uncertain whether their state will be able to sustain into the future what are perceived to be strong state economies.

Three items related to present state conditions are used to create a composite measure of state economic optimism. Perceptions of the business climate and the present state economy, as well as confidence in the ability of the state to succeed in economic competition are combined in the positive direction to create the new variable. The variable ranges from 3 through 12, with a mean of 8.6, standard deviation of 1.6, and is skewed slightly in the optimistic direction. The composite measure is related significantly to the three single indicators that make up the index (tau-b's range between .63 and .66).

Public Support for State Economic Development Programs

Despite strong support for attempts to attract new businesses into their state and much optimism about the state economy, individuals vary in the extent to which they support specific state economic development programs. In an area that many believe to be crucial to state economic competitiveness, an overwhelming majority supported improving public education programs to make the state more attractive to business and industry (94 percent strongly favor or favor). Respondents also indicated strong support for advertising that emphasizes the state's attractiveness (26 percent strongly favor and 64 percent favor).

In contrast, the public was much less positive about two other highly visible state economic development approaches: operating development offices in foreign countries (40 percent favor and 61 percent oppose) and overseas trips by the governor and state officials to encourage businesses to move to their states (48 percent favor and 52 percent oppose). More than twice as many individuals strongly opposed these two programs as those who strongly favored each (15 to 6 percent for overseas offices, and 13 to 5 percent for trips overseas).

The final SSP item relating to state economic development policies is tax incentives. One of the major controversies in state economic development policy-making is the extent to which state tax incentive policies influence economic growth. Although the experts do not agree on the desirability or effectiveness of tax incentives, by a small majority (55 percent) the public believed that raising taxes would cause businesses to leave their state. By a margin of 61 to 39 percent, they also supported using tax breaks or incentives to induce businesses to locate or expand in the state. The two variables are related in the expected direction, but the relationship is quite weak. Those supporting tax breaks as incentives to businesses were more likely than those opposed to tax incentives to believe that raising taxes would cause businesses to leave the state (tau-b = .07, p < .002).

Many advocates of increased business growth argue that taxes are antigrowth measures. Not only are high taxes alleged to discourage business investment, but lowering taxes or offering tax incentives to businesses is viewed by many as a major strategy for promoting job growth and increased business investment. Despite the debate among the experts and lack of much evidence that such incentives are cost-beneficial or that they have significant effects on business location decisions, many state and local officials continue to follow this course of action (Ambrosius 1989a; Rubin and Zorn 1985), and the public appears to agree with these officials.

A composite measure of support for state economic development programs is created by summing these five items. The variable ranges from 5 through 20, with a mean of 13.9 and standard deviation of 2.1. The composite is skewed toward support for these programs and relates to the five component items as follows (all are significant tau-b's):

Education	.44
Tax incentives	.43
Overseas trips	.60

Overseas offices   .55
Advertising   .43

Finally, the two composite measures of state economic optimism and economic development program support are not related (r = .03), indicating that they are capturing separate dimensions of state economic evaluations, namely, optimism and policy support. State economic optimists are no more likely than pessimists to support state economic development policies.[1]

Determinants of Optimism and Policy Support

Why are respondents optimistic or pessimistic about the economy and competitiveness of their state and more or less supportive of state economic development programs? To answer these questions, the multivariate model developed in previous chapters will be estimated for these two composite measures.

The contention of Weatherford (1983a) that perceptions of economic conditions are likely to be class based and contextual is discussed in chapter 4. It is hypothesized in this chapter that individuals with higher levels of education or income are more likely to have knowledge about the condition of their state economy compared with other states and consequently are more likely to judge accurately the relative condition of the state economy. In addition, these individuals are also more likely to feel secure financially and less vulnerable to changes in the economy and therefore transfer their personal confidence to the economy of their state. Together these two ideas suggest that if individuals are relatively well-off financially (individual social location) and reside in states that are more developed economically (economic context), they will be more optimistic about the economy of their state and its ability to compete economically.

For state economic development policies, more-educated and wealthy respondents are likely to be aware of these state programs and also more likely to see the results of such efforts as promoting economic growth, thereby benefiting the state and possibly benefiting them individually. In addition, these individuals might be more likely to see the benefits of foreign trips or offices overseas in this increasingly complex, global competition for economic growth. In addition to education and income, we also examine here other indicators of the social and economic conditions of individuals, namely, age, gender, and race.

Next, ideological or political factors, or what Sears et al. (1980) call symbolic predispositions, are examined. President Reagan and the Republican party agenda in the 1980s at least rhetorically were free-enterprise oriented. Their stated agenda was pro-business, pro-competition, pro-decentralization, and states' rights. These values are also identified historically with the Republican party. Do individuals who identify themselves as Republicans, rate President Reagan highly, and choose Bush over Dukakis in 1988 have more favorable views of their state's economy? Are these individuals more supportive of state economic development efforts? It is quite plausible to hypothesize positive relationships between these variables.

In addition to the more nationally oriented political variables (support for Reagan and Bush), a state-level measure of political orientation or identification is needed. As Stein (1990) demonstrates and as the data in chapter 5 support, the public holds governors at least partially responsible for state economic conditions. The indicator of state political attitudes used here is rating of the job performance of the governor. It is hypothesized that those rating their governor more highly will be more optimistic about the economy and competitiveness of their state and be more supportive of state economic development efforts.

Contextual Factors

In addition to individual-level correlates, it is hypothesized that aggregate characteristics of the states help explain individual attitudes toward state economies and policies. Individuals residing in states with relatively high levels of economic development or wealth or high rates of growth of the state's economy will be more optimistic about the economy of their state or more supportive of state economic development programs, regardless of their personal circumstances or political attitudes. In this chapter, measures of economic performance at the state level will be assessed as possible contextual determinants of individual attitudes.

The condition of a state's economy can be measured in many ways.

As noted previously, many experts gather data and attempt to evaluate state economies and business climates. These indices are based on varying aggregations and weightings of census data and often include other types of judgments about the state's economy. The GrantThornton index and the CfED index of performance discussed previously will be examined as contextual measures of economic capacity or business climate. These measures will be used to assess congruence between expert judgments and public judgments of state economies.

In addition to the expert "scorecards," the economy of a state can be measured using standard census data such as gross state product or per capita income (see chapter 5). In his assessment of state economies, Brace (1989) uses personal income per capita and value added by manufacturing to capture the dimensions of "income" and "productivity" as well as measuring the total economy and controlling for population size. In this chapter, gross state product in 1986, percentage change in gross state product from 1980 to 1986, percent of gross state product in manufacturing (1986), per capita income, jobs added in 1986, and percent of jobs added will be examined as measures of state economic context. These indicators capture the dimensions of income, productivity, size of economy, change over time, and they also control for population size. It is hypothesized that individuals residing in more prosperous states that are growing more rapidly than other states will perceive the business climate of their states as favorable and evaluate the present and future economies of their states more positively.

In addition to measures of economic development, a measure of the extent to which states have adopted innovative policies to foster economic growth is used as a contextual variable. Among the many indices developed by the Corporation for Enterprise Development (1987, 7) as part of their Development Report Card is a "Policies Index" which examines over thirty state economic development programs designed to "spur entrepreneurship, help improve the skills and adaptability of workers, speed technological innovation and strengthen the competitiveness of home-grown businesses and industries and the communities in which they are located." This index will be used to examine the extent to which individuals residing in states with more innovative economic development policies are more supportive of the state economic development programs which compose the composite index of policy support.[2]

The measure of the political conservatism of the state presented previously will be used as an indicator of the political context of the American states. It is hypothesized that individuals residing in politically conservative states will be economic optimists and economic development policy supporters.[3]

Correlates of Optimism and Support

As indicated in table 7-2 for bivariate relationships, the hypothesis that social class will be related positively to economic optimism and support for economic development programs is supported. Individual income is related positively to both state economic optimism and support for state economic development policies. Although education is not related to optimism, it is related significantly to policy support. Race is not related to either composite measure, but males and younger respondents are significantly more optimistic and supportive of these policies than are females and the elderly.

Although three of the political items are somewhat interrelated (support for Reagan, choice of Bush, and party identification), the results of the analysis are somewhat mixed. Support for Reagan and Bush and party identification vary in their relationships to economic optimism and policy support. Those who rate President Reagan's performance highly are optimistic about the economy of their state and supportive of state policies. However, those who prefer Bush over Dukakis in the 1988 election and those who identify themselves as Republicans are not more optimistic or supportive. As hypothesized, the fourth indicator of political orientation at the state level—rating of the governor—is related positively to both the composite of state economic optimism and economic development policy support.

Level of government identification is not related significantly to either state economic optimism or economic development program support. The bivariate product-moment coefficients, however, may be masking relationships between the middle group of identifiers (state level) and optimism and policy support. Recall that the level of government identification composite is a scale ranging from local to federal government identification, with state government in the middle. The composite is actually a centralization/decentralization scale. The correlation in table

Table 7-2. Correlates of State Economic Optimism and Support for Economic Development Programs

Characteristic	State Economic Optimism	Economic Development Program Support
Individual level		
Age	− .07*	− .12*
Education	.05	.16*
Income	.10*	.08*
Gender	.08*	.08*
Level of government identification	− .05	.04
Party identification	.03	.06
Presidential choice (Bush)	.05	.07
Rating of Reagan	.14*	.11*
Rating of the governor	.17*	.12*
State level		
Gross state product	.18*	− .12*
Change in gross state product	.35*	− .04
Gross state product in manufacturing	.05	.08*
Per capita income	.32*	− .14*
Jobs added (total)	.22*	− .12*
Jobs added (%)	.20*	− .07
GrantThornton index	.13*	− .04
CfED Performance Index	.25*	− .12*
CfED Policies Index	.11*	− .08
Political conservatism	− .05	.07

Note: Coefficients are product-moment. Those with an asterisk are significant at least at the .01 level.

7-2 of − .05 indicates that "centralizers" (federal identifiers) tend to be less optimistic about their state economy, and the correlation of .04 indicates that federal identifiers tend to be supportive of these economic development policies.

In order to assess whether state identifiers are more likely to be optimists and policy supporters than are local or federal identifiers, the cross-tabulations for these relationships are examined. Chi-squares indicate that state identifiers are not more likely than local or federal identifiers to be optimistic about the economy of their state or to support state economic development policies.

Table 7-2 also shows that with few exceptions, indicators of state context are related more closely than individual-level variables to the two composite measures. Except for the measure of state conservatism and gross state product in manufacturing, all the contextual variables are related significantly and in the hypothesized directions to state economic optimism. For example, individuals residing in states with higher percentage increases in gross state product, higher per capita incomes, and more jobs created are more optimistic about the economic conditions of their state.

Except for the GrantThornton index, jobs added as a percentage, state conservatism, and percent change in gross state product, the contextual measures are related significantly to support for state economic development policies, although most are in an unexpectedly negative direction. Also, the relationships are weaker than those for economic optimism. Individuals residing in states with higher per capita incomes, more jobs added, higher gross state products, and less innovative state economic development policies (according to the CfED) are less supportive of the state economic development policies used in the SSP surveys.

What might explain these perhaps unexpected or anomalous findings? Individuals in these wealthier, growing states perhaps recognize that more innovative policies are needed to sustain or increase economic growth in their state in an increasingly competitive environment, and they may feel that the traditional economic development programs used in these surveys are not sufficient.

Multivariate Models

After examining bivariate relationships between individual demographic characteristics, political attitudes, and economic and political contexts of a respondent's state of residence and public attitudes toward state economies and public policies, the next step is to assess the performance of these variables in multivariate models. Table 7-3 presents results of regression models using the two composite measures of state economic optimism and economic development policy support as dependent variables, with the individual demographic and political variables and contextual measures examined previously used as predictors.

Table 7-3. Regression Models for Economic Optimism and Support for State Development Programs

	State Economic Optimism		Economic Development Program Support	
Predictors				
Education			.15	.14
Gender	.07	.09	.11	.10
Rating of Reagan	.10	.06*		
Rating of the governor	.20	.19	.16	.15
Change in state gross product	.14	.15		
Gross state product in manufacturing	.15	.15		
Per capita income	.34	.28		
Political conservatism	.16	.10*		
CfED Policies			.12	.10*
Level of government identification	.06*		.04*	
Level for economic development		.00*		− .01*
Statistics				
Adjusted R²	.21	.21	.10	.08
F	10.7	11.1	4.9	4.5
N	650	698	650	698

Note: The coefficients are standardized regression coefficients (betas). Those with an asterisk are *not* significant. Each equation is significant at least at the .001 level. There are two separate equations for each of the two dependent variables. The first equation for each includes the measure of level of government identification as a predictor; the second uses the single measure of level preferred for regulation of economic development as a predictor instead of the composite.

State Identifiers and Optimism and Support

Before estimating the model, the role of level of government identification needs to be assessed. As one of the major concerns of this research, it is hypothesized that the extent to which individuals identify with one or another level of government helps explain their degree of optimism in their state's economy or their level of support for state economic development policies. The composite measure of level of government identification developed in chapter 3 as well as a single item from a set dealing with substantive policy areas which asks respondents which level of government is best for economic development are both used in the regression models. Level of government identification and preference for level to regulate economic development are related positively with a tau-b of .10 (p < .0001). The two regression models will be estimated with each of these measures included separately.

Table 7-3 indicates that the individual-level measures of income and age are not significant predictors for either of the composites, while education is significant only for policy support. Gender is significant for both composite measures, with males more optimistic and supportive of the policies than females. Although respondent evaluation of Reagan is significant only for state economic optimism, the measure of state political support (rating of the governor) is significant for both dependent variables.

The only contextual measure significant for policy support is the Corporation for Enterprise Development Index of Innovative Policies. In this case, the positive sign indicates that people residing in states with lower rankings for economic development policy innovativeness are more supportive of these traditional state economic development policies. Gross state product in manufacturing, change in gross state product, and per capita income are significant predictors in the expected direction of state economic optimism. The extent to which the state is conservative politically is significant for the equation that includes level of government identification, but not for the equation with the single indicator of level preferred for economic development.

Contrary to the hypothesis, neither the composite measure of level of government identification nor the single item measuring preference for level of government for economic development is related significantly to the optimism and policy composites when entered separately into the models.[4] The variance explained by the two models is not large (adjusted R^2s for economic optimism are .21, and for policy support are .08 and .10, depending on whether the overall index of level preference or the single measure of level preferred for economic development is entered in the equation). Contextual measures are somewhat stronger predictors than individual-level measures for the optimism composite and generally not significant for the policy support composite.

Conclusions

These data from the State Survey Project show that citizens believe their state economy and business climate are relatively strong, and they feel their state is likely to be among the winners in the competition to attract jobs and investments. The public is quite positive about the capacity and potential of their states to achieve future growth and prosperity (at least compared with the national economy).

A majority support the offering of incentives to entice industry or businesses to locate in their state, and they believe that raising taxes will cause businesses to leave the state. These perceptions, coupled with efforts by businesses to minimize their state taxes, could result in states' being constrained in the future from raising business taxes as a way of increasing revenues.

Individual perceptions of state economic performance correlate modestly with two separate and unrelated measures of state capacity as rated by experts. Individuals who have favorable perceptions of the business climate and economy of their state and are confident in the ability of their state to succeed in this economic competition reside in states ranked high on both the GrantThornton and CfED indices of state business or manufacturing climates.

Contextual measures of state economic and political conditions are somewhat stronger predictors of individual optimism about state economies than are individual-level measures of social class or political predispositions. It is impossible to say whether perceptions of self-interest or some broader collective interest is responsible for optimism and support; however, the extent to which the state in which individuals reside is developed economically or has experienced economic growth has independent effects on public optimism concerning the state economy and support for state economic development programs.

These findings might indicate that state officeholders (or some groups or actors in the states) are doing an effective job of making the public aware of how their states are performing. This assumption seems reasonable for those states prospering economically and having a governor (and other state officials) visible and active in promoting economic development and having economic elites interested in "boosting the economy," presumably with public support. What might be an explanation for states faring poorly in this economic competition?

Poor performance of the state "losers" in this economic competition perhaps is publicized by critics of the efforts of current state leaders, which keeps the issues and information before the public. Regardless of the explanation, the findings provide some support for the perspective that citizens have relatively accurate perceptions of the economic condition of their state. Unlike Stein (1990), however, we cannot say that voters reward or punish incumbent state officials based on these perceptions.

Although these data begin to answer certain questions about public perceptions of state economic development activity, many questions remain. On the basis of the issue of relations between state officials and private interests and public interests in the states, one can still question whether public support for state economic development policies has any impact on state policy-makers, or whether these issues are dealt with primarily at the elite level with little influence or involvement of the public. The public supports these efforts and has confidence in their state economies. We can only speculate, however, about the direction of influence.

Little is known about public perceptions or understanding of a term such as "favorable business climate," and the role of taxes, regulations, and incentives on business location decisions, and ultimately the health of a state economy. In addition, we have no direct measure of the extent to which individuals perceive that the performance of the economy of their state is due to the efforts of state officials. We know even less about public concerns with such economic development policies as right-to-work laws, new technologies, support for small businesses, public/private partnerships, and infrastructure issues. Because of the presumed low level of public concern and knowledge about these complex and less visible types of policy, it may be difficult to move beyond the broad indicators of public support for state economic development efforts and perceptions of state economies assessed here.

Most research in the area of state and local economic development examines the role of business interests and elite activity in policy-making. The role of the masses in this policy arena has been ignored. Although these data do not address directly the issue of the role of public opinion in state policy-making or direction of causality in relationships between the elite and the masses, they do suggest that state officials may be constrained by public opinion in certain program areas.

Since the public strongly favors efforts to attract business to its state, elected state officials at a minimum have to create the impression that they are making efforts to succeed in this economic competition. Also, since the public believes strongly in the desirability of advertising the virtues of its state, this may be a major tool that state officials use to assure the public of its efforts to "sell the state" and compete economically. For instance, even if empirical research casts doubt on the wisdom of offering tax incentives to businesses, the public tends to favor this approach. If business interests desire these incentives and the public is not opposed, it is understandable why state officials continue to use this controversial economic development tool.

Notes

1. The items used in the development of the composite measures are worded as follows:

Increasingly, individual states are trying to attract businesses and industries to improve their state's economy. In general, would you say you favor or oppose attempts to attract new businesses into your state? (strongly favor, somewhat favor, somewhat oppose, strongly oppose)

States have tried a number of different approaches to improve their state's economy. I am going to read you a brief list of some of these and ask you to tell me whether you strongly favor, favor, oppose, or strongly oppose each.

First, advertising that emphasizes how attractive the state is.
The second one is operating economic development offices in foreign countries such as Japan, Korea, and some European countries.
Next, how about trips overseas by the Governor and other state officials to encourage businesses to move to their state?

And what about passing special laws which give tax breaks or other incentives to industries if they will locate facilities or expand in the state?

What about improving public education programs to make the state more attractive to business and industry?

If taxes are raised in your state, do you think it is very likely, somewhat likely, not very likely, or not at all likely that it will cause businesses to leave your state?

States are now competing economically with each other. Some persons believe that if states pursue their own economic interests only a few states can succeed. How confident are you that your state will be one of those that will succeed in this competition?

Out of 1,150 responses on the third item (about raising taxes causing businesses to leave the state), 23.7 percent answered "very likely," 31.7 percent "somewhat likely," 36.2 percent "not very likely," and 8.4 percent "not at all likely." Out of 1,161 responses on the final item, 29.1 percent were "very confident" of their state's succeeding economically, 50.0 percent were "confident," 16.4 percent were "not confident," and 4.5 percent were "not at all confident."

2. The product-moment correlations between the six single indicators of the condition of the state economy and the three measures of the state economy as compiled by GrantThornton and the CfED for this sample appear in table 7-4. As might be expected, given how they were constructed, the GrantThornton and CfED performance indices are not related. They both relate significantly, however, to changes in gross state product in that states with highest rates of change tend to rank low on both indices. State per capita income is related closely to gross state product, change in GSP, and jobs added in the state from 1980 to 1986 as a total and as a percentage. The proportion of state GSP in manufacturing is related negatively to each of the other indicators except GrantThornton, indicating that in the 1980s, states more dependent on manufacturing economies had lower rates of economic growth and were ranked lower on the Grant-Thornton index.

3. The measure of political context of the state used here is related to certain of the measures of state economic conditions. For example, the product-moment correlation of state political conservatism with per capita income is −.60, with GrantThornton (−.47), with CfEDPerf (.66), and with jobs added as a percentage (.30); the correlation with gross state product in manufacturing, however, is only −.07, with total jobs added (.00), change in GSP (.06), and GSP (−.20).

Two of these contextual variables are omitted from the regression models.

Table 7-4. Correlations between Economic Conditions and Ratings of State Economies

	ChGSP	GSPMan	PcInc	Jobs	ChJobs	GT	CfED	CfEDPol
GSP	.14	−.07	.51	.88	.18	−.19	.24	.37
ChGSP		−.07	.52	.31	.63	.52	.34	.13
GSPMan			−.12	−.29	−.51	−.33	.06	.32
PcInc				.46	.30	−.02	.80	.53
Jobs					.53	.14	.14	.12
ChJobs						.65	.06	−.28
GT							−.02	−.44
CfED								.54

Note: Categories for indicating the condition of the state economy are as follows:

GSP	=	Gross state product, 1986
ChGSP	=	Percentage of change in the gross state product from 1980 to 1986
GSPMan	=	Proportion of the gross state product in manufacturing
PcInc	=	State per capita income, 1986
Jobs	=	State jobs added (total)
ChJobs	=	State jobs added (percentage)

Measures of state economies are the following:

GT	=	GrantThornton Performance Index
CfED	=	Corporation for Enterprise Development Performance Index
CfEDPol	=	CfED Policies Index

Correlations are for the sample survey, not for the fifty states. The value for each contextual measure is substituted for the state of residence of each respondent, and then correlations are calculated. The N's for each coefficient range from 1,189 to 1,197. The variables are moderately to highly correlated (product-moment coefficients of .07 are significant at least at the .01 level).

Since the correlation between Jobs and GSP is .88 and the correlation between PcInc86 and the CfED performance index is .80, Jobs and CfED are omitted from the equations.

4. There are two ways that these variables can be used. They each can be entered as predictor variables in the regression models as done in table 7-3, or they can be used to separate the samples and estimate regression models for state identifiers (or those preferring state government for economic development policy-making) and others in the sample. The latter method is used in table 7-5. One reason for using this method with level of government identification is the difficulty in interpreting coefficients for the level of government composite in table 7-3. The relationships of interest (state identifiers or the middle group of the scale with optimism and policy support) are not clear in the model as discussed above.

Table 7-5 indicates that for state economic optimism, both state identifiers and all others who are optimistic reside in states with higher per capita incomes. Only state identifiers, however, reside in politically conservative states. Those who are optimistic about the economy of their state but do not identify with state government are significantly more positive in evaluating President Reagan and their governor and more likely to reside in manufacturing states.

Table 7-5. Regression Models for Economic Optimism and Support for State Development Programs, with Separate Samples of Identifiers

	State Economic Optimism		Economic Development Program Support	
	State Identifiers	Fed./Local Identifiers	State Identifiers	Fed./Local Identifiers
Predictors				
Education			.09	.16*
Race			.21*	.00
Gender			.06	.11*
Rating of Reagan	− .01	.13*	−.21*	.07
Presidential choice (Bush)			.24*	.05
Rating of the governor	.12	.22*	.13	.17*
Gross state product in manufacturing	.08	.16*		
Per capita income	.38*	.32*		
Political conservatism	.29*	.12		
CfED Policies			.27*	.08
Statistics				
Adjusted R²	.12	.22	.08	.10
F	2.3	9.2	1.8	4.3
p <	.005	.000	.03	.000
N	161	487	161	487

Note: The coefficients are standardized regression coefficients (betas). Those with an asterisk are at least twice as large as their standard errors, which indicates significance at approximately the .05 level.

The results differ substantially for the other composite dependent variable—support for economic development policies. For this measure, state identifiers who support these state policies are significantly more likely than federal/local identifiers to reside in states ranked lower on the CfED Index of Innovative Economic Development Policies, and to be white supporters of Bush but not Reagan. The federal/local identifiers who support these policies are significantly more educated males who rate their governor highly.

The variance explained by the two models is not large (adjusted R^2s for economic optimism are .12 for state identifiers and .22 for others, and for policy support are .08 for state identifiers and .10 for others). Contextual measures are stronger predictors than individual-level measures for the optimism composite, and somewhat less strong for the policy-support composite.

The individual-level measures of income and age are not significant predictors for either of the composites, while education, race, and gender are significant only for policy support. Respondent evaluation of Reagan is significant for both composites. It is unexpectedly negative, however, for state identifiers who support state economic development policies. The only contextual measure significant for policy support is the CfED Index of Innovative Policies. Gross state product in manufacturing, per capita income, and state political conservatism are significant predictors of state economic optimism.

8
Welfare Policy

As Arendt (1963, chap. 2) notes, the social question of the modern age is the existence of poverty. Historians, social philosophers, and revolutionaries disagree over the extent to which modern revolutions have aspired to eliminate political oppression of the masses or to provide material abundance and happiness for the people. What is the relationship between bread and freedom? To what extent is a constitution a "panacea for poverty" (p. 105)? In modern America these questions usually translate into tensions between the values and principles of capitalism and democracy (McCloskey and Zaller 1984), and political and economic equality (Verba and Orren 1985).

Although few would argue that American society has ever been characterized by the huge disparities of wealth and the acute deprivation and misery of the lower classes found in prerevolutionary France or Russia, or present today in most third world or developing nations (the existence of slavery and its aftermath is a conspicuous exception to this generalization about America), poverty has been one of the most controversial issues in twentieth-century America. Presidencies have been defined by the problems of poverty and the welfare policies proposed to attack these problems. President Franklin Roosevelt developed New Deal policies to respond to the deprivations of the Great Depression. In his 1964 inaugural address, President Lyndon Johnson declared "unconditional war" on poverty in America, followed by legislation to build "The Great Society." In the decade following Johnson's declaration of war, some argue that a "welfare explosion" occurred (Dye 1987, 125).

Despite the rhetoric and symbolism of possible domestic wars and explosions, uncertainty and disagreement continue over the basic issues. Who are the poor? How many poor are there in this country, and where are they located? What can be done to eliminate or at least ease

143

this social problem? How responsible are individuals for their own poverty or welfare? To what extent are federal and state governments involved in or responsible for this policy area?

The term "welfare" itself presents problems for the analyst. Not only is the term difficult to limit and define, but many prefer other labels for this policy area. For example, very few governments use the term in identifying the agencies responsible for providing support to low-income or poor people. These agencies now provide "human services" or "social services" rather than welfare. Another example of American ambivalence toward welfare can be found in comparing social security programs including Medicare with welfare programs including Medicaid.

Social Security and Medicare (health care for the elderly) are seen as earned entitlements based on a social insurance model. Current and future workers pay into the system while still healthy and employed; later, when they are older, less healthy, or not working, the system repays them on the basis of their previous contributions. The recipients of these benefits are "beneficiaries." In contrast, welfare programs such as Aid to Families with Dependent Children (AFDC) and Medicaid (health care for the poor) are public charities primarily for women and children living in poverty. These individuals are welfare "clients." In contrast to Social Security, welfare programs means-test recipients to limit eligibility for benefits and are subject to constant, controversial policy choices and budgetary trade-offs at the state and federal levels. Medicaid will be discussed further in chapter 10.

This example of two differing types of public policies designed to deal with poverty may simply reflect the ambivalence of the American public regarding the concept of social welfare. Opinion surveys demonstrate that the public reacts more negatively to the term "welfare" than to the term "poor" or those "in need" (Smith 1987). For example, in the 1980s the average percentage of the public in the GSS (1984–88) who felt we were spending too much on welfare was 42 percent; in contrast, only 9 percent thought we were spending too much for "assistance to the poor" (Niemi, Mueller, and Smith 1989, 89). Concisely stated, "For many people welfare has come to stand for all the perceived ills of American domestic policy" (Kluegel and Smith 1986, 293).

There are many reasons for ambivalence, dissatisfaction, and conflict regarding poverty and welfare policy. Two important factors are the following: the policy area is concerned with basic American values of individualism and self-reliance, and welfare policy appears more directly redistributive than most other policy areas. The issues surrounding poverty are visible and personally applicable to many people. The widespread belief that the haves support or subsidize the have-nots and, more important, the belief that many or most of the latter may not deserve this generosity contribute to conflict and controversy. The basic conflict over the welfare state is well summarized by McCloskey and Zaller (1984, 264):

> The conservative defenders of capitalism contend that government, in trying to guarantee the welfare of its citizens, will undermine self-reliance and individual initiative, stifle the private economy, and destroy such cherished American values as competition and desire for achievement. Liberals and social reformers, however, argue with equal conviction that the promise of American democracy cannot be realized without the assistance of the welfare state. How, they ask, can a genuine democracy be achieved when powerful private interests dominate the society and millions of citizens lack the necessities for a decent and fulfilling life?

Regardless of which view predominates, there is little doubt that this nation has developed several important elements of a modern welfare state. Especially since the New Deal period, government has become involved extensively in many aspects of promoting the public welfare and devising programs to ease the burden of poverty for large numbers of people. Social Security and Medicaid discussed above are but two examples of such government welfare programs. Despite decades of policy initiatives (including Johnson's war on poverty) and the spending of billions of public dollars (the welfare explosion), it is difficult to find individuals or groups satisfied with the present system, including recipients or clients.

Welfare reform continues to be debated by federal, state, and local officials, as well as by various experts and interest groups in our society. Marmor, Mashaw, and Harvey (1990, 30–31) contend that discussions of social welfare in the United States tend to be nonideological and to focus "superficially on the means for implementing apparently agreed-on goals." Critics argue that the welfare system in America has failed to "wipe out the scourge of poverty" or remove bureaucratic barriers to "full participation by needy populations," nor has it protected all citizens from "cataclysmic medical expense." The system also is alleged to be wasteful, contradictory, oppressive, unaffordable, undesirable, and ungovernable. They contend that the focus on programs, practices, and effects without discussion of basic principles and purposes leads to these many contradictory criticisms. Also, "in the absence of continuous attempts to articulate policy in terms of principle, public understanding is almost certain to be lost." Some data on public understanding or at least public awareness and opinion concerning social welfare issues and policies will be discussed below.

Although ideology might not play a major role in the debate over the welfare state (or most political debates in American politics), and although we may have a "jumble of seemingly contradictory goals," Marmor, Mashaw, and Harvey (1990, 31) believe a "more or less coherent set of enduring commitments can be discerned," which they conceptualize as an "insurance/opportunity state." This state has a special character and structure with some "political coherence." Individual programs may be characterized by compromises and contradictions, "but those are necessary for a polity that wants to affirm *both* self-reliance and mutual support, that believes *both* in the primacy of the market and in the necessity for collective action through government, that wants to rely on *both* national fiscal capacity and local political control" (p. 47). Given contradictory goals derived from basic values of our culture and society such as equality and fairness, self-reliance and work, and families and children, and given the crazy quilt of policies and programs that make up our welfare state, how does the public view or understand poverty and social welfare issues?

McCloskey and Zaller (1984, 272–74) review survey findings since the 1930s and conclude that "Americans favor government assistance when people cannot find jobs, have no visible means of subsistence, or seriously need help." This support is qualified, however, by public denial that "society bears primary responsibility for individual welfare," or "lifetime security for all its members." Shapiro et al. (1987b, 120) echo this perspective and contend that "the American public has at best held mixed or ambivalent attitudes toward income assistance, even as the government has done more for the poor." Lane (1986, 389) quotes Rainwater, who states that "opposed to the principle that no one should live on so little money is the principle that everyone should have to work for what he gets."

Have these ambivalent attitudes been stable over time? How have public attitudes toward welfare changed? Examination of historical survey data leads Shapiro and his colleagues to conclude that the public exhibited a "modest liberalizing trend" in the 1960s, followed by a conservative shift from the 1970s to the beginning of the 1980s. Writing in 1987, they see a "striking liberal rebound" beginning in late 1981, with the public more liberal on social welfare issues than when Carter left office (Shapiro et al. 1987b, 121). Despite this broad opinion shift in the 1980s, they do not see any consensus toward assisting the poor or increasing redistribution. "More so than in the past, it appears that opinion has also shifted to a middle ground (represented by a middle response category in survey items) in which citizens want both the government and individuals to take responsibility for dealing with economic hardships" (p. 121).

Although Shapiro and his colleagues, in their review of survey findings, do not attempt to explain these changes over time or the possible ambiguities in beliefs, Kluegel and Smith (1986) develop and test a model to help explain these ambiguities. They contend that individual social and economic status, a stable "dominant ideology," and specific beliefs and attitudes shaped by recent debates and events ("social liberalism") determine public beliefs about economic inequality. Their theory is summarized as follows:

> On balance, the dominant ideology disposes people to a conservative evaluation of welfare and other redistributive programs. Such programs are perceived as unnecessary because the stratification system currently presents ample opportunity to better oneself by individual efforts. Even if the necessity of such programs is admitted, their acceptance still depends on their conformity to the dominant ideology's emphasis on individual responsibility and on the necessity of economic inequality to motivate people to achieve. On the other hand, many enduring features of social inequality, and changing beliefs and attitudes in some specific areas such as racial equality of opportunity, dispose people to what is conventionally labeled a liberal orientation (pp. 6–7).

Tensions between the dominant conservative ideology and evidence of persistent racial and other inequalities in society lead to the "inconsistency, fluctuation, and seeming contradiction" in public attitudes toward inequality and welfare (p. 6).

It is not possible here to describe the full extent of Kluegel and

Smith's theoretical development and data analysis. For policy attitudes (the focus of this research) they develop and test a causal model beginning with sociodemographic variables leading to general beliefs, then to perceptions, and finally to policy attitudes. Using national survey data and measures of support for welfare and government-guaranteed jobs and income, they find that the public supports guaranteed jobs and income but not welfare. Opposition to welfare appears to have increased over time, while attitudes toward guaranteed jobs and income "show roughly constant levels of support . . . since the 1930s" (pp. 154–55).

Regression models on these three dependent variables find "some evidence of self-interest effects (e.g., effects of income and race) on all three policies, but strongest for welfare and weakest for guaranteed incomes." Education has "strikingly different effects on the three policies, making attitudes on welfare more favorable but diminishing support for the other two" (p. 163). Elements of the dominant ideology as well as "political and racial affect" also influence policy attitudes. "Redistributive policy attitudes are thus influenced by individuals' beliefs in the dominant ideology and their self-interest and, in the case of welfare, by affective reactions to the government and to racial outgroups" (p. 175). In terms of the basic models of political opinion formation discussed previously in chapter 4—self-interest and symbolic predispositions—Kluegel and Smith find support for both in determining public attitudes toward public welfare policies.

McCloskey and Zaller (1984) take a somewhat different approach to the question of public support for welfare policies. Kluegel and Smith see the dominant ideology primarily as conservative and one-dimensional and based on individualism and economic inequality. In some contrast to the causal model approach of Kluegel and Smith and their distinction between a stable dominant ideology of conservatism and specific beliefs and attitudes that may be viewed more as social liberalism, McCloskey and Zaller (1984, 280–84) see the dominant ideology as characterized by continual conflict and tension between the two values, or "principal components," of capitalism and democracy. In their samples of elites and masses, support for welfare state principles and programs is greatest among those scoring high on democratic values and low on traditional capitalist values (pp. 280–81). They do not develop or test a causal model as do Kluegel and Smith.

In their study of equality, Verba and Orren (1985) take an approach similar to McCloskey and Zaller, including the focus on elite values and attitudes. Rather than studying the conflict between the values of capitalism and democracy in the American ethos, however, Verba and Orren examine relationships between political and economic equality, including individual and group equality, and equality of opportunity and result. The two approaches are similar in conceptualization in that economic equality appears to relate primarily to capitalist values (money), while political equality relates closely to democratic values (influence).

In terms of implications for social welfare policy, a key point made by Verba and Orren (chap. 10) is that Americans have always been more favorable to political equality than to economic equality. In contrast to economic inequalities, which are viewed as due primarily to individual effort and talent (or their lack), political inequality is viewed as unjust, although with some qualifications. Since most welfare programs are designed to ease disparities of income and wealth (at least on the surface or as stated as a goal), it follows that Americans would be somewhat unsympathetic to government programs which attempt economic equalization or redistribution of income.

With SSP data, identical tests of either the Kluegel and Smith model or the approaches of McCloskey and Zaller and Verba and Orren are not possible. We can, however, test hypotheses dealing with self-interest and symbolic identifications as determinants of welfare attitudes. For several public attitudes toward welfare programs, hypotheses on the effects of individual demographics, level of government preference, perceptions of economies and personal finances, political predispositions, and measures of the economic, political, and welfare policy context of the states will be tested.

The States and Welfare Policy

Before using the SSP date to examine public attitudes toward welfare, we describe briefly the role of the states and the federal government in this policy area. As with most domestic policy areas, welfare is complex and intergovernmental. The federal government exercises considerable leverage over the states by providing funds for major programs such as AFDC and Medicaid. Along with these federal dollars to be matched by state dollars come standards and regulations to be complied with by the states. According to Albritton (1983, 379), the effect of these formula dollars and regulations on state welfare policies is profound and "illustrates how responsive state policy is to federal policy initiatives."

The eagerness with which states seek these and other federal dollars cannot be denied; at the same time, states through their lobbying arms such as the National Governors Association and the National Conference of State Legislatures wield some influence on the policy-making and rule-making processes in the national executive and legislative branches in welfare policies as well as other intergovernmental policies. States retain discretion in several areas of public welfare policies. For example, states rather than the federal government are responsible for setting AFDC benefit levels, and as Reischauer (1989, 23) notes, there is no "simple mechanism through which the federal government can ensure that federal resources intended for benefit increase actually end up raising benefit levels." After describing how the federal government can raise the standard of living for welfare recipients by increasing food stamp benefits, he notes that some evidence exists that states responded to expanded food stamp and Medicaid programs in the 1970s by slowing the pace at which they raised AFDC benefits to offset the federal action.

States also function as innovators or policy leaders in this area. For example, along with issues of workfare, or work requirements for welfare recipients, a number of states are considering the controversial issue of denying benefits or even penalizing "welfare mothers" who have children while receiving welfare benefits. Not only are other states monitoring these issues closely, but some federal officials, including President Bush, are praising these state initiatives. The social welfare system and policy-making process is not a simplistic top-down or command and control system. Although not always a political struggle between equals, extensive bargaining and negotiation between the federal and state governments is the norm.

Despite active and sometimes effective federal influence, states vary considerably in poverty levels, spending for welfare, payment levels, eligibility standards, and adequacy of grants (Albritton 1983, 391–93). There are not fifty independent welfare policy systems, but neither is there one nationalized system. For example, in the late 1970s, the highest-ranking states spent more than five times as much for welfare (controlling for state personal income) as the lowest-ranking states. Welfare spending as a percentage of total state spending again was almost five times higher in the top states (29 percent) than those at the bottom (6 percent), while AFDC recipients per 1,000 state population ranged from 70 down to 14 (Albritton 1983). Another indicator of complexity and variation in welfare policies across the states is that they vary in rankings on all these dimensions. States low in one area are not necessarily low in other areas. The picture is one of considerable variation among the states in welfare policies.

In addition to federal mandates and dollars, what other relatively uncontrollable national or interstate economic and political forces affect the states? To what extent do states influence decisions made by the private sector as to where business or manufacturing facilities will be located, what goods or services will be produced, and what types of individuals will be hired to help produce the products? This question is discussed in more detail in the previous chapter, dealing with economic development. There is evidence that the states play a significant role in these activities and influence the movement and development of mobile capital and jobs, which relate closely to poverty and welfare.

On another dimension of the wealth-poverty question, in what ways do states influence or control decisions as to what level and types of public benefits will be provided to those not participating in or excluded from the private sector economic activities? As discussed above, although states are not autonomous and they depend on federal dollars, there is evidence that in the area of welfare policy, "states exercise considerable discretion over how the funds are spent and the level of benefits a family may receive" (Peterson and Rom 1989, 714).

Just as states compete for mobile capital and other desired resources, they also compete for presumably less-desired resources—welfare recipients. The interstate competition is based on state discretion in spending, eligibility requirements, and benefit levels. "Although the states can do a great deal to find solutions to the welfare problem, they cannot solve it themselves. As pointed out by David Reimer, author of *The Prisoners of Welfare,* if one state acted by itself to develop a comprehensive approach to combatting poverty, it would be overwhelmed by an influx of poor people. States can, however, play a vital role in experimenting with solutions, fulfilling their function as 'laboratories of democracy'" (Gold 1991, 26).

The contention that a comprehensive approach to improving a state's welfare programs would lead to an overwhelming influx of poor people is an empirical question that has yet to be answered. No state has yet volunteered to experiment with such a bold, comprehensive approach to social welfare policy that would permit testing of the mass-migration hypothesis. Peterson and Rom (1989, 712), however, do find "state-determined benefit levels distort both policy and residential choices." Using OLS regression models of changes in benefits levels and state poverty over three periods (1970–75, 1975–80, 1980–85), they conclude that state policy-makers consider the poverty rate and the interstate migration of the poor in establishing welfare policy (p. 721). They also conclude that "states that are more prosperous, more politically competitive, and culturally more disposed toward redistribution are likely to increase welfare benefits over time and in comparison to other states. But high and increasing poverty levels lead to cuts in welfare. High benefit levels also expose states to welfare-induced migration of the poor" (p. 725).

Although subject to national economic and political forces, and constrained by interstate competition, states vary in their level and types of economic activities and in their policy responses to problems of poverty. As discussed in this and previous chapters, states are consequential territorial entities for both economic development and welfare policy.

Welfare and Workfare

The SSP surveys do not address directly the issue of welfare. (In chapter 6, however, we assessed public support for several welfare-related programs.) A series of items asking respondents whether they want to increase, keep the same, or decrease spending finds a pattern of strong support for senior citizens programs, child abuse prevention, infant health care, day care, and low-income housing. A regression model on a composite measure of these human services finds minority females who have negative evaluations of Bush and Reagan to be more favorable to increased spending for these areas. Self-interest and political affect have relatively equal influence on support for welfare spending. In addition to these welfare spending items, the SSP surveys address perceptions of workfare.

Workfare, or programs requiring welfare recipients to be employed or at least to be engaged in training or education, is popular with legislators and policy experts from both parties and many ideological persuasions. This broad consensus does mask some differing perceptions about why welfare recipients are not doing more to help themselves and find jobs (Reischauer 1989, 27). Liberals, who adopt a more public orientation, tend to focus on the failings of society and the system, which provides too few jobs with adequate pay and working conditions, as well as lack of education for recipients and support services such as day care and transportation. Conservatives, adopting a more private orientation, stress behavioral and sometimes moral or value deficiencies of clients who will not work or obtain necessary training and schooling to participate in the labor force. These perceptions lead to different approaches to programs designed to move individuals from the welfare rolls to the work force. The issues include whether participation is mandatory or voluntary, the availability and extent of support services, whether health insurance can be maintained (Medicaid), whether clients should be required to accept jobs below the minimum wage, and related matters. These questions impact the costs, feasibility, and potential success of workfare programs.

Although some experts believe that required job training is as far as such workfare legislation will be able to go, the public favors actual work requirements. Harris surveys in 1972 found almost 90 percent of Americans favoring "making people on welfare go to work" (Shapiro et al. 1987a, 279). An NBC survey in 1977 found 93 percent agreeing that those on welfare "capable of working" should be required to "work at public jobs in order to receive their check" (Shapiro et al. 1987a, 279). In a 1985 ABC/*Washington Post* poll, not only did 89 percent favor legislation requiring job training for "able-bodied people" on public assistance to retain benefits, but 77 percent favored requiring these same people "to work at any minimum-wage job in return for their benefits" (Shapiro et al. 1987a, 280). Missing from many of these survey items is consideration of parents or single mothers with children. The SSP item dealing with welfare and work raises the issue of parents' staying home with preschool children.

The SSP item states: "Some persons have suggested changing the welfare system so that single parents receiving welfare must enter a job training program to continue receiving financial assistance. Other persons believe it would be better for the parent to stay home with their children. Would you strongly favor, favor, oppose, or strongly oppose requiring single parents on welfare to enter job training?" Even with consideration of children in the item, mandatory job training for single parents on welfare is strongly favored by the SSP samples in the three years the question was asked, as table 8-1 shows. Also, in this item the term "welfare" rather than "public assistance" or some other more neutral term is used.

Although the overall percentage of favorables decreased from 88 to 83 percent from 1987 to 1988 and remained at 83 percent in 1989, the percentage of those strongly favoring the policy increased from 40 to 49 to 51 percent in that same period. This trend may indicate increased levels of public dissatisfaction with the American welfare system, or perhaps it is recognition that one important way out of welfare is for welfare recipients to acquire skills sufficient to participate in the job market. Since the item does not refer specifically to the age of the children but does imply that they are preschool, it is possible that providing respondents with more information or choices dealing with the ages of these children might lead to different results.

Since the item introduces the idea of job training for welfare recipients by stating that some believe it would be better for the parent to stay home with their children, those few respondents who were strongly opposed or opposed to mandatory job training (13 to 17 percent of the samples) were asked if they would favor the proposal if the children of welfare recipients could be placed in affordable day care or school. When provided with the child care option, a majority of those opposed would change their minds and favor mandatory job training. The per-

Table 8-1. Attitude toward Mandatory Job Training for Welfare Parents

	Survey Year		
Opinion	*1987* *(%)*	*1988* *(%)*	*1989* *(%)*
Strongly favor	40	49	51
Favor	48	34	32
Oppose	11	12	14
Strongly oppose	2	5	2

centages changing their opinion to favorable range from 67 to 79 percent in the period 1987 to 1989.

Guaranteed Jobs and Incomes

Although the issue of a guaranteed income or negative income tax has faded somewhat from the legislative and public agendas over the past few decades, it continues to be a concept with some political support and appeal. Many survey items have been used in the past to attempt to tap public sentiment on this emotional issue. Because "guaranteed income" is a term that seems only to guarantee a negative response, respondents in the SSP survey were asked about a "federally guaranteed minimum payment that families would receive for food, housing, clothing, and health care." Use of the term "minimum payment" rather than "income" and the addition of qualifiers indicating necessities of life no doubt made it easier for respondents to respond affirmatively. Just as individual values and perceptions of words shape responses to survey items, these same values no doubt influence beliefs as to which of the versions of the same concept or wording of items is more likely to tap the true feelings of the public regarding income support for poor people.

In 1987 a majority of 72 percent support a guaranteed payment for certain necessities. In contrast, Kluegel and Smith (1986, 153) provide data from the 1980 NES that show that only 47 percent agree that the "federal government should guarantee an income above the poverty level to every person who works." Earlier survey data find even greater majorities opposed to a guaranteed income. Gallup polls found only 20 percent in 1965 and 28 percent in 1968 favoring a guaranteed "minimum annual income." A 1969 Harris survey, however, found 58 percent agreeing with the concept, and a 1970 CBS poll found 47 percent agreeing (Shapiro et al. 1987b, 127–28).

Another welfare-related concept is the creation of public jobs by the government. When such job creation is tied to the issue of high unemployment in rural and inner-city areas, in the 1987 SSP survey respondents favored the proposal by a margin of 67 to 33 percent. Kluegel and Smith report the 1980 NES as finding 61 percent agreeing that the "federal government should guarantee a job to every person who wants to work." Earlier, University of Michigan Survey Research

Center/Center for Political Studies (SRC/CPS) surveys in the late 1950s and in 1960 found 56–58 percent agreeing that "the government in Washington ought to see to it that everybody who wants to work can find a job." CBS polls in the 1970s found 70–74 percent agreeing with this concept; Yankelovich surveys with different question wording and different response categories, however, found somewhat lower levels of support in the 1970s (Shapiro et al. 1987a, 274–75). In contrast to the guaranteed payment item, responses to this SSP guaranteed-jobs item did not differ much from similar items in other surveys.

Respondents to the 1987 SSP survey consistently were favorable to "workfare," "guaranteed payments," and "guaranteed jobs," with all three items ranging from 72 to 88 percent support. This contrasts with some previous surveys finding differences in level of public support for these three concepts. Some of the consistency in support for the SSP items may be based on question wording and question-order effects, although the same could be said about most previous findings in this area. Another way of looking at consistency or response bias is correlational analysis. Despite the consistent high levels of support, these three SSP welfare items tend not to be related closely to one another. Although the guaranteed federal payment item and the federal jobs item are related moderately (tau-b $= .32$), the workfare item is related only weakly to the federal jobs item (tau-b $= .06$, $p < .02$) and is not related to the guaranteed payment item (tau-b $= .03$). Individuals are not consistent in their support for the three welfare items. Given these varied relationships, which groups of respondents are supporting these proposals?

Determinants of Support for Welfare

Examination of bivariate correlations between the welfare items and various individual characteristics and attitudes finds expected relationships. Those who are more favorable toward workfare are significantly more likely to be Reagan supporters, Republicans, and ideological conservatives. In addition, they are whites with higher incomes. Those favoring federal job creation differ from those favoring workfare. Those more supportive of federal job creation identify more with the federal government than with state or local government (composite measure of level of government identification); they are less positive about Reagan and are Democrat identifiers, more liberal ideologically, younger, less educated, poorer, female, and minorities. Except for level of government identification, those favoring a guaranteed payment are the same as those favoring federal job creation.

In attempting to sort out these relationships, OLS regression and discriminant models are used for the three indicators of support for welfare-related programs. The predictors include the individual social, economic, and political measures above and four measures of state context. The measures of state context are state per capita income in 1986 as a measure of the wealth and resources of the state, state welfare expenditure per $1,000 personal income in 1978 as a measure of the welfare effort of the state (Albritton 1983, 392), the percentage of the state population who are AFDC and SSI recipients in 1987, and the measure of state conservatism used in previous chapters.

The models for the workfare item are somewhat difficult to interpret. Collapsing the four categories of responses (strongly favor, favor, oppose, strongly oppose) into favorable/unfavorable categories for the discriminant model finds 87 percent of the cases are classified correctly, and evaluation of Reagan, political ideology, race, income, and the contextual measure of percentage of public aid recipients are significant discriminant function coefficients. In contrast, the regression model for the workfare item using the original four response categories with the same set of predictors is barely significant (F = 1.72, p < .05), with an adjusted R^2 of .02 and ideology the only predictor close to statistical significance. Part of the difficulty in interpretation is due to the high percentage of favorables for the item (88 percent) and the use of regression for the four-category version of the item.

The models for guaranteed payment and jobs are more consistent and interpretable than those for the workfare item. The OLS adjusted R^2 for guaranteed jobs is .12, with level of government identification, party identification, rating of the governor, education, income, and ideology significant in the expected directions. The equivalent discriminant model is similar to the OLS model, with 77 percent of the cases classified correctly and the same variables as significant coefficients with the addition of gender in the discriminant model. The OLS R^2 for guaranteed payment is .16, with age, race, income, ideology, evaluation of Reagan, and level of government identification as significant predictors in the expected directions. For the equivalent discriminant model, the significant coefficients are the same with the addition of respondent education, and 77 percent of the cases are classified correctly. None of the contextual measures are significant in any of the models for guaranteed payments and jobs.

Conclusions

Although previous empirical research demonstrates low to moderate public support for social or public welfare programs in general, the SSP data show relatively high public support for certain welfare programs: workfare, guaranteed payment for necessities, and guaranteed jobs. Despite the overall high level of support, the SSP data also suggest the ambivalence and value conflict found in other survey results. Respondents support a "conservative" proposal (workfare), as well as the "liberal" proposals of guaranteed jobs and payments.

Despite high levels of support for all three welfare programs, people are not consistent in their support. Some of the inconsistency or ambivalence of the public is explained by the fact that different groups support different programs. The data show that individuals vary in expected ways in their support for workfare, guaranteed jobs, and guaranteed payments. Political liberals, those with lower incomes, and Democrats support the "liberal" policies. Political conservatives, those with higher incomes, and Republicans support the "conservative" policy. Multivariate models find both self-interest and political affect variables related significantly to the dependent variables for welfare policies. In addition to indicators of possible self-interest such as age, race, and income, party identification and level of government identification are significant predictors of support for guaranteed jobs and payments.

To what extent does level of government identification affect attitudes toward welfare? The answer is mixed. For policy or political items that contain an intergovernmental reference, level of government identification is significant when controlling for numerous other variables. For example, the items of support for federally provided jobs or a payment for necessities are related significantly to the composite measure of level of government identification, controlling for other variables in the model.

For issues of public welfare, a fundamental social, political, and economic question is, What is private and what is public? How are self-interest (private?) and symbolic predispositions (public?) as used in these models related to the values of capitalism and democracy in the political ethos of McCloskey and Zaller, or the concepts of political and economic equality as elaborated by Verba and Orren? At best, it can be said that they do not appear to be incompatible.

In regard to public support for welfare policies, what are the relationships between rational self-interest and values such as altruism, commitment, or public-regardingness? As measured at least indirectly by age, income, race, attachments to political parties, ideologies, or levels of government, these data demonstrate that self-interest and symbolic predispositions are difficult to disentangle or separate in the public mind. Analysis of items relating to public welfare from the SSP illustrates the complexities and ambiguities in this controversial policy area.

What are some implications of these findings for federal and state welfare policies? Since the survey data suggest that Americans are supportive of welfare programs that are tied to work and employment, to what extent do some of the latest welfare reforms reflect these values? The Family Support Act of 1988, although not a major reform (at least when compared with Nixon's proposed Family Assistance Plan of the 1970s or the many guaranteed income or negative income tax proposals of the 1960s and 1970s), does appear to bring welfare policy more into the mainstream of American life. In the past, welfare policies have been perceived by most Americans as separate from work and education, which are based on values of commitment, independence, responsibility, and obligation. By emphasizing self-sufficiency and people helping themselves through education, training, and employment, the Family Support Act reflects public opinion and mainstream American values. It remains to be seen whether this most recent policy-opinion congruence will lead to increased levels of public support for more generous welfare programs.

9
Public Education, Families, and Values

The States and Education Policy

There are many indicators of the importance of public education to the American people. The policy area consumes a larger proportion of state and local government budgets than any other service. In 1988 approximately $309 trillion was spent on schooling in this nation, and 55 percent of the U.S. population is either enrolled in an educational institution or employed in an educational system (Bowman and Kearney 1990, 426). Why is so much money invested and so many people involved in the area? One reason is the expanded mission of the public schools. Dye (1987, 170) contends that American schools are now expected to do far more than simply provide basic education for our children. Public schools also are expected to help build a racially integrated society, promote good citizenship, offer recreation and entertainment, fight disease and poor health, produce scientists and technologists, help fight drug abuse, provide sex education, and supply other services and promote numerous other socially desirable goals. All of these difficult and often conflictual goals require extensive resources.

What is the role of the American states in this gigantic enterprise? As Wirt (1983, 305) states, "Public education is a state responsibility administered by a special local education district." There is no mention of education in the U.S. Constitution, and virtually no federal involvement in the area until after World War II. Federal involvement has increased during this period but is still modest compared with that of the states. Dye (1987, 171) contends that the federal government is mostly "an interested spectator" in education policy, with its share of education spending in the postwar period not exceeding more than 10 percent of the total. Despite lip service and symbolism concerning local control of the schools, most observers agree that since the 1960s, states have increased their control over local schools to the degree that "local control is meaningless" (Wirt 1983, 305). Wirt goes on to say that "it is difficult today to find a local school issue that has not been escalated to the state level by lobbying or litigation" (p. 306).

As in other policy areas and despite the overall trend toward centralization at the state level, there is substantial diversity across the states in degree of centralization as well as other aspects of public education. For example, states vary substantially in education spending as a proportion of state per capita income and spending per pupil, as well as in the percentage of total state and local spending from state sources (Wirt 1983; Bowman and Kearney 1990).

As a context to assessment of public opinion data relating to education policies, it is important to note that education reform was high on the agenda of many state governments, as well as the federal government, in the decade of the 1980s. The period was characterized by major reform efforts in many states. The reforms of the 1980s followed years of study and sporadic attempts to change the system in earlier decades. A major study in 1983 entitled *A Nation at Risk,* which described a crisis in our system of elementary and secondary education, was an important catalyst to change. Many governors and other state officials, especially in the southern states, initiated large-scale efforts to improve their schools. Some of these policy efforts died soon after conception; some have succeeded, and some continue to struggle for resources and support. The reforms center on issues of management, curriculum, and financing and include such concepts as performance standards for students and teachers, professionalization and accountability of teachers, and increased and more equitable funding of schools. In terms of analysis of public opinion in the late 1980s, it is important to note that education problems and reforms were highly visible and controversial during this period.

Public Education Reforms

In contrast to its feelings about welfare and poverty, the public has more positive and perhaps consistent views of public education. As discussed in chapter 6, although the public supports increased spending for most state programs, it is most supportive of spending increases for public education improvements. Examination in chapter 7 of the role of education in economic development also finds strong public support for public education.

It is not surprising that the public supports education. In comparing economic and political equality in modern democracies, Verba and Orren (1985, 12) see this public support as compatible with certain components of American ideology and the concept of equality of opportunity. More important, they see education as an important source of inequality.

> One area in which governmental spending in the United States has exceeded that in other nations is education. The United States ranks first in per capita spending on schooling and first in the percentage of the population that has received higher education. But educational expenditure differs from other outlays in that it promotes equal opportunity rather than equal results. Support for public education harmonizes perfectly with American ideology. The educational system has been the main channel for upward mobility. In that sense, it is a source of economic inequality rather than equality.

It should be emphasized that the relatively high ranking of the United States for education spending compared with other nations masks great extremes between and within the American states. Not only is public education in this country a cause of economic inequality, as Verba and Orren note, but the system itself is based on or is the result of economic disparities. Public education policies, spending patterns, and student performance vary substantially across the states and local school districts. Despite these inequities, researchers generally have been unable to demonstrate any significant relationships between student achievement and school resources such as spending, class size, and facilities (Hanushek 1981).

In addition to the items dealing with education spending and economic development analyzed in previous chapters, a series of items in the 1989 SSP provides more specific and detailed findings concerning public education in this country. First, to what extent do people have positive views of the American system of public education? In 1989, by a margin of 60 to 40 percent, people expressing an opinion were very or somewhat satisfied with the job being done by the public schools. As a comparison, another way to assess satisfaction or support for public schools is to ask respondents to grade their schools. For over twenty years the Gallup organization has conducted yearly polls of public attitudes toward schools, and one long-standing item asks respondents to give the grades of A, B, C, D, or FAIL to denote the quality of their local schools.

From 1980 through 1990 for these Gallup surveys, the percentage of respondents giving a grade of A or B ranged from 31 to 43, with a slight upward trend in the latter part of the decade. If one includes a grade of C as indicating satisfaction (most educators would regard this as a "passing" score), then another one-third of the respondents could be added to the roughly 40 percent choosing an A or B, resulting in approximately two-thirds to three-quarters satisfaction. In the ten-year period, less than 15 percent gave the grade of D, and less than 8 percent gave a failing grade (Elam 1990, 50–51).

In an interesting variation on this item, if respondents are asked to grade the public schools "in the nation as a whole" rather than their local schools, they are much less positive. In 1990, the percentage giving an A or B for national schools was 21 percent (versus 41 percent for their local schools), while the percentage giving a grade of C was 49 percent (versus 34 percent for local schools). In yet another variation, those who have children in the public schools gave even higher grades to the school attended by their oldest child (72 percent gave an A or B in 1990), in contrast to their local schools. Although not without some ambiguity, limited evidence from the annual Gallup polls suggests reasonable public satisfaction with the nation's education system. This is supported by the 1989 SSP item dealing with satisfaction with the schools.

Despite the moderately high level of overall satisfaction in the 1989 SSP survey, people favored reforms of public education. Table 9-1 shows that the following proposed improvements were favored by more than 85 percent of the SSP sample:

increased emphasis on the "basics"
competency testing for students
competency testing for teachers
giving teachers more control over classroom activities
increased school discipline

Table 9-1. Support for Education Improvements

Proposal for Improving Public Schools	Favor (%)	Oppose (%)
Increase the emphasis on basic reading and arithmetic skills and knowledge	97.7	2.3
Competency testing for teachers	94.2	5.8
Competency testing for students	91.5	8.5
Give teachers more control over their classroom activities	91.1	8.9
Increased school discipline	86.7	13.3
Higher salaries for teachers	78.1	21.9
Merit pay for teachers	77.6	22.4
Require students to stay in school until age 18	77.5	22.5
Mandatory homework	74.4	25.6
Allow parents to choose public schools for their children	70.4	29.6
Provide vouchers for parents to allow them to send children to private schools if desired	66.2	33.8
Deny drivers licenses to students who drop out of high school	61.9	38.1
Increase taxes to provide money for public schools	60.8	39.2
Lengthen the school year	35.7	64.3
Lengthen the school day	30.1	69.9

Note: Figures under "Favor" and "Oppose" are based on responses to the following survey item: "Many ideas have been proposed about how we might improve our public schools. I am going to read you a list of some of these ideas. For each one, please tell me if you favor or oppose it." The N's for individual items range from 969 to 1,020.

Somewhat smaller majorities favored merit pay for teachers (78 percent), mandatory homework (74), higher salaries for teachers (78), allowing parents to choose public schools for their children (70), and requiring students to stay in school until they reach eighteen years of age (78). Majorities favored increasing taxes to provide money for schools (61 percent), providing vouchers to allow parents to send their children to private schools (66), and denying drivers licenses to high school dropouts (62). The only two proposals that did not receive at least majority support were to lengthen the school day (30 percent favor) and to lengthen the school year (36 percent favor). Some traditions apparently die very hard.

The annual Gallup polls on public schools have some items comparable to the SSP items in table 9-1. In 1982, by a margin of 53 to 37 percent (10 percent don't knows), the Gallup sample opposed extending the school year by one month, and by a margin of 55 to 37 percent (8 percent don't knows) opposed extending the school day by one hour. These findings are comparable to the 1989 SSP results. The 1985 Gallup survey found a large majority favoring competency testing for teachers (89 percent) and a somewhat smaller majority (60 percent) favoring merit pay for teachers. These findings also are comparable to those from the SSP survey.

In 1988, the Gallup poll found 64 percent willing "to pay more taxes to help raise the standards of education in the U.S." (Gallup and Elam 1988, 38). This figure is close to that for the comparable item in the SSP survey (where it is worded quite differently), in response to which 61 percent indicated that they favored increased taxes for the public schools. Although the findings of the two surveys differ for teacher salaries, the differences may be due more to question wording or response categories than actual perceptions. In the 1990 Gallup poll, 50 percent believed salaries for teachers were too low, while 31 percent believed salaries were "just about right" and only 5 percent thought they were too high. The 1989 SSP survey found 78 percent favoring higher salaries for teachers, with 22 percent opposed.

Although most of the above results demonstrate some consistency across the separate surveys and different years, items dealing with the issue of parental choice and vouchers show contrasting results. There are many variations of the concept of choice as applied to public education, but the basic idea is that parents would be given a voucher each year to spend on schooling for their elementary and secondary school-age children. Parents could then choose which schools (private as well as public) their children would attend. This empowerment of parents and school children would lead to schools' competing to offer education programs desired by consumers. A comprehensive, theoretically based elaboration of institutional perspectives (politics, bureaucracies, and markets) on American schools with an emphasis on "choice" and "effective organization" is presented in Chubb and Moe 1990 (especially chap. 2).

The impacts of such market-based approaches are subject to much debate. Some believe this type of competition would encourage innovation, increase parental involvement in education, improve the quality of most schools, and cause the worst schools either to change or to close. Others argue that such a system would perpetuate or even exacerbate existing inequities between rich and poor districts, public schools would suffer at the hands of the private schools, and poor children or those most in need would be least likely to benefit from such a system. Chubb and Moe (1990) contend that the real issue is not public versus private school systems but the extent to which schools are organized effectively; that is, they are autonomous and relatively free of bureaucracy. They conclude that such autonomy is not likely to occur without true institutional reform—that is, market alternatives based on competition and choice.

In contrast to the 1989 SSP sample, which favored both vouchers and parent choice by at least 2-to-1 margins, a Gallup sample in 1987 was mixed on these two reforms. Although a voucher system was favored only by 44 percent and opposed by 41 percent in the 1987 Gallup poll, with 15 percent not expressing an opinion, 71 percent believed parents should have "the right to choose which local schools their children attend" (Gallup and Clark 1987, 20). The school choice item responses are almost identical in the SSP and Gallup surveys, while the voucher item responses are quite different.

The differences are most likely due to question wording, but the sequencing of survey items and the different survey periods might also be affecting the findings.[1] Also, as Chubb and Moe (1990, 306) conclude, the public "endorses the general concept of parental choice." When discussing the various groups of supporters of the concept, however, they also conclude that "choice means many different things to its supporters" (p. 207). It is one thing for Americans to respond favorably to a survey item on parental choice; it is another for them to understand and favor a particular implementation of that basic value.

Patterns of Support for Reforms

Given the range of support, from virtual unanimity to two-thirds opposition to the various proposals in the 1989 SSP survey, it is appropriate to assess the extent to which people are consistent in their support for these improvements, and whether different groups support different reforms. Examination of bivariate correlations and the use of factor analysis find similar patterns for the fifteen items. The fifteen items described in table 9-1 form six factors corresponding to the categories below, with the factors accounting for 57 percent of the variance in the structure. The items within each category are moderately to strongly related to one another, but not to the items in the other categories. On the basis of the patterns found using the two methods, the following summed variables are created:

Money/Taxes Index:
  teacher salaries
  merit pay for teachers
  increase taxes
  range 3–6, mean 5.2, s.d. .94
Basics/Discipline Index:
  school discipline
  teacher control of classroom
  emphasize basics
  mandatory homework
  range 4–8, mean 7.5, s.d. .76
School Length Index:
  lengthen school year
  lengthen school day
  range 2–4, mean 2.7, s.d. .79
Competency Testing Index:
  testing for teachers
  testing for students
  range 2–4, mean 3.9, s.d. .41
Public Choice Index:
  parents choose schools
  vouchers for school choice
  range 2–4, mean 3.4, s.d. .73
Student Incentives Index:
  deny driver's license to dropouts
  mandatory attendance until 18
  range 2–4, mean 3.4, s.d. .70

In addition to the six indices, an overall composite measure of support for education reform is created by summing responses to all fifteen items. This education reform composite ranges from 15 to 30, with a mean of 26.0 and s.d. of 2.21. As would be expected, given the overall percentages of favorable responses, except for the school length index the indices are skewed positively.

Table 9-2 provides the correlations among the six indices and the overall index of support for education improvements. As expected, given the method of index construction, the overall index is related significantly to each of the other six indices, with the weakest relationship with competency testing (tau-b = .31), while the six separate indices are correlated only weakly to each other. The summary indices for public choice and student incentives have the weakest relationships with the other summary measures.

Multivariate Models of Education Reforms

What types of individuals are more or less supportive of these education reforms? Table 9-3 presents results of regression models for each of the six indices and the overall index of support for education reform. The predictor variables include those used in previous chapters (demo-

Table 9-2. Support for Education Reform: Correlations among Composite Measures

Support for Improvements	Mon./ Taxes	Bas./ Disc.	Sch. Lgth.	Comp. Test.	Pub. Ch.	Stud. Inc.
Overall support	.48	.43	.46	.31	.34	.38
Money/taxes		.09	.15	.10	.01	.09
Basics/discipline			.17	.15	.09	.14
School length				.10	−.02	.10
Competency testing					.11	.04
Public choice						.04
Student incentives						

Note: Figures are tau-b's. Coefficients of .09 and above are significant at least at the .002 level.

Table 9-3. Regression Models of Support for Education Reforms

	Reform Indices[a]						
	Over. Sup.	Mon./ Taxes	Bas./ Disc.	Sch. Lgth.	Comp. Test.	Pub. Ch.	Stud. Inc.
Predictors							
Age		−.14	.13	.16			
Education		.13		−.12		−.12	
Income	.12	.16					
Race				.14	−.09	.09	−.09
Party identification				.12	.10	.17	
Rating of the governor					.13		
Personal finances						.10	
School satisfaction	−.09				−.09		
Per capita income	−.15						
Statistics							
Adjusted R^2 (without contexts)	.01	.04	.02	.04	.02	.02	.00
Adjusted R^2 (with contexts)	.01	.07	.01	.05	.03	.02	.02

Note: Coefficients are standardized regression coefficients that are significant at least at the .05 level. (Coefficients are approximately twice as large as their standard errors.)

[a]See table 9-2 for spelling in full of the reform indices abbreviated here.

graphic characteristics, perceptions of economies and personal finances, level of government identification, political predispositions) and five additional variables. Four of these additional variables are contextual measures of state per capita income (resources), the political conservatism of the state, the percentage change in public elementary and secondary school student enrollment from 1980 to 1986 (representing the need or demand), and the amount of education spending per student in 1988 (representing the state's effort). The fifth additional predictor is the attitudinal measure of overall satisfaction with the public schools. Table 9-3 includes only the predictor variables significant in at least one equation.

On the basis of the low R^2s, the models are not very successful in explaining public support for education reforms. The individual coefficients, however, are relatively understandable or explainable. The effect of age on support for education conforms to conventional wisdom. The elderly were significantly less likely to support increased taxes and spending but more likely to favor increased discipline and a return to basics, and to favor lengthened school days and school years. Those with higher levels of education favored more taxes and spending but opposed lengthening the school day or year and opposed more parental choice of schools or vouchers. Those with higher incomes were more, rather than less, favorable to the summary measure of reform, and they favored more spending and taxing for the schools. Minorities favored lengthening the school experience and parent choice but were opposed to competency testing and student incentives (deny driver's license to dropouts and mandatory attendance until age eighteen).

The results for party identification also were as expected in that Republican identifiers favored lengthening the school experience, competency testing, and parent choice. These categories of reform are quite compatible with Republican rhetoric and policy proposals over the past decade. The attitudinal measure of overall satisfaction with the public schools is related negatively to the overall index of support for reforms and to competency testing. Those more satisfied with the schools were less likely to favor reforms in the aggregate. It is not clear, however, why the only other reform measure they opposed was competency testing.

The only contextual variable related significantly to education reform is that individuals residing in wealthier states were significantly less likely to favor reforms. The model for the overall education reform index finds that individuals with higher incomes who were less satisfied with the schools and who lived in poorer states were more likely to favor all the proposed reforms. The other measures of context, including educational need and resources in the state, display little or no effect on the reform variables. Level of government identification is not related to public attitudes toward education reforms. It may be that most Americans, regardless of a general preference for a level of government, understand and accept public education as a state and local function. Federal identifiers are no less likely than state and local identifiers to favor state and local control of public education.

Schools and Values

With schools involved with racial integration, good citizenship, sex education, and the like, it is difficult to deny the involvement of schools in social and moral values. There is little doubt that a public school experience promotes certain social values. Although not necessarily taught in any overt way, most students learn obedience, discipline, conformity, respect for authority, and related values in the public schools, or at least they usually "go along" and learn to pretend to accept these values. In some contrast, many argue that these values or traits are and should be the primary responsibility of the family, with the schools free to focus on academic learning and skills. Before examining these issues related to the American family, let us consider how the public views the involvement of public schools in values education.

Although a large majority wanted the public schools to teach moral values to children (82 percent), respondents were evenly divided over satisfaction with what they perceived to be the moral values being taught (only 50 percent were very or somewhat satisfied with the moral values being taught). The SSP survey did not attempt to assess what values respondents believed were being taught in the public schools, although people were asked to judge whether the schools were doing an excellent, good, not so good, or poor job in certain areas that have very broad value content. The sample is divided closely on all five areas, with people rating the schools somewhat higher in providing a safe and secure school environment (57 percent said excellent or good), developing self-reliance (52 percent), and teaching good citizenship (51 percent), than in teaching values of trust and honesty (57 percent said not so good or poor) or in preparing children for challenges of the future (57 percent not so good or poor).

Evaluating the American Family

Although a consensus has not yet emerged, many of the current advocates of reforms of the schools have begun to focus on the role of the family as the primary locus of education of our young. Historically, the family has usually been regarded as the first or most natural locus for socialization and education, although perhaps mostly in symbolic terms. Some current critics of American society argue that the family as an educational and socializing institution has been supplanted by huge, impersonal, undemocratic, technocratic, remote education bureaucracies. The family has been ignored or excluded from effective participation in this policy arena. The supporters of parental choice of schools usually promote this viewpoint.

There is dispute over whether the education establishment has developed this greatly expanded mission on the basis of its own interests and purposes, or whether public schools have simply reacted to the breakdown of the so-called traditional family in contemporary society. Have the schools expanded their educational reach and now attempt to fill a void left by the changing and disappearing traditional American family, or have they consciously sought to establish and protect their dominion over an ever-expanding, self-perpetuating system? Proponents of the expanded education mission believe the public school is the primary institution, if not the only viable one, to fill the gaps in socialization, education, and well-being of our children resulting from the collapse of the family. Others contend that regardless of what might be happening with family structure in this country, the schools are not equipped to, and should not, deal with all the social, health, and economic problems related to the breakdown of the family. Although few convincing answers exist to the question of why the mission of the public schools has expanded so much in recent decades, the SSP data do permit examination of public opinion on the two institutions of public education and the family.

Before looking at public opinion, it is useful to consider some changes in the American family, especially since World War II. Family structure has changed dramatically, and children appear to have paid a heavy price for this change. The "1950s family" has disappeared. First, the average American family is now one person smaller than in 1950 (Hodgkinson 1989, 3). The increased rate of divorce is suggested by the fact that "over one-third of all marriages performed in 1988 were second marriages for at least one partner." Also, among the more than 91 million households in the United States in 1988, nonfamily households (one-person households and those living with unrelated others) outnumbered by over 1.3 million the family households (married couples) with children. This fact suggests an explanation for the "striking decline" in birthrate in this country.

We have 15.3 million children living with one parent (the mother, in more than 90 percent of the cases), and 23 percent of children born today are born outside of marriage. Out-of-wedlock births as a percentage of all births increased to this 23 percent level in 1986 from 5.3 percent in 1960, while the figures for blacks in the same period show an increase of 21.6 to 61.2 percent. The proportion of female-headed families with children increased from 8.5 percent in 1960 to 19.3 percent in 1986, while the rate for blacks increased from 24.2 to 47.6 in the same period (Reischauer 1989, 15–16). Reischauer contends that divorce, female-headed families, and out-of-wedlock births are not as unusual or stigmatized as in the past.

These demographic figures relate closely to the high rate of youth poverty. Reischauer (pp. 14 and 314–15) notes that 20 percent of all children were poor in 1987, which is a large increase since 1970 (14.9 percent), but a slight decline since 1983 (21.8 percent). Also, the percentage of the poor who were children in 1987 (38.2 percent) declined slightly from 1970 (40.3 percent), but increased slightly from 1983 (37.9 percent). Regardless of which of these measures one focuses on, the incidence of poverty among children is a sad commentary on our society and also suggests a potentially bleak economic future for this nation. As Reischauer (p. 14) suggests, "Today's poor children will be the American workers of tomorrow, who will not only need to compete with the Koreans, Taiwanese, Japanese, and Germans, but will also have to support the retirement benefits of the baby boom generation."

A crucial concern for our society is the linkage between family structure, especially as this structure has changed over the past few decades, and various social problems such as poverty, crime, substance abuse, teenage pregnancies, teen suicides, AIDS, and the like. These linkages are being rediscovered, reemphasized, and reassessed, but now within the confusing and conflictual contexts of feminism, racism, multiculturalism, seeming deadlock among government institutions, and economic stagnation and restructuring. Also, although the focus has tended to be on poverty and the "underclass," many observers contend that these social problems, changing family structures, and issues of the transmission of cultures and values across the generations transcend class and race. Traditional or middle-class families now face many of these same pressures and problems of child-rearing and family preservation.

Given these many, potentially profound changes, how does the American public feel about the institution of the American family? Steiner (1981, 6) cites data from the 1975 NORC survey that most people were not discontented with their family life—88 percent reported either a very great deal, a great deal, or quite a bit of satisfaction, while less than 9 percent reported either a fair amount or no satisfaction. These data relate to feelings about one's own family life, but how do people perceive the institution of the American family in general?

In addition to evaluating public schools and values, respondents in the SSP also were asked to assess the extent to which the American family is doing a good or poor job in these same five areas discussed above. As table 9-4 shows, majorities rated the family negatively in four of five areas, and they rated the family as doing a worse job than the public schools in all five areas. People were evenly divided over whether the American family was providing a safe and secure home environment, but majorities ranging from 54 to 63 percent perceived that the family was doing a not so good or poor job in instilling values of trust and honesty, developing self-reliance, preparing children for the future, and teaching them to be good citizens. Although most of the differences were not large, the public believed the American family was doing a poorer job than the public schools in these five areas, at least some of which historically have been viewed as the primary responsibility of the family.

Survey data comparable to these SSP items are not abundant; the Gallup Polls on Public Schools, however, have dealt with the issue of "character education." The 1987 Gallup poll asked whether "courses on values and ethical behavior should be taught in the public schools, or do you think this should be left to the students' parents and the churches?" (Gallup and Clark 1987, 23–24). A plurality of 43 percent said the schools, while 36 percent said it should be left to parents and churches (13 percent volunteered both, and 8 percent were don't knows). Although the items in the SSP and Gallup polls are not identical, the findings suggest support for the schools in conducting "character" or "values" education. Moving beyond this unsurprising finding poses difficulties. Numerous groups in American society are only too eager to

Table 9-4. Comparisons of Schools and Families

Issue Involving Children	Excellent (%)	Good (%)	Not So Good (%)	Poor (%)
Teaching children to be good citizens				
Schools	5	46	34	15
Families	3	37	43	17
Instilling in children values of honesty and trust				
Schools	4	39	42	15
Families	2	37	42	19
Providing a safe and secure school (home) environment				
Schools	7	50	31	12
Families	2	49	38	12
Developing self-reliance				
Schools	4	48	35	13
Families	3	43	41	13
Preparing children to face the challenges of the future				
Schools	5	38	40	17
Families	3	34	47	16

Note: Figures in the four columns are based on responses to the following survey item: "Would you say the public schools (American families) are doing an excellent, good, not so good, or poor job in the following areas?" The N's for individual items range from 949 to 1,010.

suggest what those values should or should not be. Consensus on values education will not come easily, if at all.

The aggregate percentages for the SSP items indicate slightly more positive views of schools than families, but to what extent can individuals be identified as supporters of schools or families as doing a good job in these areas? To measure an individual's relative support for families or schools, responses to the five schools "values" items are summed for each respondent to give a measure of overall evaluation of school performance in this broad area. The measure ranges from 5 to 20, with a mean and median of 12, and a s.d. of 3.1. Next, the same items for individual evaluations of families are summed to give a composite with the same range as for the schools items (5–20) and a mean of 11.5, median of 11, and s.d. of 3.1. The summed variables correlate very highly with each of the five items composing the summed index for both schools and families.

Once summary measures of evaluations of schools and of families are computed, the sums for family evaluations are subtracted from those for school evaluations to give a composite measure of the extent to which the individual evaluates families or schools more positively. This overall composite variable ranges from − 15 to 14, with a mean of .5, median of .0, and s.d. of 3.1. Nineteen percent of respondents had a value of 0, indicating they do not believe one institution is doing a better job than the other in these five areas. Forty-seven percent had positive values, indicating more favorable evaluations of schools than families, while 34 percent had negative values, indicating more positive evaluations of families than the schools. The values tend to cluster about the mid-point of 0. Eighty-six percent of the sample are in the categories from − 4 to + 4. Because of the method of calculation, the overall composite is related moderately in the positive direction to the separate schools composite (r = .495) and negatively to the families composite (r = − .499), while the family and schools composites are related positively (r = .51).

Multivariate Models of School and Family Evaluations

What types of individuals are more or less positive in their evaluations of schools and families in these five areas? Table 9-5 presents results of regression models for the composites of evaluations of families, schools, and the combined index as three dependent variables, with the predictors of demographics, assessment of the economies and personal finances, level of government preference composite, political predispositions, overall satisfaction with the public schools, satisfaction with the teaching of values in the schools, and certain contextual measures used previously. The table includes only the predictors that were significant in at least one of the three equations.

The explained variance in these measures of support for schools or families is moderately high, ranging from 8 to 38 percent. Standardized

Table 9-5. Regression Models of Evaluations of Family and School Performance

Predictor	Dependent Variables		
	Family	Schools	Composite
Age	− .17	− .09	
Gender	− .12	− .12	
Overall satisfaction with public schools	.16	.33	.16
Satisfaction with the teaching of values in the schools	.20	.36	.16
Party identification		− .08	
Personal finances		.09	
Adjusted R^2	.16	.38	.08

regression coefficients indicate that those evaluating families more positively are younger females who are satisfied with the schools and satisfied with the values being taught in the schools. Those evaluating schools more positively also are younger females who are satisfied with the schools and the values being taught, but in addition they are Democrat identifiers with positive views of their present financial conditions.

Since women historically have been identified with (or pushed or exploited into, depending on one's ideology) the role of family caregiver, with primary responsibility for child-rearing, this finding is not surprising. Despite recent changes in the role of females in American society, younger women continue to bear the major responsibilities for family and child-rearing, and these data show they have a more positive view of schools and family than males. One difference between school and family evaluations is that young females with more confidence in their present financial situation are more positive about the public schools than are young females with less confidence in their financial situation. Females with financial concerns may feel less ability to influence school policies and practices than their family situations.

For the composite measure which combines both these indices, the only significant predictors are the attitudinal measures of satisfaction with the schools and satisfaction with the values being taught. Attitudinal measures are obviously the more important predictors of the assessments of school and family performance. Although the two attitudinal measures of satisfaction with schools and values taught behave similarly in the three models, they are only correlated moderately (tau-b = .38).

Levels of Government and Public Education

As we saw in chapter 6, respondents prefer that certain educational activities be regulated more by state governments than by federal or local governments. As table 9-6 indicates, a majority of 55 percent in 1989 preferred state regulation of teacher certification and training to federal (28) or local regulation (17), while 46 percent preferred state regulation of textbook selection to federal (25) or local regulation (29). In some contrast, only 20 percent preferred state regulation of prayer in the public schools versus 31 percent for federal and 33 percent for local regulation.

In chapter 6 these three items are included in a composite measure of preferred level of government regulation, and regression models are estimated. In this section the items are estimated separately using multivariate models and the contextual measures of state education as well as the attitudinal measure of overall support of the schools. The explained variance for all three measures is quite low, ranging from .02 to .06, and the only consistently significant predictor for each equation is level of government identification. Gender also is significant for teacher certification, income for textbook selection, and party identification for school prayer. In addition, two contextual measures are significant for school prayer: the per capita income of the state and the political conservatism of the state. Those who prefer school prayer to be regulated by the federal government are Democrats who prefer the federal government over the other levels and who reside in politically conservative, higher income states.

Conclusions

Although not discussed in detail in this chapter, the evidence is relatively clear and consistent that state governments are the major actors in

Table 9-6. Level Preferred for Regulation of Selected Activities

Activity	Federal (%)	State (%)	Local (%)
Teacher certification and training			
1989	28	55	17
1987	27	57	16
Selection of textbooks for public schools			
1989	25	46	29
1987	25	47	26
Regulation of prayer in public schools			
1989	31	20	33
1987	31	27	30

Note: Figures in the three columns are based on responses to the following survey item: "Do you feel that laws and standards regulating the following activities should be set at the federal, state, or local level?" N's range from 990 to 998 in 1989 and from 958 to 980 in 1987.

public education in this country. The decade of the 1980s also established state governments as major reformers or innovators in the field. Many states engaged in some type of education reform effort in that decade. Despite interstate emulation, including themes and goals common to all reform proposals, states continued to vary in approaches to change and in education spending and program performance. Attempts to reform the schools and controversy over the relative success of the 1980 efforts continues in the 1990s. The public, however, remains relatively positive about schooling in America.

Although the public is positive about the job being done by the public schools, large proportions of people favor reform proposals, including competency testing for students and teachers, emphasizing basic skills and knowledge, increased school discipline, and giving teachers more control over their classroom activities. Other reform proposals have less public support. When the various reform proposals are combined into six different composite measures, multivariate models show self-interest and political affect relate significantly to support for reforms in expected directions. The explained variance for all seven models, however, is quite small. Party identification is significant for three of seven indices, while evaluation of the governor is significant for only one index. Age and education are significant predictors of three indices, while income is significant for two, and race is significant for four of seven indices. Perceived satisfaction with the schools is significant for two of seven indices.

People want values taught in the public schools, but they are divided over satisfaction with the values being taught. By small margins, the public believes the schools are doing a better job than the family in instilling values of trust and honesty, developing self-reliance, teaching children to be good citizens, providing a safe and secure environment, and preparing children to face the challenges of the future. When these items are combined into composite measures of support for schools and families, younger females who are favorable to the schools and the values being taught are more likely to be positive about school and family functioning in these areas. These same individuals who identify with the Democratic party and are confident about their present financial condition are more positive about the functioning of the schools in these areas. Once again, the data show the influence of both self-interest and political affect for these school and family variables.

To what extent does level of government identification affect attitudes toward education? The answer is mixed. As with welfare programs, for policy or political items that have an intergovernmental reference, level of government identification is usually significant when controlling for numerous other variables. Level of government identification is a significant predictor of the items asking which level should regulate teacher certification, textbook selection, and school prayer, but not of support for school reforms or evaluation of school functioning in certain areas.

Issues of family breakdown and related problems of teen pregnancy, drug and alcohol abuse, youth poverty, unemployment, and a host of other social ills are virtually impossible to separate from American schools. Since family structure has changed so dramatically since the 1950s, many are debating the extent to which the public schools can and should replace or at least support legitimate family authority and functioning. How far can and should the schools go in attempting to lessen these problems of families and youths?

State governments over the past decade have been at the forefront of education reform and are now forging ahead of the federal government in health care reform. Although both areas have tremendous impact on family well-being, the states have not been very active or visible regarding problems of the American family. As the federal government continues to be unable or unwilling to act in the areas of child care, maternity leave, child support payments, child and family allowances, and other family support issues, state governments perhaps will again take the lead and initiate reforms to attempt to strengthen the American family. They would be wise to consider Steiner's (1981, 8) advice: "The design of policies that can positively affect the quality of family life challenges the inventive capacity of any government. Problems of design present only the first difficulty. In a libertarian democracy that prizes privacy and rejects the primacy of the state, further constraints stem from constitutional limits to permissible government action. In addition, good inventions that are within constitutional boundaries may pose insuperable difficulties of delivery."

Note

1. Although certain percentages from the Gallup poll differ from the comparable SSP figures, in addition to different years for the surveys and sometimes different item wording, it should be remembered that the SSP results are only for those expressing an opinion, while the Gallup data include the "don't knows" in the results.

10
Health Care

Public Opinion and Health Care

This chapter focuses on several issues related to American health care policy. Because of a complex set of interrelated factors, health care is a relatively unique policy area. The life-and-death immediacy of the field distinguishes it from most other areas of domestic public policy. In contrast to the more long-run and somewhat indirect effects of poor education or poverty, the consequences to the individual or to a family of a major illness are immediate, direct, and potentially catastrophic. To make the field even more difficult for policymakers, an immediate, major catastrophic illness may be the result of years of poor health behaviors on the part of the individual or effects of the environment on the individual, or poorly understood interactions of these two factors. Complex ethical issues of who shall live and who will have access to what types of treatments and care are pervasive and intense components of debates over health care policy.

The issue of risk behavior and individual responsibility for poor health continues to complicate decision-making in this policy area. If life-style is a major cause of illness and disease, what if anything should the government do to influence or alter individual behavior? To what degree should government punish unhealthy behavior or reward healthy behavior? The financing and delivery of medical services is a complex mix of private and public components including private insurance, fees for service, and government payment of some services provided to the poor and elderly. The major providers of services, especially doctors and hospitals, are powerful political actors with significant economic resources. These providers of services compete quite successfully with the major payers of services—individuals, businesses, and government.

Since the policy area is characterized by many unique and complex features, it is expected that public opinion on health care issues will be complex, volatile, and difficult to assess and understand.

The second major issue of this chapter concerns the extent to which citizens are self-interested or public-interested (altruistic) in their assessments and policy preferences regarding health care. The question of whether people want "something for nothing" in terms of government spending and taxing policies or whether they only prefer policies that benefit them or those like them has been discussed previously in other policy areas (Sanders 1988; Citrin 1979; Welch 1985). Some see similar complexities or possible contradictions in the health care area. In their assessment of public opinion on health care, Gabel, Cohen, and Fink (1989, 107) contend that Americans are satisfied with their health care but very dissatisfied with the cost of this care. This dichotomy "distinguishes American health care from other products and services."

As further evidence of ambiguity, despite this overall dissatisfaction with the cost of health care, Americans believe society should spend more on health care. Citing data from a Peter Hart poll in 1987, Gabel, Cohen, and Fink (1989, 110) conclude that "health care is the public spending area that Americans are most willing to pay higher taxes to support." This apparent contradiction may be based on differences between what the public fear they might have to pay for health care out of their own pocket versus what they believe society or government should be investing in this area. Evidence for this is that when cost-containment proposals that involve "personal sacrifice of one's own demand for care" or that suggest lower quality of care are presented to individuals, support for the proposals declines (p. 114). These findings support the notion that the public is motivated by self-interest or desires "something for nothing" in the health care area.

In contrast to this view, Shapiro and Young (1986, 418) in their review of public opinion on medical care see public support for government assistance in medical care as "virtually on par with Social Security as an entitlement." They suggest that support for government spending in this policy area has been high because of the elderly and poor, who are perceived to be truly needy. "The public appears to be motivated by compassion and altruism toward all citizens, although some broadly defined private interests cannot be ruled out" (pp. 418–19).

The views of Shapiro and Young contrast with Gabel, Cohen, and

Fink and raise the basic question whether the public supports increased (or not decreased) spending in health care primarily because of altruism or self-interest. Are people supportive in order that their level or quality of care in the future would not be diminished or they would not have to pay excessive amounts out of pocket for such care, or does the public support increased government spending for health care because of a desire to help other, less fortunate individuals—the poor and the elderly with health problems?

In addition to questions of the uniqueness of the health care policy area and the extent to which the public is self-interested or altruistic about health care costs, this chapter analyzes the importance of the American states in responding to health care problems. If, as some claim, the federal government has failed to deal in any important way with American health care problems since the enactment of Medicaid and Medicare legislation in the 1960s, are the states filling this policy void? If so, does the public recognize and support these efforts?

The American Health Care System

The American health care industry has undergone major changes in the past two decades. New delivery systems such as health maintenance organizations (HMOs) and preferred provider organizations (PPOs) have grown rapidly. For example, there were 33 HMOs serving approximately 3 million enrollees in 1970 (2 percent of the population); by 1987 there were 662 HMOs serving 29 million people (11 percent of the population). From 1984 to 1986, the number of persons enrolled in a health plan including a PPO grew from 1.3 to over 17 million persons.

The days of the independent hospital may be waning, as the nation experiences rapid growth in multihospital systems, especially investor-owned or for-profit systems. The "corporatization" of health care has grown concurrently with the push for more competition and less regulation in the system. The development of a prospective payment system in Medicare has increased pressures on hospitals to be more efficient. This pressure has affected disproportionately smaller, rural hospitals that do not have the resources and patient base to compete.

To control their health care costs, payers such as large businesses are putting increased pressures on providers to cut costs of medical treatment. The pressures on employers to cut labor and production costs to be more competitive in the global economy means that more and more marginal employees are losing health benefits, or having their health insurance coverage decreased, or having to pay more out-of-pocket expenses for the same level of coverage. In addition, many Americans fall in the gap between employer-provided insurance and public-provided health care for the poor through Medicaid. Estimates of those without insurance range as high as 15 percent of the population.

The States and Medicaid

Because of escalating costs, states and the federal government are now viewing Medicaid (government health care for the poor) as "the king of the budget busters." In many states in the 1980s, the Medicaid budget has grown at twice the rate of other state spending. For example, despite enacting numerous cost control measures, Michigan's spending for Medicaid increased at an annual rate of 8 percent, while other spending increased by 3–4 percent in the 1980s (Hutchison 1990, 15). States are projected to spend almost $25 billion of their own fiscal-year 1990 funds on Medicaid programs, and this spending has increased by 107 percent from 1980 to 1988, with some states experiencing growth rates in excess of 200 percent in this period (p. 15).

Regardless of the magnitude of spending on Medicaid programs, it is estimated that fewer than one-half of the poor people in this country are eligible for the program as it now exists in the fifty states (Hansen 1989, 12). Despite the claims advanced by advocates of health care for the poor that major inequities and undercoverage exist in Medicaid, many state officials continue to resist efforts to expand this program, especially when many of these efforts at expansion are perceived as "unfunded or partially funded" mandates by the federal government.

As with welfare, discussed in chapter 8, health care for the poor is a complex intergovernmental policy area. Medicaid is a federal grant-in-aid program with numerous rules and regulations imposed on the states "from above." Despite this appearance of a top-down system, the states exert much control over eligibility requirements, benefit levels, and reimbursement to providers of care. As Schneider (1988, 757) shows, states vary substantially in Medicaid program costs which reflect these decisions. For example, although Texas and New York have roughly the same population size, in 1985 New York spent more than five times as much on Medicaid ($7.5 billion versus $1.4 billion for Texas). Wisconsin and Oklahoma have about the same numbers of individuals living in poverty, but Wisconsin spent about twice as much for Medicaid ($942 million). On the basis of regression models for state medicaid spending in the period 1975–85, Schneider shows that state-level factors as well as the change in presidential administration in 1980 both had significant effects on spending.

Many other issues face the American health care industry. As the population ages, there is increased demand for long-term care and treatment of chronic illnesses. Although the federal Medicare program was designed originally as the health insurance plan for the elderly, Medicaid has become a major payer of long-term care or nursing home services. Medicaid was intended to be a joint federal/state program to provide health care for poor women and children, the disabled, and poor elderly. The Social Security Amendments of 1972, however, have shifted dramatically the balance between the two categorical groups entitled to Medicaid: recipients of Aid to Families with Dependent Children (AFDC) and Supplemental Security Income (SSI) for those who are aged, blind, or disabled (Oberg and Polich 1988, 87). In 1987, AFDC recipients composed 66 percent of the Medicaid population but accounted for only 25 percent of Medicaid expenditures. In contrast, SSI recipients composed 28 percent of the Medicaid population, but 73 percent of expenditures (Oberg and Polich 1988, 88–89).

As health care technology advances, costs continue to rise. AIDS and drug-testing add to the strains on the system. Physicians face rising medical malpractice costs and pressures from third-party payers to control costs. All these factors interrelate in many complex and not well understood ways but can be summarized as the three basic health care issues of access, cost, and quality of care. Who will have access to what types of care, and who will pay for that care? In this chapter, questions of health care access and costs will be examined from the complementary perspectives of the individual as consumer and as citizen. Although not correlated perfectly, the relationships between (1) self-interest and the consumer perspective and (2) altruism and the citizen perspective are related closely. Finally, because of the increased role of the states in health care, public understanding of and support for this increased state role will also be assessed in this chapter.

State Health Policies

Many states have begun to take the initiative in improving access to health care for the poor and uninsured. States such as Florida, Massachusetts, Wisconsin, New York, Oregon, and Washington are experimenting with diverse approaches to increased access to health care. Massachusetts implemented the Health Security Act of 1988, which requires employers to provide health insurance for employees and also provides insurance pools and tax credits for small businesses to help meet the cost of the mandate.

The Florida Health Care Access Act of 1984 (Jones 1989) levies a tax on hospitals and then uses the revenue for an expanded Medicaid program. The approach attempts to blend market and regulatory strategies, as well as achieve several interrelated goals, including increased access and cost-containment. The approach taxes the revenues of all hospitals and then redistributes these revenues (primarily through Medicaid) back to the hospitals that are more heavily involved in providing care to the poor. The Florida approach is viewed as an alternative to the rate-setting, or regulatory, system as enacted by states such as Maryland.

The state of Oregon has attempted perhaps the boldest and most controversial step in dealing with the many complexities of cost and access to health care. In 1989, the state adopted the Oregon Basic Health Services Act. Although many factors led to this landmark legislation, a major precipitating event was a legislative decision in 1987 to discontinue Medicaid funding for certain organ transplants, potentially affecting 30 individuals, in order to expand prenatal care to 1,200 women and 1,800 children (Kitzhaber 1990, 20). This legislative decision was followed by the emotional and highly publicized death of a seven-year-old from leukemia while awaiting a bone marrow transplant. The legislative action to discontinue funding transplants followed by the child's death precipitated an intense policy debate over allocation of scarce resources. If limited public dollars were going to be spent for health care, which individuals, groups, treatments, or services should be funded? As Kitzhaber, an emergency room physician and state senator, and the architect of the Oregon policy, explains: If Americans accept the fact that the health care budget is finite, then an explicit decision to allocate money for one service means that an implicit decision has also been made to withhold money from other services. That, in essence, constitutes health care rationing, and legislative bodies do it every budget cycle. But it is rationing done implicitly, with no accountability (p. 22).

The Oregon law defines the population for whose health care the state is responsible as all those with a family income below the federal poverty level (this includes more than the population eligible for Medicaid). The private sector is mandated to provide for the health care of those above the poverty level. These two policies therefore guarantee access of all Oregonians to at least some minimal level of health care. The next step is defining which services and procedures will be provided at a minimum to all Oregonians.

To define these services, a Health Services Commission, which includes consumer and provider representatives, will prioritize health services "using criteria based on accepted social values and (within the context of those social values) in accord with the effect each service or procedure is expected to have on the health of the entire population being served" (Kitzhaber 1990, 23). An actuarial firm will then review the priority list and determine costs of each service provided through managed care. The legislature then must begin at the top of the list and work down as far as revenue will allow and ensure that the same package of services is available to the defined populations.

There are many questions and implications of the Oregon approach that will not be discussed here. The brief description, however, does focus attention on the major issues involved in health care: Who will have access to what health care services, and who will pay for these services? There is certain to be continued debate over the Oregon approach, and one critic argues that unless significantly more money is appropriated to the program, services will be cut disproportionately to poor women and children; that is, benefits will be transferred from "some poor Oregonians to other poor Oregonians," and "benefits will be taken from poor Oregonians to give more money to the state's nonpoor providers" (Dougherty 1990, 29). Dougherty's basic criticism is that the base or minimum level of care available to all Oregonians will be inadequate.

A Right to Health Care

As has been found in other health care surveys of Americans, the public believes there is a "right to health care regardless of ability to pay." In the 1989 SSP survey, only 7 percent somewhat or strongly disagreed with this statement. As an example from other surveys, over 90 percent of respondents to a 1987 Harris poll agreed that everybody has a right to the "best possible heath care." An item from the Roper survey, which asked whether individuals thought adequate medical care was a right to which people were entitled as citizens or a privilege to be earned, found somewhat less support for health care as a right in the period 1968–78. Those stating that it was a privilege ranged from 14 percent in 1968 to 19 percent in 1978 (Shapiro and Young 1986, 421). In the mid-1960s, three out of four Americans favored a constitutional amendment guaranteeing every American a "right to adequate health care if he or she cannot pay for it." Ironically, another survey found that 42 percent of the public already believes that the U.S. Constitution guarantees the right to health care (Gabel, Cohen, and Fink 1989, 111). Legislators in at least one state have filed bills calling for a right to health care in state constitutions.

Further evidence of public belief in greater public responsibility for health care is an item from the General Social Survey (GSS-NORC) which found that the proportion of the public agreeing that people should take care of their own health care declined from 13 percent in 1975 to 8 percent in 1984 (Shapiro and Young 1986, 421). These diverse national survey data suggest that support for a right to health care has increased in the past decade. Some contend, however, that these types of broad items asking about health care as a right may simply be eliciting "reflexive responses to a platitudinous statement" (Rochefort and Boyer 1988, 656).

As a further caution about right to care, Gabel, Cohen, and Fink (1989) contend that survey data show support both for more spending for health care and dissatisfaction over high costs. They suggest the reason for this apparent contradiction may be concern over future personal costs rather than some type of social concern. How would the public operationalize a right to health care in terms of services provided, and who would pay for health care for the poor?

Who Should Pay for Health Care?

Despite strong support for health care as a right, data from the 1989 SSP show that the public wants health care providers, employers, or governments rather than individuals with health insurance to pay for health care for the poor. As table 10-1 demonstrates, large majorities favored requiring businesses, doctors, hospitals, or state and federal governments to bear the financial burden of care for the uninsured. In contrast, a substantial majority (79 percent) opposed having insured individuals pay higher premiums to cover costs of indigent care. One explanation for this difference may be that people see insurance cost-shifting as affecting their pocketbooks directly, while the alternatives are not viewed as having such obvious or immediate effects. Such an interpretation supports the view of the public as being more self-interested consumers or potential consumers of health care than altruistic citizens, but it also suggests that people may not understand how costs are passed on indirectly to consumers by health care providers and insurers.

An alternative explanation for opposition to increased insurance premiums may be that although a majority of the 1989 sample (87 percent) were covered by health insurance, many of those covered (32 percent) did not have the insurance paid by an employer, and of those who did, most (59 percent) had policies that were only partially paid by the employer. Despite these possible gaps in insurance coverage, most respondents were very or somewhat confident that their insurance would meet the cost of a major illness (85 percent). The relationship of insurance coverage to support for these health care reforms will be examined in a later section.

Concern with paying for medical care raises many related issues. National Health Insurance (NHI) has been debated for many decades in this country. Critics of American health care point out that most other Western democracies, including Canada, Germany, and Great Britain, have developed national health plans that appear to offer improved ac-

Table 10-1. Support for Health Care Reform Proposals, 1989

Proposal for Health Care Reform	Favor (%)	Oppose (%)
Require all businesses to provide health insurance for all employees and their families	78.8	21.2
Require doctors to provide more services without charge to help cover cost of care for the uninsured	76.2	23.8
Require hospitals to provide more services without charge to help care for the uninsured	80.8	19.2
Have individuals with health insurance pay higher premiums to cover costs for uninsured people	20.7	79.3
Have state government provide more money to help pay for the health care of the uninsured	82.7	17.3
Have the federal government develop a national health insurance program to provide care for all citizens	85.4	14.6

Note: Figures under "Favor" and "Oppose" are based on responses to the following survey item: "Many persons cannot afford to pay for their health care. A number of proposals have been suggested for dealing with this problem. I am going to read you a list of some of these proposals. For each one, please tell me if you favor or oppose it." The N's for individual items range from 994 to 1,008.

cess to care while spending less of their GNPs on health care than does the United States. It is estimated that Americans spend almost 50 percent more per capita on health care than Canadians, and 100 percent more than the Japanese, although the United States ranks far behind these and other nations in life expectancy and infant mortality (Hutchison 1990, 16). Many advocates of improved quality and access to health care for the poor believe that a comprehensive, government-funded, national health insurance program is needed.

National Health Insurance

As with many issues, public support for NHI is relatively high when expressed in general or abstract terms. As table 10-1 shows, 85 percent of the SSP sample favored a national health insurance program for all citizens. Despite this high level of support, other surveys show that when financing alternatives such as taxes or alternatives such as private insurance are mentioned, support for NHI declines. NBC polls in the late 1970s found the public favored NHI by 2 to 1 (approximately 60 versus 30 percent) when no alternative was offered (Shapiro and Young 1986, 423).

When the public has been asked to choose between a "government health insurance plan" and "private health insurance," with answers spread along a seven-point scale, the percentage of those choosing either extreme of the scale has declined over time (Shapiro and Young 1986, 423). Support for private insurance plans declined from 24 percent in 1970 to 12 percent in 1984, while support for government insurance plans declined from 29 to 16 percent in that same period. As the extremes decreased, the percentages of those choosing intervals between the extremes increased in this period. For example, those choosing the midpoint of the scale increased from 15 to 20 percent in this period.

Other variations in items on NHI versus private insurance (or the present system) find support for government insurance in the 40 to 50 percent range from the 1970s to the mid-1980s. Surveys from Yankelovich, Skelly, and. White/Health Insurance Association of America (YSW/HIAA) in the late 1970s and early 1980s find percentages ranging from 34 to 41 favoring strongly or somewhat national health insurance with a tax increase, with percentages of 20 to 28 opposing strongly or somewhat (Shapiro and Young 1986, 424). A plurality still favor national health insurance, even with the addition of the presumably negative qualifier "tax increase." Gabel, Cohen, and Fink (1989, 111) also raise another qualification to the issue of public support for national health insurance. They contend that public support in this area is more for expansion of federal coverage of individuals or increased regulation of doctors and hospitals than it is for "government-owned and operated health insurance."

Additional evidence of contradictions and possible ambiguities in public support for national health insurance comes from Jajich-Toth and Roper (1990). They contend that public support for national health insurance actually reflects frustration with the current system rather than support for a "government-run health insurance system." When items dealing with the possible effects on the individual of a government-run health insurance system are used, they find the public believes their freedom of choice would be adversely affected, health care would become impersonal, quality of care would suffer, and the system would not save money (p. 153).

Jajich-Toth and Roper (p. 156) argue further that preference for the Canadian national health insurance system as an alternative to the present American system is not as clear and extensive as reported by Blendon and Taylor (1989). First, preference for the Canadian system versus the American system is much less in the Roper (45 percent) than in the Harris survey (61 percent), with the differences related to the "don't know" responses (2 percent in Harris and 18 percent in Roper). Although the time periods and interviewing techniques differ, they contend that the difference in support is due to the context or question order effects in the respective surveys. In addition, when specific components of the Canadian system were presented to respondents in the Roper survey, either some aspects of the Canadian system were not supported, or support became ambivalent. They conclude, "The American people desire change, but they are either ambivalent or undecided about what that change would entail" (p. 157). When combined with the political power of providers and private insurers, these ambiguities in public opinion help explain why this nation has no national health plan.

Although national health insurance has faded somewhat from the public policy-making agenda, employer-mandated coverage has risen in prominence. Should employers be required to provide health insurance for all employees and their dependents? Legislation has been proposed in the U.S. Congress to require employer-paid health insurance coverage, legislation which some believe could be as far-reaching as the Medicare program enacted in the mid-1960s. More significantly, Massachusetts and several other states have already implemented versions of this approach to solving the problems of indigent care and health care costs. The significance of this approach lies in the fact that the largest group of Americans without health insurance are working men and women and their dependents.

Regardless of the exact magnitude of the problem, 81 percent of those surveyed in 1987 and 79 percent surveyed in the 1989 SSP strongly favored or favored legislation to require employee health insurance. This finding coincides with survey data from the Health Insurance Association of America showing over 60 percent favoring employer-mandated health insurance coverage (Gabel, Cohen, and Fink 1989, 112–13). (It appears from their table that the percentage favoring the mandate would be higher if only those having an opinion were included in the calculations.) These researchers say that "undoubtedly, the seemingly 'free-lunch' facet of employer-mandated coverage appeals to the public," and they predict that with increased scrutiny of this alternative, "we can expect support for mandated coverage to decline" (p. 112).

Determinants of Public Opinion on Health Care Reforms

Despite extensive survey data on public attitudes toward health care, there is little explanation of why Americans hold these views. Although numerous researchers speculate on ambiguities and contradictions in attitudes of Americans toward health care issues and argue whether these attitudes are based on altruism or self-interest, it is difficult to find tests of hypotheses in this area of research. A self-interest perspective suggests that poorer, economically vulnerable individuals or uninsured individuals would be more likely to support government health insurance or having providers provide more "free care" to the indigent or uninsured. A symbolic politics perspective suggests that Republican identifiers who support Reagan and Bush would be less likely to support the alternatives which call for increased government intervention in the health care market.

Table 10-2 provides selected demographic and political correlates of support for the six reforms of the health care system used in the 1989 SSP survey. Recalling that the public supports strongly all the proposals except having individuals pay higher insurance premiums, note that minorities support this proposal as well as the proposals requiring businesses to provide health insurance, and having the federal government develop a national health insurance program.

More educated, higher-income, white male Republican supporters of Bush are opposed to requiring businesses to provide health insurance for all employees and their families. More educated, higher-income Republicans are opposed to requiring doctors and hospitals to provide more free care. Republican supporters of Bush also are opposed to national health insurance. Younger minorities who identify with the

Table 10-2. Demographic and Political Correlates of Support for Health Care Reforms, 1989

	Correlates[a]						
Reform Proposal	Age	Educ.	Income	Gender	Race	Party ID	Pres. Choice
Businesses provide insurance	−.03	−.17	−.16	−.11	.14	−.12	−.08
Doctors provide free care	.05	−.13	−.12	−.02	.04	−.12	−.04
Hospitals provide free care	−.00	−.08	−.11	−.03	.03	−.13	−.06
Individuals pay higher insurance premiums	.00	−.02	.02	.05	.08	−.05	−.03
State government provide more care	−.04	−.04	−.07	−.03	.06	−.05	−.04
Federal government provide national health insurance	−.07	−.05	−.06	.01	.07	−.12	−.12

[a]Coefficients are tau-b's. Those .07 and higher are significant at least at the .01 level.

Democratic party and are more negative about President Bush favor national health insurance.

The bivariate relationships suggest support for both the self-interest (vulnerability) perspective and the symbolic politics perspective; neither theory, however, has been tested adequately. Some would contend that location in the social class system (age, education, etc.) is less satisfactory a measure of self-interest than perceptions of economic vulnerability (present and future). Others might contend that the extent to which one has health insurance is a better measure of self-interest or perceived vulnerability. Finally, as a measure of symbolic predispositions, in addition to party identification or support for a Republican president, the extent to which one views health care as a right should relate significantly to support for certain health care reform proposals.

Table 10-3 presents correlations between support for reform proposals and respondent perceptions of present personal finances and belief in health care as a right. The additional measures of perceptions of present and future economic conditions and insurance coverage were not related significantly to support for these reform proposals. The only two exceptions are that those who view the present national economy positively do not support requiring businesses to offer health insurance to employees (tau-b $=-.09$), and those with health insurance do not favor national health insurance (tau-b $=-.08$).

Table 10-3 shows that those who believe health care is a right regardless of ability to pay favor all six proposals, although the relationships are very weak for mandated business insurance and for individuals paying higher insurance premiums. Perceptions of present personal financial conditions are related significantly to four of the six proposals. Those who are positive about their present financial condition are opposed to mandated business insurance, requiring doctors to provide more free care, having state governments provide more care, and enacting a national health insurance program. Although the symbolic attitude of right to health care appears to have a somewhat stronger relationship to support for reforms, the perception of one's financial condition also demonstrates moderately strong relationships.

Table 10-3. Personal Finances and Right to Health Care: Relationships with Support for Health Care Reforms

| | Correlates[a] | |
| | Personal Finances | Right to Health Care |
Reform Proposal		
Businesses provide insurance	−.12	.07
Doctors provide free care	−.08	.13
Hospitals provide free care	−.06	.16
Individuals pay higher insurance premiums	.04	.07
State government provide more care	−.08	.15
Federal government provide national health insurance	−.11	.22

[a]Coefficients are tau-b's. Those .07 and higher are significant at least at the .01 level.

Multivariate Models of Health Care Reforms

The next step is to attempt to sort out these relationships using multi-variate models. In addition to the individual-level variables discussed above, several contextual variables are entered into the equations. Two measures of health care resources available in the state are used: the number of short-term hospital beds, and the number of active nonfederal physicians per population, both in 1987. A measure of the overall health status of the state is the rate of premature death, which is from the Northwestern National Life Insurance Company State Health Rankings (1989). This variable is calculated from mortality tables and measures the effects of ill-health and injury on the population of that state before that population reaches sixty-five years of age.

Since the six dependent variables are all dichotomous, discriminant analysis is used. The results in table 10-4 are mixed, with none of the models explaining much variance (adjusted R^2s ranging from .01 to .08), but all performing reasonably well in classifying cases correctly (77 to 84 percent). For individual-level variables, the status of insurance coverage is not significant in any of the models. Rating the performance of the governor is significant only for support for having individuals pay more in insurance premiums, while race is significant only for support for businesses providing coverage for all employees.

The individual-level variable most important for predicting support for health care reforms is whether people believed there is a right to health care for all, regardless of ability to pay. Finally, level of government identification is significant for wanting doctors to provide more free care and support for a national health insurance program. It was expected that those who identified more with the federal government would also prefer a health care reform identified with that level.

At the contextual level, both number of physicians in the state and per capita income of the state are significant for several of the reform proposals. Individuals residing in states with more physicians were supportive of having individuals pay more through insurance premiums and having a national health insurance plan. Individuals residing in states with higher incomes supported having doctors and hospitals provide more free care, but not having state government pay for more care for the poor.[1]

Table 10-4. Multivariate Models of Support for Health Care Reforms

	Health Care Reforms[a]					
	Bus.	Doc.	Hosp.	Ind. Insur.	State Gov.	NatHlth Insur.
Predictors						
Age			.22			−.18
Education	.65	.50				
Income	.31		.33		−.35	
Gender	.33			.60		
Race	−.37					
Personal finances						−.21
Level of government identification		.31				.21
Party identification		.36	.38	−.37		−.32
Rating of the governor				.43		
Right to health care		−.60	−.73	.54	.83	.83
Living in a state with more physicians				.42		.27
Living in a state with higher income		.44	.41		−.44	
Statistics						
Eigenvalue	.078	.092	.103	.036	.037	.097
Canonical correlation	.268	.290	.305	.187	.190	.297
OLS adjusted R^2	.08	.06	.06	.01	.02	.06
F	4.0	3.3	3.4	1.4	1.7	3.2
Percentage of grouped cases classified correctly	79	77	81	79	83	84

[a]Coefficients are standardized canonical discriminant function coefficients. All are significant at least at the .05 level.

Recall from chapter 6 that in 1989 an item asked respondents which level of government should set laws and standards for hospitals to decide whether to accept or reject patients who could not afford to pay. A plurality of 42 percent chose the federal government, while 30 percent chose state and 22 percent chose local. The same regression model used for the health care reform proposals shows that those choosing the federal level to regulate in this area are more-educated whites who identify with the Democratic party and the federal government. The explained variance of .05 in the model is quite low.

Conclusions

The intergovernmental complexity of health care policy is undeniable. States remain heavily dependent on federal dollars to help provide care for the elderly, poor, and disabled in their jurisdictions. Despite this dependence, states have been active and innovative in searching for solutions to the problems of providing decent health care for those unable to afford it in the marketplace and have been sensitive to the high and ever-increasing costs of care for all citizens. These solutions range from the explicit rationing of health care proposed by Oregon to rate-setting in Maryland to employer-mandated health insurance in Massachusetts. If the federal government moves to enact major reform in the health care system in the 1990s, it will have the benefit of numerous state experiments carried out over the past two decades.

If the American public continues to indicate its dissatisfaction with the current system, a national solution may be possible. Unfortunately, despite public dissatisfaction with the current system, there does not appear to be a public consensus regarding solutions to the interrelated problems in health care. Given the power of special interests in health care, public opinion may be nothing more than a catalyst that eventually spurs action by the federal government, resulting in a policy based on the interest-group struggle.

Previous survey research suggests ambiguity as to whether people are self-interested consumers or public-spirited, altruistic citizens regarding health care. SSP data echo this ambiguity and suggest both self-interest and public interest are important determinants of public attitudes toward health care. Evidence for self-interest is that most respondents want businesses, physicians, hospitals, state government, or the federal government rather than individuals with health insurance to pay for health care for the poor. The underlying logic seems to be to have someone else pay, at least directly. When characteristics of individuals favoring or opposing these alternatives are examined in multivariate models, however, there also is support for a political affect as well as a rational or self-interested explanation.

The most important predictor of support for health care reform proposals is the extent to which people believe health care is a right, regardless of ability to pay. Other significant political-affect predictors are party identification and level of government identification. Support for a rational perspective is found in that certain demographic variables such as education, income, age, and gender also are significant predictors of these reform proposals. Both self-interest and political affect influence public attitudes on health care issues, at least for these SSP data on paying for health care for the poor.

Further research is needed to determine the extent to which the public understands that individuals and groups, payers and providers involved in health care are interconnected in many complex and somewhat hidden ways. Each proposed action leads ultimately to increased costs for individuals through tax increases, higher fees for provider services, or higher insurance premiums. Until this issue is addressed somehow in survey items, it will be difficult to ascertain the extent to which the public is compassionate and altruistic or merely looking for "something for nothing" in health care policy.

Note

1. Although results of discriminant models are presented here, probit/logit models were estimated for the same equations. Also, OLS regression models were estimated to derive the adjusted R^2s. As most data analysts recognize, the type of model estimated sometimes affects results. Although the probit and logit estimates were virtually identical to each other, they differed somewhat from regression estimates and discriminant estimates. Although the overall fit of the models tended to be the same, the significant coefficients differed for some of

the models. The differences between models are for variables close to the cutoff for significance. Because of the overall poor fit of the models and the somewhat differing results depending on the estimation procedure, one cannot be overly confident of the findings for these policy questions.

11
Public Opinion and
the American States

Evidence from many studies indicates that state governments emerged in the 1980s as innovative, activist policy-makers and problem-solvers. Some contend that after federal activism and state quietude in the 1960s and 1970s, in this recent period the states have performed successfully in the role characterized by Brandeis as laboratories of democracy. Some analysts go even further and contend that the states have emerged as the entrepreneurs or even the heroes of the federal system.

The previous chapters provide evidence that the public recognizes and supports a strong, active role for the states in the intergovernmental system. Data from the State Survey Project show considerable public support for state policy leadership as well as positive evaluations of state governmental leaders and institutions. On the basis of single-item ratings, the public perceives their governors and state legislatures more favorably than the Congress and the president. For an item requiring a choice among these institutions, however, respondents choose the president as doing the best job, followed by local government and governors. Congress and state legislatures are at the bottom of the list of choices. Comparisons with single-item ratings from earlier periods suggest that support for state leaders and institutions increased in the 1980s.

For several policy areas, people prefer state or state and local control to federal government control. When asked their preference for turning over control of eight different programs or functions to state and local governments, majorities have favored returning control of all of them to state and local government. Three-fourths favor state/local control of public schools, day care and social services, school lunch programs, and public service jobs. Two-thirds favor control of hospitals and of highways and mass transit. The lowest margin is 62 percent favoring state/local control of welfare.

In another set of items, people are asked which level of government is best for dealing with selected policy areas. Although the responses are mixed, state government fares reasonably well in the preferences. Majorities believe state government is best for dealing with education, while by very narrow margins the federal government is preferred over state government for control of public health and pollution control. By a slight margin, state government is preferred over local government for dealing with homeless individuals, and local government is preferred to the state level for dealing with crime. In contrast to these somewhat mixed preferences, by a 2-to-1 margin, people prefer federal to state government for economic development.

When asked which level of government should set laws or standards for regulating certain activities, the public displays interesting variations. Majorities or pluralities favor state regulation of teacher certification, selection of school textbooks, and setting highway speed limits. State government comes a close second to the federal government for the level preferred for licensing physicians, setting legal drinking age, controlling pornography, and providing health care to indigents. Regulation of hazardous waste disposal by the federal government is favored strongly over state regulation, while the public is virtually evenly divided over which level should regulate school prayer. Although the public prefers federal regulation of the death penalty and abortion, state government is preferred by large minorities for these areas (37 and 32 percent respectively).

With few exceptions, the SSP data demonstrate that people hold favorable views of state government. For policy responsibilities and control and regulation of activities, the public favors a strong state role, although the patterns of support are not completely consistent or positive. For some policy and program areas the public is closely divided over which level is preferred, while in other areas either the federal or local governments are preferred to the state level. The data suggest that the public is not clear and consistent in choosing which levels of government are preferred for dealing with certain policy issues and problems and in their evaluations of leaders and institutions at those levels. What explains these patterns?

One hypothesis is that the public is expressing understandable or explainable preferences between levels based on some underlying logic. Although no standard exists to judge whether people are making comprehensible distinctions between levels of government and policy responsibilities, there is no clear indication of the structure or logic of the meaning attached to the choices. There is some evidence in these data that preferences and evaluations are based on rational self-interest. There also is support, however, for an alternative view that these political and policy attitudes are based on an emotional or symbolic attachment to a level of government.

Level of Government Identification

In addition to questions of public support for state policy leadership and activism, this book began with the hypothesis that the American state is an important referent for public attitudes toward politics, government, and public policies. The state was hypothesized as being meaningful in a psychological way, with individuals forming attachments or identifications with state government as well as with other levels of government.

The SSP data provide support for the concept of individual identification with levels of government. In the late 1980s, when national samples of adults were asked to compare the three levels of government for responsiveness to the public, efficiency in service provision, honesty of public officials, and leadership in solving social problems, state government was ranked in the middle for all four items. The national level was ranked first for leadership, while local government was ranked first for the other three items.

Because of the complex and ambiguous policy responsibilities which characterize the American intergovernmental system, and the location of the states between the national and local jurisdictions, it might seem obvious that contrary to the assertion of James Madison, state governments would not be first in the hearts and minds of their citizens. Despite the middle position for the states, do these findings indicate consistent and stable attachments or loyalties? Is there a state electorate, or at least a potential state electorate? If so, what are their characteristics and political and policy attitudes?

Relationships between the level of government identification items indicate the public is moderately consistent for responsiveness, efficiency, and honesty, although the relationships of the leadership items with the other items are weak. A composite measure of level of government identification using three of the items is created to distinguish individuals who identify consistently with one level of government and those who have mixed identifications. Although only one in five respondents is fully consistent in identifying with one level for three items, an additional 60 percent are relatively consistent in identifying with one level for two of three items. In total, 86 percent of respondents are relatively or completely consistent in identifying with a level of government. Of these, 20 percent are federal identifiers, while 25 percent identify with the level of state, and 39 percent with local government. These percentages changed little over the three years of surveys, suggesting a relatively stable psychological construct. What are some characteristics of these identifiers?

Respondent education, reported income, and race are related weakly to the composite measure of level of government identification. By small margins, federal government identifiers are nonwhite with less education and lower incomes. Level of government identification is not highly class based, at least for the demographic or social location characteristics used in the SSP. Contrary to expectations, the symbolic political predispositions of party identification and political ideology are not related significantly to level of government identification. Democrats and liberals are not more likely than Republicans and conservatives to identify with the federal government.

Does level of government identification relate to other political and policy attitudes? When respondents are asked to rate Congress, their governor and state legislature, and their local government in single and separate items, consistent state identifiers rate their governor and legislature much higher than do other identifiers, while consistent federal identifiers rate Congress more positively, and local identifiers rate their local government more positively than other identifiers. When asked in a single item to choose the one individual or institution doing the best job, the level of government identification composite is related significantly and in the expected directions to the choices.

Level of government identification also is related significantly to public preferences for state/local control of selected policy areas and desires to return control of certain programs to state and local control. Regardless of whether single items or summed composites in these areas are used, this relationship holds almost without exception. When individuals are asked which level of government should regulate certain programs, only one of nine program areas is not related significantly to level of government identification, and the summed index of these preferences is related significantly to level of government identification ($r = .19$).

In contrast to these positive relationships, level of government identification is not related to evaluations of state program performance or to state spending preferences. State identifiers are no more likely than are federal or local identifiers to evaluate state programs more positively (or negatively) or to prefer increased (or decreased) levels of spending for numerous public programs. Relationships between level of government identification and policy attitudes in several substantive areas are mixed or inconsistent.

Do the significant bivariate relationships between level of government identification and political and policy attitudes hold when other plausible determinants are considered? Other predictors of public attitudes toward politics and policy are party identification, political ideology, demographic characteristics indicating social location or class, and perceptions of economic conditions.

Competing hypotheses based on self-interest models and symbolic models of attitude formation are tested. Previous research finds that some individuals prefer policy alternatives or candidates because it is perceived to be in their personal interest to do so. For example, individuals more vulnerable economically will prefer policies believed to provide income or other support to poor people. In contrast, some individuals develop political or policy attitudes because of altruism or concern for interests much different or larger than their own, a process some call sociotropy. These individuals make choices based more on symbolic identification with a political party or an ideology, or they choose based on feelings about a social group such as labor or business which might be important to them.

Multivariate models for numerous policy attitudes find mixed support for the importance of level of government identification when controlling for these other factors. For ratings of government institutions and political leaders, level of government identification has independent and significant effects on four of seven dependent variables. For two of the ratings of individuals (Reagan and Bush), level of government identification is significant; party identification, however, is a much stronger predictor. Level of government identification is significant for the in-stitutional ratings of Congress and local government, while party identi-fication is significant only for rating Congress.

For the evaluations of political leaders and government institutions, numerous other attitudinal and demographic predictors are also signifi-cant. Still, even with party identification, demographic characteristics, and perceptions of personal finances and economic conditions in the models, level of government identification is a significant predictor of four of seven ratings of political institutions and leaders. Knowing a person's identification with a level of government adds to one's ability to predict that person's opinion on certain political issues beyond what is known about his or her demographic characteristics, party identifica-tion, perceptions of economic conditions, and other factors.

Although level of government identification as well as other variables are significant predictors for attitudes toward institutions and leaders, with some exceptions the multivariate models do not do a very good job in explaining variance in several policy attitudes or preferences. This is especially the case for the policy attitudes relating to economic de-velopment, health care, welfare, and education examined in chapters 7 through 10. Results of the multivariate analyses are not uniformly strong and unambiguous, although there is support for level of government identification having some independent influence on individual policy attitudes. For some models it performs as well or better in predicting policy attitudes than does party identification or political ideology. Al-though perhaps not as intense or pervasive as the emotional attachment to a political party, or even to an ideological label, people identify with levels of government, and these identifications influence other political attitudes and opinions.

Rather than a changeable, issue-oriented predisposition, level of gov-ernment identification appears to be a relatively stable attachment that is more affective than rational. In some contrast to Dahl's (1967, 968) assertion, states do "tap strong sentiments of loyalty or likemindedness among their citizens." At least the sentiments of loyalty appear compa-rable to those for local governments or the federal government. The answer to the question raised by Erikson, McIver, and Wright (1987, 798) is that the states of the United States do matter; they are of some "political consequence," at least for substantial numbers of the public.

Is identification with a level of government a form of pride or attachment that has little or no ideological content? If the contention of Bennet and Bennet (1990, 27–28) is accurate that views on the role of the federal government are at the core of ideological cleavages between liberals and conservatives, why is the SSP measure of political ideology not related to the composite measure of level of government identification? Why is party identification also not related to level of government identification? Why in the late 1980s are liberals no more likely than conservatives, or Democrats no more likely than Republicans, to identify with the federal government? Bennet and Bennet suggest that the answer may be found in the concept of party identification as well as perceptions of Ronald Reagan by conservatives and Republicans. "Partisanship and ideology have become enmeshed in their impact on big government opinions and now the party, or the person, in the White House is the most important" (Bennet and Bennet 1990, 134). They also suggest a major role in this complex issue for age or cohort differences.

Do people identify with the federal government primarily because of vague feelings of patriotism? Do people identify with state governments because of some form of state pride? For example, the CSEP found 63 percent of a national sample agreeing that their state "is the best place in the United States to live in." The responses in the thirteen states ranged from 43 to 82 percent, indicating large variation in state pride. The relative ranking of the states on this variable tends to look very much like responses to many of the other CSEP items dealing with evaluations of institutions and leaders; it is therefore difficult with the CSEP data to disentangle the relationship of state pride to other attitudes with perhaps more political content or meaning.

In this research, the concept of primary interest is the composite measure of level of government identification. The concern is not with a particular state or pride in one's state of birth or residence. The SSP data suggest a generalized identification with a level of government rather than pride in one's own state (or locality); this latter possibility, however, cannot be eliminated on the basis of these data.

Party Identification

If level of government identification is a relatively stable symbolic predisposition and exhibits some independent effects on political and policy attitudes, how does it compare with party identification? There are many reasons to think that level of government identification would be much less salient to the American people than party identification. Except for some local elections and a few state elections, political parties are actively and regularly involved in attempting to win adherents to their cause. Large amounts of money, emotion, and energy are expended in promoting the causes of the two major political parties. The two party labels are quite pervasive in the mass media and political communications, even in nonelection periods and even in this era of increased candidate-centered elections.

Despite evidence that American political parties have declined somewhat in importance over the past few decades (having experienced a process of dealignment), they continue as active and powerful social organizations with millions of dedicated adherents. Much policymaking in America reflects the ways legislatures and executives are organized by political parties. An indirect (and perhaps misleading) measure of the importance of political parties is the large amount of time and energy devoted by political scientists to discovering and analyzing numerous aspects of the concept of party identification.

Weatherford (1983c, 184) summarizes the importance of political parties as follows: "First, party loyalty is the major source of stability in aggregate voting patterns over a series of elections. Second, parties are the primary articulators of the political relevance of economic events, and party identification provides voters with important cues about which policies are most likely to serve their interests."

In contrast to parties, levels of government are not mass-based social organizations with periodic calls to battle to energize and engage people in the electoral enterprise. Organizations advocating on behalf of state and local governments are relatively small, elite-oriented groups spending most of their time and energy lobbying for their interests quietly and sometimes very effectively in the nation's capital. Although individual states or localities from time to time engage in conflicts with neighboring jurisdictions or with the federal government, most conflicts between levels and types of governments are sporadic, remote from public view, and too complex to become a campaign or media slogan.

The one possible exception to this view of limited visibility of levels of government may be nationalism or patriotism. In times of war or external threat, elites and masses engage in extensive patriotic and nationalistic fervor. Riker (1962, 104–8) suggests that the transfer of patriotism from state to nation has been a major factor in increased nationalization and consequent diminishing of the role of state governments.

Although the impact of all three levels of government on individual lives cannot be ignored or denied, the pervasiveness and visibility of political parties would appear to be significantly greater and more constant in the eyes of the public. There is little evidence that loyalty to levels of government has as much impact on election outcomes as party identification or that levels of government function as "articulators of the political relevance of economic events." Some evidence has been provided here, however, that level of government identification does provide people with important cues about political and policy choices.

Symbolic Predispositions Compared

Although level of government identification may not be a pervasive or continual influence on policy attitudes and preferences, we can ask whether political ideology and party identification, major symbolic predispositions on which political scientists focus much attention and effort, exert a significant influence on these same areas. For some political attitudes such as evaluation of presidential job performance or choice of candidates for this national office, party identification is a significant and important predictor. This has been documented by numerous researchers and is confirmed with these SSP data. For other political and policy attitudes, party identification and political ideology are not always strong, consistent predictors.

For example, neither party identification nor level of government identification is related to state economic optimism or support for state economic development programs (chapter 7). Although both party identification and political ideology are related significantly to support for workfare and guaranteed income while level of government identification is not, all three symbolic predispositions are related to support for federal job creation (chapter 8).

Neither party identification nor level of government identification is related significantly to support for schools or families as doing a good job in several areas (chapter 9). For several composite measures of support for school reforms, party identification and level of government identification are each related to only one of the six summed measures. For health care reforms, party identification is related significantly to support for having businesses, hospitals, and doctors provide more uncompensated care and for national health insurance, while level of government identification is significant only for support for national health insurance (chapter 10).

Overall, the symbolic predispositions of party identification and level of government identification have mixed relationships with the policy attitudes of the public. The point in these comparisons is that a symbolic predisposition proposed here for the first time—level of government identification—has independent effects on several policy and political attitudes and is distinct empirically from party identification and political ideology, two important predispositions that have been previously studied.

Just as analysts have raised conceptual and measurement issues about party identification and political ideology, there are similar questions about level of government identification. Why do 50 to 70 percent of the public have positive opinions about state government or choose state government over the other levels of government for numerous policy or regulatory responsibilities when only 25 percent identify with state government, based on the items and measurement strategy used with the SSP surveys? In contrast, why is level of government identification sometimes not related or only related weakly to certain policy attitudes, especially in the areas of health, education, and welfare?

One possible answer to these questions is measurement error. People do not give much thought to these issues and offer "doorstep" or "phoneline" opinions. One could infer that much of the variation in responses to the policy items is random and due to the lack of attention on the part of the public to many of the less visible and controversial intergovernmental issue areas. Since the issues are not very salient to them, individuals are not much "constrained," consistent, or logical in their political and policy attitudes. The policy items may be measuring "nonattitudes."

Error, however, may be due to the survey items rather than the respondents. The items used are perhaps not adequate to capture the complexity of the policy issues. The policy issues being investigated are too complicated to be reduced meaningfully to a few items with limited choices prefaced by brief introductions. This problem might be magnified by the difficulty in providing an intergovernmental dimension to certain policy issues. If most individuals are not much aware of the policy issues, let alone the intergovernmental complexities of the policy area, and the survey items and responses categories do not provide sufficient information in an understandable form, then any underlying patterns of meaning may be difficult to discern. The problem with these two competing explanations for inconsistencies and errors is that as Neuman (1986, 48) asserts, "There is no independent basis for determining whether response instability is a result of vagueness of the respondent's thinking or the vagueness of the survey question."

To better assess public attitudes toward intergovernmental policy issues, researchers will need to devise alternative survey items including simple but informative introductions and meaningful response categories. For example, using the 1986 GSS, Iyengar (1990) analyzes public attitudes toward issues of poverty and shows how detailed framing of the issues by using vignettes affects responses to survey items.

Also, improvements in conceptualization of level of government identification may be needed. This initial SSP effort hypothesized four dimensions of level of government identification: efficiency, leadership, honesty of officials, and responsiveness to the public. The honesty item presented some analysis problems, so it was not used in the composite measure. Further analysis is needed to understand better why people are less willing to choose or prefer a level of government based on the perceived honesty of its public officials. Can other plausible dimensions be developed for the concept? For example, one could make a case that confidence or power are relevant and important dimensions of individual identifications with a level of government.

Rationality and Choice

Issues of measurement error and sophistication of respondents relate to rationality and public choice. The data do not clarify whether individuals are aware of differences between state and national interests, and whether they can relate their personal interests to the interests of the levels of government. This view of rationality for level of government identification can be related to the concept of political ideology and how it has evolved over time in political behavior research.

Political ideology began as a somewhat "rational" concept with researchers' concerns for attitude constraint and consistency (Converse 1964). Later research suggests the concept has become more "symbolic" (Conover and Feldman 1981). In this research, level of government identification is conceptualized as a symbolic predisposition or an emotional attachment, although some logical or rational components may actually underlie the concept. Do individuals comprehend issues of decentralization, intergovernmental conflict and power, competition between states, and substantive questions in various policy areas, and do they also perceive some personal benefits arising from different power arrangements or relationships between the federal and state governments in these policy areas? Such requirements of sophistication and knowledge would appear to impose a heavy burden on citizen information processing. If certain levels of knowledge and sophistication are not present among the public, then questions must be raised about basic assumptions of the public choice models and the hypothesized behaviors of exit, voice, loyalty, and neglect.

Another issue relating to unidimensionality of the concept is conflicting identifications. If individuals have varying degrees of national or state loyalties, what happens when these two perspectives conflict? Although this analysis has focused primarily on level of government identification as a symbolic or emotional attachment, this question implies rationality or calculation in dealing with the cognitive dissonance.

Public and Private Interests

To what degree do individuals assess political leaders, government institutions, and policy alternatives on the basis of private concerns (rational self-interest) or public interests (altruism or sociotropy)? How do people decide what is private and what is public, and how does this dimension differ from economic versus political influences? Can a private/public interest dimension be distinguished from an economic/political dimension? How do these perspectives relate to levels of government? The distinction between private and public values or preferences does not appear to be much studied, but the analogous values of capitalism and democracy have been the subject of some research.

McCloskey and Zaller (1984) argue that the American ethos comprises two traditions of belief or values—capitalism and democracy—related in complex ways among elites and the public. After examining the relationship between two scales of democratic and capitalist values and finding them significantly and inversely related (correlation of −.44 for the public and −.52 for opinion leaders [p. 174]), they go on to explore in some detail the relationships of the two scales to support for welfare principles and issues such as economic exploitation, distribution of rewards, private property, and limiting profits.

Despite the negative correlations of the two scales, they find that "highly prodemocratic respondents give no indication of being opposed to capitalism as such," although there is some evidence of "resentment toward the advantages enjoyed by corporations and the wealthy" (pp. 176–77). The explanation for the seeming anomaly of conflict and consensus regarding capitalism and democracy is that the conflict is played out within a relatively narrow range of alternatives that "presuppose widespread popular support for the basic values of each tradition" (p. 186). Since many of the basic questions relating to these two broad traditions are translated into specific policy and program issues in an intergovernmental context with a major role for state governments, research on state public opinion and public policy must incorporate concepts and findings relating to the basic values of capitalism and democracy.

These issues are most prominent in the areas of health, education, and welfare, three areas of domestic policy where state governments have substantial influence and extensive responsibilities. The SSP data show support for existing systems and programs, but they also show desire for reforms. Self-interest and more symbolic concerns also appear to be influencing public attitudes in all three of these policy areas. One question in these policy areas is, If people think times are better at least for them personally, are they therefore more willing to be generous or redistributive in their policy choices or vice versa?

Political Socialization and the States

Wright, Erikson, and McIver (1987) demonstrate that the American state is a consequential territorial division beyond the demographic characteristics of its citizens. If the state is meaningful to individuals, does it matter how long one has lived in a state or whether one was "socialized" or educated in a state, or is the state perspective a temporary political identification that operates only when there is some type of conflict between national and state interests?

In an assessment of political culture in the states, Lowery and Sigelman (1982) examine the question of differences in their model between one's present state of residence and the state where one grew up and was socialized. When separate regression models are run for measures of political efficacy, sense of citizen duty, and two other scales, no significant differences are found in the regressions based on state of residence and state of socialization of the respondents. Whether people are categorized in terms of their present state political culture or the one in which they grew up makes no difference in predicting these political attitudes. Despite the purported high mobility of Americans, it is likely that the measures of state of birth and state of socialization are highly correlated.

Elites, Masses, and State Policies

Much current activity in comparative state policy research concerns relationships among political parties, ideologies, elite/mass interactions, and public policies. Despite many questions about whether a relatively inattentive American public thinks ideologically or organizes and processes political information on a liberal/conservative dimension, Wright, Erikson, and McIver (1987, 996–97) find that state public opinion as measured by political ideology is related strongly to the liberal/conservative content of "sometimes obscure and invisible state policies."

The mechanisms linking public opinion and government policies include elections, recruitment for public office, and other "sharing" mechanisms. Lowery, Gray, and Hager (1989, 28) also focus attention on linkage mechanisms and suggest "multiple forms of individual opinion-policy linkages" may be operative. These forms would seem to depend on issue salience and elite mass communication. In later work, Erikson, Wright, and McIver (1989) argue that state electoral politics (including party and ideology) are responsible for the relationship between public opinion and policy.

This analysis of SSP data suggests that level of government identification might play a role in helping to sort out and understand linkages between masses and elites and public policies, especially in an intergovernmental context. In an earlier work, Erikson, McIver, and Wright (1987) conclude that one's state of residence contributes to one's political attitudes, but it is not clear why that is so. It may be that level of government identification operating at the individual level helps explain the varying aggregate impacts of the state on political attitudes.

The State as Context

In addition to a psychological identification or emotional attachment, it was hypothesized initially that state of residence also affects individual attitudes and beliefs. Do the economic, political, or policy contexts of the state have any effects on public attitudes toward government and policy? Although not pervasive or consistent, certain characteristics of an individual's state of residence are related to political attitudes, independent of possible attachment to a particular level of government and other individual-level characteristics.

In chapters 5 through 10, several contextual measures are examined in multivariate models of political and policy attitudes. The contextuals can be categorized into three broad groups. First, analogous to individual-level characteristics of financial well-being, aggregate indicators of state economies are examined. These contextual measures include gross state product, state income per capita, jobs created, and the like, as well as changes over time for these variables. Although three contextual political variables are examined, a measure of state conservatism is used in most of the models. Finally, for the chapters dealing with the substantive policy areas of health, welfare, and education, characteristics of the states in these areas such as physicians per capita or the proportion of the state population who are welfare recipients are included in the multivariate models. When possible, time periods are

sequenced so that a contextual or aggregate state characteristic is measured prior to the individual attitude being predicted or so that change
over time in the state context occurs prior to the individual attitude.
One significant area for contextual measures is state economic development (chapter 7). Individuals who are optimistic about their state
economies are significantly more likely to reside in states with higher
per capita incomes, larger increases in gross state product, and larger
numbers of jobs created. Two of these contextual measures of the state
economy are significant in the multivariate model for state economic
optimism, controlling for individual demographic characteristics and
political attitudes. Both optimistic and pessimistic individuals seem to
be making accurate assessments about the status or performance of their
state economy, at least relative to other states. In contrast to state economic optimism, the contextual measures are much less important in the
multivariate models for economic development program support.

Another example of the impact of contextual factors is the multivariate model for evaluations of state programs in chapter 6. Individuals
residing in politically conservative states are significantly more likely to
rate state programs negatively, controlling for individual-level variables.
Since the programs being evaluated are liberal in orientation or directed
to vulnerable populations, this relationship is not unexpected. Again,
the relationship remains when controlling for other contextual and
individual-level predictors of program evaluation. In chapter 10, the
number of physicians per capita and personal income per capita are
significant contextual predictors of certain proposed health care reforms
in the multivariate models. Although several contextual measures are
significant predictors of political and policy attitudes and the direction of
the relationships are plausible, with few exceptions such as economic
development, the contextual variables do not contribute much to the
overall fit or successful prediction of the models.

Despite the lack of strong and consistent evidence of the state's playing a major role as a contextual determinant of individual political and
policy attitudes, the analysis suggests questions and issues for future
research. Analysis is needed of the degree to which individuals recognize and understand the relative position of their state in regard to many
of these policy areas. What are the mechanisms by which congruence is
achieved between public opinion and the actual condition of the state?

The issue of direction of relationships between state context and public opinion is important. What is the role of opinion-elites in this relationship? Officeholders have a stake in educating the public about the status of the state economy or welfare policy or education. This information can be either positive or negative, critical or supportive of the existing situation. If the state is performing well in a particular area, incumbents will try to inform constituents. If it is performing badly, challengers also will attempt to inform the public. Presumably the most effective message will determine who wins the contest. This implies a two-way flow of communication between elites and masses, which also implies some concern for media coverage in the states and concern for the differential attention paid by masses and elites to politics and policies at the various levels of government.

What are possible differential effects of context on individual behaviors? It is not likely that all individuals in a state will be affected the same by these varying contexts. One might expect individuals with more education and higher levels of sophistication to be more aware of state contexts, or those more directly affected by a context to be more attentive to that area. In the areas examined here, it is not possible to do much more than speculate about these issues. It is important to emphasize that this analysis does not include a detailed presentation of the "mechanisms by which characteristics of the context affect the attitudes and behaviors of individuals embedded in it" (Prysby and Books 1987, 243).

Government Power over Time

Is the nation in the late 1980s and early 1990s experiencing only a brief lull in the inexorable rise in centralized federal government power, or are states and localities increasing their autonomy and independence in a relatively permanent way, or are all levels increasing their power and responsibilities concurrently? Surveys dealing with this issue over longer time periods are needed to assess whether the public recognizes, understands, or supports these changes. The SSP survey data suggest that the public is aware of differences between levels of government and has opinions about the distribution of power and responsibility between them. The data, however, are examined over a relatively limited time period.

Problems and Opportunities for State Leaders

What are the problems and the opportunities facing state government leaders? Although the direction of causality has not been established, the public appears quite favorable to the present level of policy activism and leadership of the American states. If state elites are leading more than following their constituents, the challenge for these officials in the future is whether they can continue to be responsive, effective, and innovative in the face of exceptionally difficult domestic problems and sporadic challenges from the federal government to promote national solutions to these problems. If states do not somehow manage to ameliorate certain of these problems or at least be perceived as doing more than the federal government, will citizens turn to the federal government for relief, as they have in the past?

This question implies that people want more from government or perhaps that the public is now more liberal on domestic programs. Bennet and Bennet (1990, 161) conclude that "Americans have come to terms with big government" and "expect their government to provide the services that are the heart of a large national establishment." If that is the case, what do they want from government, and what level of government do they feel is most desirable for providing these desired goods and services?

In more abstract terms, there are two related questions concerning big government and centralization: What are public attitudes toward overall government power, and what are attitudes toward the relative power of the three levels of government? Bennet and Bennet conclude that the public has come to accept Leviathan. These SSP data, however, show that the public also supports decentralized government. Are these contradictory or paradoxical findings? I believe these are two separate but related issues. The public wants more and better government services, which have come to be viewed as entitlements (Huntington 1981). At the same time, they prefer more state and local control of these programs. To invite even greater complexity, the question of overall government power also should be assessed relative to the market. Neither the concept of big government nor that of intergovernmental power appears to be a zero-sum concept; rather, they are positive or negative-sum concepts.

Although there is little evidence for political sophistication or ideological thinking by the public, is there a consensus or bias for the private provision of goods and services and "local" responsibility for delivery of public goods and services? Bennet and Bennet (1990) believe that Americans have come to terms with big government. If so, is our national culture or ideology no longer based primarily on private-regardingness and decentralization, or do we favor these concepts symbolically, but their opposites programmatically? To what extent are Americans free-enterprise and decentralized in their outlooks, and how do these values interrelate? How do these values relate to values of capitalism and democracy (McCloskey and Zaller 1984) and economic and political equality (Verba and Orren 1985)? Do the decentralized and private-regarding orientations explain why people might be less willing to identify with the federal or central government but still want the goods and services provided by "big government" programs? Recall that a substantial majority of respondents in the SSP (approximately 2 out of 3) identify with state and local governments, with the remainder either mixed or federal identifiers.

Extensive energy and resources have been devoted by social scientists and others to assessing or trying to understand how people think about politics, government, and public policy. Most of this effort has been devoted to analyzing the symbolic predispositions of party identification and ideological identification and their relationships to political issues and policy attitudes and behaviors. Analysis of these questions relative to a fundamental element of the American political system—federalism or intergovernmental relations—has been neglected. The primary question in this research is whether individuals hold variable and consequential identifications, attitudes, and preferences concerning levels of government. The answer is yes. People vary in their attachments to one or another level of government, and these symbolic identifications appear to be relatively stable and to have independent effects on certain political and policy attitudes.

Level of government identification is certainly not the philosophers' stone of political and policy attitude research. It does show promise, however, of being as selectively useful as the concepts of party identification or political ideology, especially relative to research on the relationships between state public opinion and public policies. Just as party identification explains much about individual attitudes toward, or choices of, alternative political actors and public policies, level of government identification appears to be a useful explanatory concept for values and attitudes relating to issues of decentralization and intergovernmental politics and policies.

References

Achen, Christopher. 1979. "Issue Voting: What Counts as Evidence." In *Public Policy and Public Choice,* ed. Douglas Rae and Theodore Eismeier. Beverly Hills, Calif.: Sage Publications.

Advisory Commission on Intergovernmental Relations. 1989. *Changing Public Attitudes on Governments and Taxes, 1989.* Washington, D.C.: Government Printing Office.

Albritton, Robert B. 1983. "Subsidies: Welfare and Transportation." In *Politics in the American States,* ed. Virginia Gray, Herbert Jacob, and Kenneth N. Vines. 4th ed. Boston: Little, Brown.

Aldrich, John, and Charles Cnudde. 1975. "Probing the Bounds of Conventional Wisdom: A Comparison of Regression, Probit, and Discriminant Analysis." *American Journal of Political Science* 19:571–608.

Alvarez, R. Michael. 1990. "The Puzzle of Party Identification." *American Politics Quarterly* 18:476–91.

Ambrosius, Margery M. 1989a. "The Effectiveness of State Economic Development Policies: A Time-Series Analysis." *Western Political Quarterly* 42:283–300.

———. 1989b. "The Role of Occupational Interests in State Economic Development Policy-Making." *Western Political Quarterly* 42:53–68.

AmeriTrust/SRI. 1986. *Indicators of Economic Capacity.* Cleveland: AmeriTrust/SRI.

Arcelus, Francisco, and Allan H. Meltzer. 1975. "The Effect of Aggregate Economic Variables on Congressional Elections." *American Political Science Review* 69:1232–39.

Arendt, Hannah. 1963. *On Revolution.* New York: Viking Press.

Beaumont, Enid, and Harold A. Hovey. 1985. "State, Local, and Federal Economic Development Policies: New Federal Patterns, Chaos, or What?" *Public Administration Review* 45:327–32.

Beer, Samuel. 1978. "Federalism, Nationalism, and Democracy in America." *American Political Science Review* 72:9–21.

223

Bell, Daniel. 1989. "'American Exceptionalism' Revisited: The Role of Civil Society." *Public Interest* 95:38–56.

Bennet, Linda L. M., and Stephen Earl Bennet. 1990. *Living with Leviathan: Americans Coming to Terms with Big Government.* Lawrence: University Press of Kansas.

Bibby, John F., Cornelius P. Cotter, James L. Gibson, and Robert J. Huckshorn. 1983. "Parties in State Politics." In *Politics in the American States,* ed. Virginia Gray, Herbert Jacob, and Kenneth N. Vines. 4th ed. Boston: Little, Brown.

Black, Merle, David M. Kovenock, and William C. Reynolds. 1974. *Political Attitudes in the Nation and the States.* Chapel Hill, N.C.: Institute for Research in Social Science.

Blendon, Robert J., and Karen Donelan. 1989. "The 1988 Election: How Important Was Health?" *Health Affairs* 8:6–15.

Blendon, Robert J., and Humphrey Taylor. 1989. "Views on Health Care: Public Opinion in Three Nations." *Health Affairs* 8:149–57.

Bloom, Howard S., and H. Douglas Price. 1975. "Voter Response to Short-Run Economic Conditions: The Asymmetric Effect of Prosperity and Recession." *American Political Science Review* 69:1240–54.

Books, John, and Richard Prysby. 1988. "Studying Contextual Effects on Political Behavior: A Research Inventory and Agenda." *American Politics Quarterly* 16:211–38.

Bowman, Ann O., and Richard C. Kearney. 1986. *The Resurgence of the States.* Englewood Cliffs, N.J.: Prentice-Hall.

————. 1990. *State and Local Government.* Boston: Houghton Mifflin.

Brace, Paul. 1989. "Isolating the Economies of States." *American Politics Quarterly* 17:256–76.

Burstein, Paul. 1981. "The Sociology of Democratic Politics and Government." In *Annual Review of Sociology,* vol. 7, ed. Ralph H. Turner and James Short. Palo Alto, Calif.: Annual Reviews.

Campbell, Angus, Philip E. Converse, Warren E. Miller, and Donald E. Stokes. 1964. *The American Voter: An Abridgement.* New York: Wiley and Sons.

Chubb, John E. 1988. "Institutions, the Economy, and the Dynamics of State Elections." *American Political Science Review* 82:133–54.

Chubb, John E., and Terry M. Moe. 1990. *Politics, Markets, and America's Schools.* Washington, D.C.: Brookings Institution.

Citrin, Jack. 1979. "Do People Want Something for Nothing? Public Opinion on Taxes and Government Spending." *National Tax Journal,* June Supplement, 113–29.

Cohen, Jeffrey E. 1983. "Gubernatorial Popularity in Nine States." *American Politics Quarterly* 11:219–35.

Conover, Pamela J. 1985. "The Impact of Group Economic Interests on Political Evaluations." *American Politics Quarterly* 13:139–66.

Conover, Pamela Johnson, and Stanley Feldman. 1981. "The Origins and Meaning of Liberal/Conservative Self-Identifications." *American Journal of Political Science* 25:617–45.

Converse, Philip E. 1964. "The Nature of Belief Systems in Mass Publics." In *Ideology and Discontent,* ed. David E. Apter. New York: Free Press.

Corporation for Enterprise Development. 1987. "Making the Grade: The Development Report Card for the States." In *The Entrepreneurial Economy.* Washington, D.C.: CfED.

Council of State Governments. 1987. "Public Opinion and Policy Leadership in the American States: A National Survey." Presented at the Annual Meeting, Boston, December 1987.

———. 1988. "Public Opinion and Policy Leadership in the American States 1988." Presented at the Annual Meeting, Kansas City, December 1988.

———. 1989. "Public Opinion and Policy Leadership in the American States 1989." Presented at the Annual Meeting, Salt Lake City, December 1989.

Dahl, Robert. 1967. "The City in the Future of Democracy." *American Political Science Review* 61:953–70.

Derthick, Martha. 1987. "American Federalism: Madison's Middle Ground in the 1980s." *Public Administration Review* 47:66–74.

Diamond, Martin. 1961. "What the Framers Meant by Federalism." In *A Nation of States,* ed. Robert A. Goldwin. Chicago: Rand McNally.

Dougherty, Charles. 1990. "The Proposal Will Deny Services to the Poor." *Health Progress* 71:21–32.

Dye, Thomas R. 1969. "Executive Power and Public Policy in the States." *Western Political Quarterly* 22:926–39.

———. 1980. "Taxing, Spending, and Economic Growth in the American States." *Journal of Politics* 42:1085–1107.

———. 1987. *Understanding Public Policy.* Englewood Cliffs, N.J.: Prentice-Hall.

———. 1990. *American Federalism: Competition among Governments.* Lexington, Mass.: Lexington Books.

Elam, Stanley M. 1990. "The Twenty-second Annual Gallup Poll of the Public's Attitudes toward the Public Schools." *Phi Delta Kappan* 72 (September): 41–55.

Elazar, Daniel J. 1972. *American Federalism: A View from the States.* 2d ed. New York: Thomas Y. Crowell.

Elling, Richard C. 1983. "State Bureaucracies." In *Politics in the American States,* ed. Virginia Gray, Herbert Jacob, and Kenneth N. Vines. Boston: Little, Brown.

Erikson, Robert S. 1976. "The Relationship between Public Opinion and State Policy: A New Look Based on Some Forgotten Data." *American Journal of Political Science* 20:25–36.

Erikson, Robert S., John P. McIver, and Gerald C. Wright, Jr. 1987. "State Political Culture and Public Opinion." *American Political Science Review* 81:797–813.

Erikson, Robert S., Gerald C. Wright, Jr., and John P. McIver. 1989. "Political Parties, Public Opinion, and State Policy in the United States." *American Political Science Review* 83:729–49.

Feldman, Stanley. 1982. "Economic Self-Interest and Political Behavior." *American Journal of Political Science* 26:446–66.

Fiorina, Morris. 1978. "Economic Retrospective Voting in American National Elections: A Microanalysis." *American Journal of Political Science* 22:426–43.

Free, Lloyd, and Hadley Cantril. 1986. *The Political Beliefs of Americans*. New York: Simon and Schuster.

Gabel, Jon, Howard Cohen, and Steven Fink. 1989. "Americans' Views of Health Care: Foolish Inconsistencies?" *Health Affairs* 8:103–18.

Gallup, Alec M. 1985. "The Seventeenth Annual Gallup Poll on the Public's Attitudes toward the Public Schools." *Phi Delta Kappan* 67:35–47.

Gallup, Alec M., and David L. Clark. 1987. "The Nineteenth Annual Gallup Poll of the Public's Attitudes toward the Public Schools." *Phi Delta Kappan* 69:17–30.

Gallup, Alec M., and Stanley M. Elam. 1988. "The Twentieth Annual Gallup Poll of the Public's Attitudes toward the Public Schools." *Phi Delta Kappan* 70:33–46.

Gallup, George H. 1982. "The Gallup Poll of the Public's Attitudes toward the Public Schools." *Phi Delta Kappan* 64:31–44.

———. 1983. "The Fifteenth Annual Gallup Poll of Public Attitudes toward the Public Schools." *Phi Delta Kappan* 65:33–47.

Gilbert, Dennis A. 1988. *A Compendium of American Public Opinion*. New York: Facts on File Publications.

Ginsberg, Benjamin. 1986. *The Captive Public: How Mass Opinion Promotes State Power*. New York: Basic Books.

Goggin, Malcolm L., Ann O. Bowman, James P. Lester, and Laurence J. O'Toole. 1990. *Implementation Theory and Practice: Toward a Third Generation*. Glenview, Ill.: Scott, Foresman.

Gold, Steven D. 1991. "Replacing an Impossible Dream." *State Legislatures* 17:24–26.

GrantThornton. 1987. *The Eighth Annual Study of General Manufacturing Climates*. Chicago: GrantThornton Accountants and Management Consultants.

Gray, Virginia. 1973. "Innovation in the States: A Diffusion Study." *American Political Science Review* 67:1174–85.

Gray, Virginia, Herbert Jacob, and Kenneth N. Vines, eds. 1983. *Politics in the American States*. 4th ed. Boston: Little, Brown.

Gray, Virginia, and David Lowery. 1988. "Interest Group Politics and Economic Growth in the U.S. States." *American Political Science Review* 82:109–31.

Grumm, John. 1971. "The Effects of Legislative Structure on Legislative Performance." In *State and Urban Politics,* ed. Richard Hofferbert and Ira Sharkansky. Boston: Little, Brown.

Gulick, Luther. 1933. "Reorganization of the State." *Civil Engineering* 3:420–22.

Hamilton, Alexander, John Jay, and James Madison. 1937. *The Federalist.* Introduction by E. M. Earle. New York: Random House.

Hansen, Karen. 1989. "The Ethical Dilemma of Health Care." *State Legislatures* 15:9–13.

Hanushek, Eric A. 1981. "Throwing Money at Schools." *Journal of Policy Analysis and Management* 1:19–41.

Herbers, John. 1990. "In the Briar Patch of Federalism, States Struggle with Change." *Governing* 3:11.

Herzik, Eric B., and Brent W. Brown, eds. 1991. *Gubernatorial Leadership and State Policy.* New York: Greenwood Press.

Hill, Kim Quaile, and Roger Durand. 1988. "The Growth Machine Revisited: Public and Private Sector Elites' Assessments of Growth and Growth Policies." *Social Science Quarterly* 69:737–45.

Hodgkinson, Harold L. 1989. *The Same Client: The Demographics of Education and Service Delivery Systems.* Washington, D.C.: Institute for Educational Leadership.

Hofferbert, Richard I. 1974. *The Study of Public Policy.* Indianapolis: Bobbs-Merrill.

Hofferbert, Richard I., and Ira Sharkansky. 1971. "The Nationalization of State Politics." In *State and Urban Politics,* ed. Hofferbert and Sharkansky. Boston: Little, Brown.

Holbrook-Provow, Thomas, and Steven C. Poe. 1987. "Measuring State Political Ideology." *American Politics Quarterly* 15:399–416.

Hudson, William E., Mark S. Hyde, and John J. Carroll. 1987. "Corporatist Policy-Making and State Economic Development." *Polity* 20:402–18.

Huntington, Samuel P. 1981. *American Politics: The Promise of Disharmony.* Cambridge: Harvard University Press.

Hutchison, Tony. 1990. "The Medicaid Budget Tangle." *State Legislatures* 16:15–19.

Iyengar, Shanto. 1990. "Framing Responsibility for Political Issues: The Case of Poverty." *Political Behavior* 12:19–40.

Jajich-Toth, Cindy, and Burns W. Roper. 1990. "Americans' Views on Health Care: A Study in Contradictions." *Health Affairs* 9:149–57.

Jennings, M. Kent, and Harmon Zeigler. 1970. "The Salience of American State Politics." *American Political Science Review* 64:523–35.

Jewell, Malcolm E., and David M. Olson. 1982. *American State Political Parties and Elections*. Homewood, Ill.: Dorsey Press.

Jones, Bryan D. 1990. "Public Policies and Economic Growth in the American States." *Journal of Politics* 52:219–33.

Jones, Katherine R. 1989. "The Florida Health Care Access Act: A Blended Regulatory-Competitive Approach to the Indigent Health Care Problem." *Journal of Health Politics, Policy and Law* 14:261–85.

Karnig, Albert, and Lee Sigelman. 1975. "State Legislative Reform and Public Policy: Another Look." *Western Political Quarterly* 28:548–52.

Kee, James Edwin, and John Shannon. 1992. "The Crisis and Anticrisis Dynamic: Rebalancing the American Federal System." *Public Administration Review* 52:321–29.

Kemp, Kathleen A. 1978. "Nationalization of the American States: A Test of the Hypothesis." *American Politics Quarterly* 6:237–47.

Kenney, Patrick J. 1983. "The Effect of State Economic Conditions on the Vote for Governor." *Social Science Quarterly* 64:154–62.

Key, V. O. 1964. *Politics, Parties, and Pressure Groups*. New York: Crowell.

———. 1967. *Public Opinion and American Democracy*. New York: Alfred Knopf.

Kinder, Donald R. 1983. "Diversity and Complexity in American Public Opinion." In *Political Science: The State of the Discipline*, ed. Ada Finifter. Washington, D.C.: American Political Science Association.

Kinder, Donald R., Gordon S. Adams, and Paul W. Gronke. 1989. "Economics and Politics in the 1984 American Presidential Election." *American Journal of Political Science* 33:491–515.

Kinder, Donald R., and D. Roderick Kiewet. 1979. "Economic Discontent and Political Behavior: The Role of Personal Grievances and Collective Economic Judgments in Congressional Voting." *American Journal of Political Science* 23:495–527.

Kinder, Donald R., and David O. Sears. 1985. "Public Opinion and Political Behavior." In *Handbook of Social Psychology*, vol. 2, ed. Gardner Lindzey and Elliot Aronson. New York: Random House.

Kitzhaber, John A. 1990. "Oregon Act to Allocate Resources More Efficiently." *Health Progress* 71:20–27.

Klingman, David, and William W. Lammers. 1984. "The 'General Policy Liberalism' Factor in American State Politics." *American Journal of Political Science* 28:598–610.

Kluegel, James R., and Eliot R. Smith. 1986. *Beliefs about Inequality.* New York: Aldine De Gruyter.

Knight, Kathleen. 1984. "The Dimensionality of Partisan and Ideological Affect." *American Politics Quarterly* 12:305–34.

Kramer, Gerald H. 1971. "Short-Term Fluctuations in U.S. Voting Behavior, 1896–1964." *American Political Science Review* 65:131–43.

Kuklinski, James H., and Darrell M. West. 1981. "Economic Expectations and Voting Behavior in United States House and Senate Elections." *American Political Science Review* 75:436–47.

Ladd, Everett C., Jr., and Charles D. Hadley. 1978. *Transformation of the American Party System.* 2d ed. New York: Norton.

Landau, Martin. 1969. "*Baker v. Carr* and the Ghost of Federalism." In *Empirical Democratic Theory,* ed. Charles F. Cnudde and Deane E. Neubauer. Chicago: Markham.

Lane, Robert E. 1962. *Political Ideology: Why the American Common Man Believes What He Does.* New York: Free Press.

———. 1986. "Market Justice, Political Justice." *American Political Science Review* 80:383–402.

Legge, Jerome S., and Herbert Zeigler. 1979. "Utilizing Discriminant Analysis in Social Research." *Public Data Use* 7:27–35.

Levitin, Teresa E., and Warren E. Miller. 1979. "Ideological Interpretations of Presidential Elections." *American Political Science Review* 73:751–71.

Lipset, Seymour M., and William Schneider. 1987. *The Confidence Gap.* Baltimore: Johns Hopkins University Press.

Lowery, David, Virginia Gray, and Gregory Hager. 1989. "Public Opinion and Policy Change in the American States." *American Politics Quarterly* 17:3–31.

Lowery, David, and Lee Sigelman. 1982. "Political Culture and State Public Policy: The Missing Link." *Western Political Quarterly* 35:376–84.

Lyons, William, and David Morgan. 1976. "Multi-Level Analysis in State Politics." *American Political Science Review* 70:159–63.

McCloskey, Herbert, and John Zaller. 1984. *The American Ethos: Public Attitudes toward Capitalism and Democracy.* Cambridge: Harvard University Press.

McConnell, Grant. 1966. *Private Power and American Democracy.* New York: Random House.

Marmor, Theodore R., Jerry L. Mashaw, and Philip L. Harvey. 1990. *America's Misunderstood Welfare State.* New York: Basic Books.

Martinez, Michael D., and Michael M. Gant. 1990. "Partisan Issue Preferences and Partisan Change." *Political Behavior* 12:243–64.

Nardulli, Peter F. 1990. "Political Subcultures in the American States: An Empirical Examination of Elazar's Formulation." *American Politics Quarterly* 18:287–315.

Neuman, W. Russell. 1986. *The Paradox of Mass Politics: Knowledge and Opinion in the American Electorate*. Cambridge: Harvard University Press.

Nie, Norman H., with Kristi Anderson. 1974. "Mass Belief Systems Revisited: Political Change and Attitude Structure." *Journal of Politics* 36:540–91.

Nie, Norman H., Sidney Verba, and John R. Petrocik. 1979. *The Changing American Voter*. Cambridge: Harvard University Press.

Niemi, Richard G., John Mueller, and Tom W. Smith. 1989. *Trends in Public Opinion: A Compendium of Survey Data*. New York: Greenwood Press.

Northwestern National Life Insurance Company. 1989. *The NWNL State Health Rankings: Results, Methodology, and Discussion*. Minneapolis.

Oberg, Charles N., and Cynthia Longseth Polich. 1988. "Medicaid: Entering the Third Decade." *Health Affairs* 7:83–96.

Orren, Gary R. 1988. "Beyond Self-Interest." In *The Power of Public Ideas*, ed. Robert B. Reich. Cambridge, Mass.: Ballinger.

Osborne, David. 1988. *Laboratories of Democracy*. Boston: Harvard Business School Press.

Page, Benjamin I., and Robert Y. Shapiro. 1983. "The Effects of Public Opinion on Policy." *American Political Science Review* 77:175–90.

Peterson, Paul E. 1981. *City Limits*. Chicago: University of Chicago Press.

Peterson, Paul E., and Mark Rom. 1989. "American Federalism, Welfare Policy, and Residential Choices." *American Political Science Review* 83:711–28.

Pollack, Ervin H. 1956. *The Brandeis Reader*. New York: Oceana Publications.

Prysby, Charles L., and John W. Books. 1987. "Modeling Contextual Effects on Political Behavior: Static versus Dynamic Models." *Political Behavior* 9:225–45.

Reich, Robert B., ed. 1988. *The Power of Public Ideas*. Cambridge, Mass.: Ballinger.

Reichley, James. 1964. *States in Crisis*. Chapel Hill: University of North Carolina Press.

Reischauer, Robert D. 1989. "The Welfare Reform Legislation: Directions for the Future." In *Welfare Policy for the 1990s*, ed. Phoebe H. Cottingham and David T. Ellwood. Cambridge: Harvard University Press.

Riker, William H. 1964. *Federalism: Origin, Operation, Significance*. Boston: Little, Brown.

Rochefort, David A., and Carol A. Boyer. 1988. "Use of Public Opinion Data in Public Administration: Health Care Polls." *Public Administration Review* 48:649–60.

Roeder, Phillip W. 1979. "State Legislative Reform: Determinants and Policy Consequences." *American Politics Quarterly* 7:51–70.

Rose, Douglas D. 1973. "National and Local Forces in State Politics: The Implications of Multi-Level Policy Analysis." *American Political Science Review* 68:1162–73.

Rosenstone, Steven J., John Mark Hansen, and Donald R. Kinder. 1986. "Measuring Change in Personal Economic Well-Being." *Public Opinion Quarterly* 50:176–92.

Rubin, Barry, and Kurt Zorn. 1985. "Sensible State and Local Economic Development." *Public Administration Review* 45:333–39.

Salmore, Barbara G., and Stephen A. Salmore. 1989. "The Transformation of State Electoral Politics." In *The State of the States*, ed. Carl Van Horn. Washington, D.C.: Congressional Quarterly Press.

Sanders, Arthur. 1988. "Rationality, Self-Interest, and Public Attitudes on Public Spending." *Social Science Quarterly* 69:311–24.

Sanford, Terry. 1967. *Storm over the States.* New York: McGraw-Hill.

Schneider, Saundra K. 1988. "Intergovernmental Influences on Medicaid Program Expenditures." *Public Administration Review* 48:756–63.

Sears, David O., and Jack Citrin. 1982. *Tax Revolt.* Cambridge: Harvard University Press.

Sears, David O., Richard R. Lau, Tom R. Tyler, and Harris M. Allen, Jr. 1980. "Self-Interest vs. Symbolic Politics in Policy Attitudes and Presidential Voting." *American Political Science Review* 74:670–84.

Sen, Amartya K. 1977. "Rational Fools: A Critique of the Behavioral Foundations of Economic Theory." *Philosophy and Public Affairs* 6:317–44.

Shapiro, Robert Y., Kelly D. Patterson, Judith Russell, and John T. Young. 1987a. "The Polls—a Report: Employment and Social Welfare." *Public Opinion Quarterly* 51:268–81.

———. 1987b. "The Polls: Public Assistance." *Public Opinion Quarterly* 51:120–30.

Shapiro, Robert Y., and John T. Young. 1986. "The Polls: Medical Care in the United States." *Public Opinion Quarterly* 50:419–28.

Sharkansky, Ira. 1969. "The Utility of Elazar's Political Culture: A Research Note." *Polity* 2:66–83.

———. 1972. *The Maligned States: Policy Accomplishments, Problems, and Opportunities.* New York: McGraw-Hill.

Sigelman, Lee. 1976. "The Quality of Administration: An Exploration in the American States." *Administration and Society* 8:107–44.

Sigelman, Lee, and Yung-Mei Tsai. 1981. "Personal Finances and Voting Behavior: A Reanalysis." *American Politics Quarterly* 9:371–99.

Smith, Tom W. 1987. "That Which We Call Welfare by Any Other Name Would Smell Sweeter." *Public Opinion Quarterly* 51:75–83.

Stein, Robert M. 1990. "Economic Voting for Governor and U.S. Senator: The Electoral Consequences of Federalism." *Journal of Politics* 52:29–53.

Steiner, Gilbert Y. 1981. *The Futility of Family Policy.* Washington, D.C.: Brookings Institution.

Stillman, Richard J., II. 1991. *Preface to Public Administration.* New York: St. Martins.

Sundquist, James L., with David W. Davis. 1969. *Making Federalism Work.* Washington, D.C.: Brookings Institution.

Tufte, Edward R. 1978. *Political Control of the Economy.* Princeton: Princeton University Press.

Van Horn, Carl E., ed. 1989. *The State of the States.* Washington, D.C.: Congressional Quarterly Press.

Verba, Sidney, and Gary R. Orren. 1985. *Equality in America: The View from the Top.* Cambridge: Harvard University Press.

Vertz, Laura L., John P. Frendreis, and James L. Gibson. 1987. "Nationalization of the Electorate in the United States." *American Political Science Review* 81:961–66.

Walker, Jack. 1969. "The Diffusion of Innovations among the American States." *American Political Science Review* 63:380–99.

Wanat, John, and Phillip W. Roeder. 1976. "The Relative Impact of State and National Forces: A Comment on Rose's 'National and Local Forces in State Politics.'" *American Political Science Review* 70:163–66.

Weatherford, M. Stephen. 1983a. "Economic Voting and the 'Symbolic Politics' Argument: A Reinterpretation and Synthesis." *American Political Science Review* 77:158–74.

———. 1983b. "Evaluating Economic Policy: A Contextual Model of the Opinion Formation Process." *Journal of Politics* 45:866–88.

———. 1983c. "Parties and Classes in the Political Response to Economic Conditions." In *The Political Process and Economic Change,* ed. Kristen Monroe. New York: Agathon.

Weber, Ronald, and William R. Shaffer. 1972. "Public Opinion and American State Policy-Making." *Midwest Journal of Political Science* 16:633–99.

Weisberg, Herbert. 1983. "A New Scale of Partisanship." *Political Behavior* 5:363–76.

Welch, Susan. 1985. "The 'More for Less' Paradox: Public Attitudes on Taxing and Spending." *Public Opinion Quarterly* 49:310–16.

Welch, Susan, and Kay Thompson. 1980. "The Impact of Federal Incentives on State Policy Innovation." *American Journal of Political Science* 24:715–29.

Wilson, James Q., and Edward C. Banfield. 1964. "Public-Regardingness as a

Value Premise in Voting Behavior." *American Political Science Review* 58:876–87.

Wirt, Frederick M. 1983. "Institutionalization: Prison and School Policies." In *Politics in the American States,* ed. Virginia Gray, Herbert Jacob, and Kenneth N. Vines. Boston: Little, Brown.

Wright, Gerald C., Jr., Robert S. Erikson, and John P. McIver. 1987. "Public Opinion and Policy Liberalism in the American States." *American Journal of Political Science* 31:980–1001.

Index

About the Author

Phillip Roeder is Associate Professor of Political Science and Public Administration, University of Kentucky. He received his B.A. and M.A. from the University of Delaware, and his Ph.D. from Florida State University.

About the Institute

The University of Alabama established the Institute for Social Science Research in 1984 to promote and conduct social science research. The Institute seeks to advance the theory and methodology of social science disciplines and to respond to society's needs by applying social science to the study of social problems. ISSR is composed of three units: the Center of Social and Policy Analysis, the Capstone Poll, and the Research and Consulting Laboratory. Correspondence should be addressed to:

> Institute for Social Science Research
> 319 ten Hoor Hall
> The University of Alabama
> Box 870216
> Tuscaloosa, Alabama 35487-0216

About the Social Science Monograph Series

The Institute for Social Science Research and The University of Alabama Press publish the Social Science Monograph Series through a cooperative agreement. The Series includes analyses of social problems and theoretical or methodological works that significantly advance social science research in the judgment of Institute social scientists and of two or more anonymous referees. Conclusions expressed in the monographs are those of the authors and do not necessarily reflect the views of ISSR, The University of Alabama, or organizations that provide funds to support Institute research.